新世纪双语系列
New Century Bilingual Series

国际贸易实务

International Trade Practice

（第二版）

主　编 郭　琛
副主编 袁自国 任雪梅

HEUP 哈尔滨工程大学出版社
Harbin Engineering University Press

内容简介

本书是以国内外国际贸易实务研究和教材建设的最新进展为主线组织编写而成的，对第一版进行了大规模的修订和完善。全书分为10章：第一章介绍了最新版本的国际贸易术语；第二章到第九章介绍了国际贸易合同的主要条款，如货物的品名、品质、数量、包装、价格、运输、保险、货款支付、检验、索赔、不可抗力及仲裁；第十章介绍了国际货物销售合同的商订。附录介绍了国际贸易实务常用词汇和单证样本。

本书可以作为普通高等学校国际贸易、国际经济、国际金融及工商管理等专业本科阶段的国际贸易实务课程双语教材，也可以作为跨国公司、银行及保险公司等金融机构的培训教材。

图书在版编目(CIP)数据

国际贸易实务/郭琛主编. —2 版. —哈尔滨：哈尔滨工程大学出版社，2011. 12
ISBN 978 - 7 - 5661 - 0294 - 2

Ⅰ. ①国… Ⅱ. ①郭… Ⅲ. ①国际贸易 - 贸易实务 - 教材 Ⅳ. ①F740. 4

中国版本图书馆 CIP 数据核字(2011)第 256902 号

出版发行 哈尔滨工程大学出版社
社　　址 哈尔滨市南岗区东大直街 124 号
邮政编码 150001
发行电话 0451 - 82519328
传　　真 0451 - 82519699
经　　销 新华书店
印　　刷 黑龙江省地质测绘印制中心
开　　本 787mm × 960mm 1/16
印　　张 17
字　　数 348 千字
版　　次 2012 年 1 月第 1 版
印　　次 2012 年 1 月第 1 次印刷
定　　价 32. 00 元
http://press. hrbeu. edu. cn
E - mail:heupress@ hrbeu. edu. cn

前　言

本书第一版已出版近4年，得到了广泛的好评。众多师生在使用本教材的过程中，给我们提出了非常富有建设性的意见和建议，在此我们表示衷心的感谢。根据国内外教材建设的最新进展、我们在教学第一线所积累的经验以及众多同行师生的意见和建议，我们对第一版进行了大规模的修订和完善。

"国际贸易实务"是高等院校国际经济与贸易等专业的一门主干课，适宜采用外语讲授。《国际贸易实务（第二版）》正是为了适应入世后国际化竞争的需要而编写的，其目的是为有志于从事国际经贸事业的人员，提供适应新形势要求的必备理论知识和实践技能，以提高国际经贸人员的理论水平和实际操作能力，不断增强其国际竞争力。

编者借鉴了国内外学者的研究成果，在教材结构上作了一些尝试性的创新，既有简单基本常识的阐述，又有重点难点的讲解；既有理论知识的框架体系，又注意理论联系实际，用案例分析，着力于事务操作、技能训练。这种结合我国对外经贸实践，利用外资和外贸实务的引导式学习方式，必将有助于读者提高分析问题和解决问题的能力。全书结构完整，内容详实，简明易懂，符合国情。

本书撰写的分工如下：哈尔滨理工大学经济学院郭琛负责第一章、第五章、第八章（共约180千字）；哈尔滨师范大学西语学院袁自国负责第二章至第四章、第十章（共约90千字）；哈尔滨师范大学西语学院任雪梅负责第六章、第七章、第九章（共约80千字）。

本书主编对修订稿进行了全面、细致的审订。国际贸易的理论与实践正在不断发展完善之中，加之作者水平有限，书中错误或疏漏之处在所难免，恳请同行专家和广大读者批评指正。

编　者

2011年9月

CONTENTS

目录

English Part

Chapter 1　International Trade Terms

1.1　Summary of International Trade Terms

1.1.1　Role of Trade Terms

Trade terms, also known as price terms or delivery terms, are standardized terms used in sales contracts that describe the place and manner for the transfer of goods from the seller to the buyer. These trade terms, such as Free on Board (FOB) and Cost, Insurance, and Freight (CIF), may also define a variety of other matters, including the price, the time when the risk of loss shifts from the seller to the buyer, and the costs of freight and insurance. The use of trade terms greatly simplifies the process of negotiation of contract, thus saving time and cost for businessmen.

1.1.2　International Rules & Practices on Trade Terms

Trade terms have been developed in practice for many years. However, different countries might have different interpretations of the terms, misunderstandings occurred frequently. To clear up the confusion, some commercial organizations drew up sets of rules or standard definitions.

1. Warsaw-Oxford Rules 1932

This rule was drafted by the Association of International Law in 1932. It contains 21 clauses, which only stipulate the nature of CIF contract, and the charges, risks and obligations which should be born by the seller or the buyer.

2. Revised American Foreign Trade Definitions 1941

This rule was made out by nine American commercial organizations in 1941. It is a set of foreign trade terms which are considered obsolete, but still sometimes is used in domestic U. S. trade. It contains 6 trade terms.

3. International Rule for the Interpretation of Trade Terms 2000

The International Chamber of Commerce (ICC) developed INCOTERMS (International Commercial TERMS). It was first published in 1936 and has been periodically revised. The INCOTERMS 2000 came into force on Jan. 1, 2000. In this rule, there are totally 13 trade terms, which have been divided into 4 different groups.

(1) The "E" term (EXW). The only term where the seller/exporter makes the goods available at his or her own premises to the buyer/importer.

(2) The "F" terms (FCA, FAS and FOB). Terms where the seller/exporter is responsible to deliver the goods to a carrier named by the buyer.

(3) The "C" terms (CFR, CIF, CPT and CIP). Terms where the seller/exporter is responsible for contacting and paying for carriage of the goods, but not responsible for additional costs or risk of loss or damages to the goods once they have been shipped. C terms evidence "shipment" (as opposed to "arrival") contracts.

(4) The "D" terms (DAF, DES, DEQ, DDU and DDP). Terms where the seller/exporter is responsible for all costs and risks associated with bringing the goods to the place of destination. D terms evidence "arrival" contracts.

4. International Rule for the Interpretation of Trade Terms 2010

The global economy has given business broader access than ever before to markets all over the world. Goods are sold in more countries, in large quantities, and in greater variety. But as the volume and complexity of global sales increase, so do possibilities for misunderstandings and costly disputes when sale contracts are not adequately drafted.

The INCOTERMS rules, the ICC rules on the use of domestic and international trade terms, facilitate the conduct of global trade. Reference to an INCOTERMS 2010 rule in a sale contract clearly defines the parties' respective obligations and reduces the risk of legal complications.

Since the creation of the INCOTERMS rules by ICC in 1936, this globally accepted contractual standard has been regularly updated to keep pace with the development of international trade. The INCOTERMS 2010 rules take account of the continued spread of customs-free zones, the increased use of electronic communications in business transactions, heightened concern about security in the movement of goods and consolidates in transport practices. INCOTERMS 2010 update and consolidate the 'delivered' rules, reducing the total number of rules from 13 to 11, and offers a simpler and clearer presentation of all the rules. INCOTERMS 2010 are also the first version of the INCOTERMS rules to make all references to buyers and sellers gender-neutral.

The broad expertise of ICC's Commission on Commercial Law and Practice, whose membership is drawn from all parts of the world and all trade sectors, ensures that the INCOTERMS 2010 rules respond to business needs everywhere.

ICC would like to express its gratitude to the members of the Commission, chaired by Fabio Bortolotti (Italy), to the Drafting Group, which comprised Charles Debattista (Co-Chair, France), Jens Bredow (Germany), Johnny Herre (Sweden), David Lwee (UK), Lauri Railas (Finland), Frank Reynolds (US), and Miroslav Subert (Szech Republic), and to Asko Raty (Finland) for assistance with the images depicting the 11 rules.

1.2 International Practice

1.2.1 Purpose and Scope of INCOTERMS

The purpose of INCOTERMS is to provide a set of international rules for the interpretation of the most commonly used trade terms in foreign trade. Thus, the uncertainties of different interpretation of such terms in different countries can be avoided or at least reduced to a considerable degree.

Frequently, parties to a contract are unaware of the different trading practices in their respective countries. This can give rise to misunderstandings, disputes and litigation, with all the waste of time and money that this entails. In order to remedy these problems, the International Chamber of Commerce first published in 1936 a set of international rules for the interpretation of trade terms. These rules were known as "INCOTERMS 1936". Amendments and additions were later made in 1953, 1967, 1976, 1980, 1990, 2000 and presently in 2010 in order to bring the rules in line with current international trade practices. It should be stressed that the scope of INCOTERMS is limited to matters relating to the rights and obligations of the parties to the contract of sale with respect to the delivery of goods sold (in the sense of "tangible", not including "intangibles" such as computer software).

It appears that two particular misconceptions about INCOTERMS are very common. First, INCOTERMS are frequently misunderstood as applying to the contract of carriage rather than the contract of sale. Second, they are sometimes wrongly assumed to provide for all the duties which parties may wish to include in a contract of sale.

First of all, as has always been underlined by ICC, INCOTERMS deal only with the relation between sellers and buyers under the contract of sale, and moreover, only do so in some very distinct respects. While it is essential for exporters and importers to consider the very practical relationship between the various contracts needed to perform an international sales transaction where not only the contract of sale is required, but also contracts of carriage, insurance and financing. INCOTERMS relate to only one of these contracts, namely the contract of sale. Nevertheless, the parties' agreement to use a particular INCOTERMS would necessarily have implications for the other contracts. To mention a few examples, a seller having agreed to CFR or CIF contract cannot perform such a contract by any other mode of transport than carriage by sea, since under these terms he must present a bill of lading or other maritime document to the buyer which is simply not possible if other modes of transport are used. Furthermore, the document required under a documentary credit would necessarily depend upon the means of transport intended to be used.

Second, they deal with the obligations to clear the goods for export and import, the packing of the goods, the buyer's obligation to take delivery as well as the obligation to provide proof that the respective obligations have been duly fulfilled. Although INCOTERMS are extremely important for the implementation of the contract of sale, a great number of problems may occur in such breaches as well as exemptions from liability in certain situations. It should be stressed that INCOTERMS are not intended to replace such contract terms that are needed for a complete contract of sale either by the incorporation of standard terms or by individually negotiated terms. Generally, INCOTERMS do not deal with the consequences of breach of contract and any exemptions from liability owing to various impediments. These questions must be resolved by other stipulations in the contract of sale and the applicable law. INCOTERMS have always been primarily intended for use where goods are sold for delivery across national boundaries, hence, it is a set of international commercial terms. However, INCOTERMS are in practice at times also incorporated into contracts for the sale of goods within purely domestic markets. Where INCOTERMS are used, the A2 and B2 clauses and any other stipulation of other articles dealing with export and import do, of course, become redundant.

1.2.2 Reasons of INCOTERMS' Revision

The main reason for successive revisions of INCOTERMS has been the need to adapt them to contemporary commercial practice. Thus, in the 1980 revision the term Free Carrier (now FCA) was introduced in order to deal with the frequent case where the reception point in maritime trade was no longer the traditional FOB point (passing of the ship's rail) but rather a point on land, prior to loading on board a vessel, where the goods were stowed into a container for subsequent transport by sea or by different means of transport in combination (so called combined or multimodal transport).

Further, in the 1990 revision of INCOTERMS, the clauses dealing with the seller's obligation to provide proof of delivery permitted a replacement of paper documentation by EDI messages provided the parties had agreed to communicate electronically. Needless to say, efforts are constantly made to improve upon the drafting and presentation of INCOTERMS in order to facilitate their practical implementation.

1.2.3 INCOTERMS 2000

During the process of revision, which has taken about two years, ICC has done its best to invite views and responses to successive drafts from a wide ranging spectrum of world traders, represented as these various sectors are on the national committees through which ICC operates.

The result of this dialogue is INCOTERMS 2000, a version which when compared with INCOTERMS 1990 may appear to have effected few changes. It is clear, however, that INCOTERMS now enjoy world wide recognition and ICC has therefore decided to consolidate upon that recognition and avoid change for its own sake. On the other hand, serious efforts have been made to ensure that the wording used in INCOTERMS 2000 clearly and accurately reflects trade practice. Moreover, substantive changes have made in two areas:

(1) the customs clearance and payment of duty obligations under FAS and DEQ;

(2) the loading and unloading obligations under FCA.

All changes, whether substantive or formal have been made on the basis of thorough research among users of INCOTERMS and particular regard has been given to queries received since 1990 by the Panel of INCOTERMS Experts, set up as an additional service to the users of INCOTERMS.

1.2.4 Incorporation of INCOTERMS into the Contract of Sale

In view of the changes made to INCOTERMS from time to time, it is important to ensure that where the parties intend to incorporate INCOTERMS into their contract of sale, an express reference is always made to the current version of INCOTERMS. This may easily be overlooked when, for example, a reference has been made to an earlier version in standard contract forms or in order forms used by merchants. A failure to refer to the current version may then result in disputes as to whether the parties intended to incorporate that version or an earlier version as a part of their contract. Merchants wishing to use INCOTERMS 2000 should therefore clearly specify that their contract is governed by "INCOTERMS 2000".

1.2.5 Structure of INCOTERMS

In 1990, for ease of understanding, the terms were grouped in four basically different categories: namely starting with the term whereby the seller only makes the goods available to the buyer at the seller's own premises (the "E" term Ex works); followed by the second group whereby the seller is called upon to deliver the goods to a carrier appointed by the buyer (the "F" terms FCA, FAS and FOB); continuing with the "C" terms where the seller has to contract for carriage, but without assuming the risk of loss of or damage to the goods or additional costs due to events occurring after shipment and dispatch (CFR, CIF, CPT, and CIP); and, finally, the "D" term whereby the seller has to bear all costs and risks needed to bring the goods to the place of destination (DAF, DES, DEQ, DDU, and DDP). Table 1.1 sets out this classification of the trade terns.

Table 1.1 INCOTERMS 2000

Group E	**Departure**	
	EXW	Ex Works (... named place)
Group F	**Main carriage unpaid**	
	FCA	Free Carrier (... named place)
	FAS	Free Alongside Ship (... named port of shipment)
	FOB	Free On Board (... named port of shipment)
Group C	**Main Carriage Paid**	
	CFR	Cost and Freight (... named port of destination)
	CIF	Cost, Insurance and Freight (... named place of destination)
	CPT	Carriage Paid To (... named port of destination)
	CIP	Carriage and Insurance Paid To (... named place of destination)
Group D	**Arrival**	
	DAF	Delivered At Frontier (... named place)
	DES	Delivered Ex Ship (... named port of destination)
	DEQ	Delivered Ex Quay (... named port of destination)
	DDU	Delivered Duty Unpaid (... named place of destination)
	DDP	Delivered Duty Paid (... named place of destination)

Further, under all terms, as in INCOTERMS 2000, the respective obligations of the parties have been grouped under 13 headings where each heading on the seller's side "mirrors" the position of the buyer with respect to the same subject matter.

1.2.6 Terminology

While drafting INCOTERMS 2000, considerable efforts have been made to achieve as much consistency as possible and desirable with respect to the various expressions used throughout the thirteen terms. Thus, the use of different expressions intended to convey the same meaning has been avoided. Also, whenever possible, the same expressions as appear in the 1980 *UN Convention on Contracts for the International Sale of Goods* (CISG) have been used.

1. Shipper

In some cases it has been necessary to use the same term to express two different meanings simply because there has been no suitable alternative. Traders will be familiar with this difficulty both in the context of contracts of sale and also of contracts of carriage. Thus, for example, the term "shipper" signifies both the person handing over the goods for carriage and the person who makes the contract with the carrier: however, these two "shippers" may be different persons, for example, under a FOB contract where the seller would hand over the goods for carriage and the buyer would make the contract with the carrier.

2. Delivery

It is particularly important to note that the term "delivery" is used in two different senses in INCOTERMS. First, it is used to determine when the seller has fulfilled his delivery obligation which is specified in the A4 clauses throughout INCOTERMS. Second, the term "delivery" is also used in the context of the buyer's obligation to take or accept delivery of the goods, an obligation which appears in the B4 clauses throughout INCOTERMS. Used in this second context, the word "delivery" means first that the buyer "accepts" the very nature of the "C" terms, namely that the seller fulfils his obligations upon the shipment of the goods and, second that the buyer is obliged to receive the goods. This latter obligation is important so as to avoid unnecessary charges for storage of the goods until they have been collected by the buyer. Thus, for example, under CFR and CIF contracts, the buyer is bound to accept delivery of the goods and to receive them from the carrier and if the buyer fails to do so, he may become liable to pay damages to the seller who has made the contract of carriage with the carrier or, alternatively, the buyer might have to pay demurrage charges resting upon the goods in order to obtain the carrier's release of the goods to him. When it is said in this context that the buyer must "accept delivery", this does not mean that the buyer has accepted the goods as conforming with the contract of sale, but only that he has accepted that the seller has performed his obligation to hand the goods over for carriage in accordance with the contract of carriage which he has to make under the A3 a) clauses of the "C" terms. So, if the buyer upon receipt of the goods at destination were to find that the goods did not conform to the stipulations in the contract of sale, he would be able to use any remedies which the contract of sale and the applicable law gave him against the seller, matters which, as has already been mentioned, lie entirely outside the scope of INCOTERMS.

Where appropriate, INCOTERMS 2000 have used the expression "placing the goods at the disposal of the buyer" when the goods are made available to the buyer at a particular place. This expression is intended to bear the same meaning as that of the phrase "handing over the goods" used in the 1980 *United Nations Convention on Contracts for the International Sale of Goods.*

3. Usual

The word "usual" appears in several terms, for example, in EXW with respect to the time of delivery (A4) and in the "C" terms with respect to the documents which the seller is obliged to provide and the contract of carriage which the seller must procure (A8, A3). It can, of course, of course, be difficult to tell precisely what the word "usual" means, however, in many cases, it is possible to identify what persons in the trade usually do and this practice will then be the guiding light. In this sense, the word "reasonable", which requires an assessment not against the word of practice, but it may against the more difficult principle of good faith and fair dealing. In some circumstances it may well be necessary to decide what is "usual" has been generally preferred to the word "reasonable".

4. Charges

With respect to the obligation to clear the goods for import, it is important to determine what is meant by "charges" which must be paid upon import of the goods. In INCOTERMS 1990 the expression "official charges payable upon exportation and importation of the goods" was used in DDP A6. In INCOTERMS 2000 the word "official" has been deleted, the reason is that this word gave rise to some uncertainty when determining whether the charge is "official" or not. No change of substantive meaning is intended through this deletion. The "charges" which must be paid only concern such charges as are a necessary consequence of the import regulations. Any additional charges levied by private parties in connection with the import are not to be included in these charges, such as charges for storage unrelated to the clearance obligation. However, the performance of that obligation may well result in some costs to customs brokers or freight forwarders if the party bearing the obligation does not do the work by himself.

5. Ports, Places, Points and Premises

So far as concerns the place at which the goods are to be delivered, different expressions are used in INCOTERMS. In the terms intended to be used exclusively for carriage of goods by sea—such as FAS, FOB, CFR, CIF, DES and DEQ—the expressions "port of shipment" have been used. In all other cases the word "place" has been used. In some cases, it has been deemed necessary also to indicate a "point" within the port or place as it may be important for the seller to know not only that the goods should be delivered in a particular area like a city but also where within that area the goods should be placed at the disposal of the buyer. Contracts of sale would frequently lack information in this respect and INCOTERMS therefore stipulate that if no specific point has been agreed within the named place, and if there are several points available, the seller may select the point which best suits his purpose (as an example see FCA A4). Where the delivery point is the seller's place the expression "the seller's premises" (FCA A4) has been used.

6. Ship and Vessel

In the terms intended to be used for carriage of goods by sea, the expressions "ship" and "vessel" are used as synonyms. Needless to say, the term "ship" would have to be used when it is an ingredient in the trade term itself such as in "free alongside ship" (FAS) and "delivery ex ship" (DES). Also, in view of the traditional use of the expression "passed the ship's rail" in FOB, the word "ship" has had to be used in that connection.

7. Checking and Inspection

In the A9 and B9 clauses of INCOTERMS the headings "checking-packaging and marking" and "inspection of the goods" respectively have been used. Although the words "checking" and "inspection" are synonyms, it have been deemed appropriate to use the former word with respect to the seller's delivery obligation under A4and to reserve the latter for the particular case when a "pre-shipment inspection" is performed, since such inspection normally is only required when the buyer or the authorities of the export or import country want to ensure that the goods conform with contractual or official stipulations before they are shipped.

1.2.7 Seller's Delivery Obligation

INCOTERMS focus on the seller's delivery obligation. The precise distribution of functions and costs in connection with the seller's delivery of the goods would normally not cause problems where the parties have a continuing commercial relationship. They would then establish a practice between themselves ("course of dealing") which they would follow in subsequent dealing in the same manner as they have done earlier. However, if a new commercial relationship is established or if a contract is made through the medium of brokers—as is common in the sale of commodities, one would have apply the stipulations of the contract of sale and, whenever INCOTERMS 2000 have been incorporated into that contract, apply the division of functions, costs and risks following therefore.

It would, of course have been desirable if INCOTERMS could specify in as detailed a manner as possible the duties of the parties in connection with the delivery of the goods. Compared with INCOTERMS 1990, further efforts have been made in this respect in some specified instances (such as FCA A4). But it has not been possible to avoid reference to customs of the trade in FAS and FOB A4 ("in the manner customary at the port"), the reason is that particularly in commodity trade the exact manner in which the goods are delivered for carriage in FAS and FOB contracts vary in the different sea ports.

1.2.8 Passing of Risks and Costs Relating to the Goods

The risk of loss of or damage to the goods, as well as the obligation to bear the costs relating to the goods, pass from the seller to the buyer when the seller has fulfilled his obligation to deliver the goods. Since the buyer should not be giver the possibility to delay the passing of the risk and costs, all terms stipulate that the passing of risk and costs may occur even before delivery, if the buyer does not take delivery as agreed or fails to give such instructions (with respect to time for shipment and/or place for delivery) as the seller may require in order to fulfill his obligation to deliver the goods. It is a requirement for such premature passing of risk and costs that the goods have been identified as intended for the buyer or, as is stipulated in the terms, set aside for him (appropriation).

This requirement is particularly important under EXW, since under all other terms the goods would normally have been identified as intended for the buyer when measures have been taken for their shipment or dispatch ("F" and "C" terms) or their delivery at destination ("D" terms). In exceptional cases, however, the goods may have been sent from the seller in bulk without identification of the quantity for each buyer and, if so, passing of risk and cost does not occur before the goods have been appropriated as aforesaid (cf. also article 69.3 of the 1980 *United Nations Convention on Contracts for the International Sale of Goods*).

1.2.9 Terms

1. "E" Term

The "E" term is the term in which the seller's obligation is at its minimum: the seller has to do no more than place the goods at the disposal of the buyer at the agreed place, usually at the seller's own premises. On the other hand, as a matter of practical reality, the seller would frequently assist the buyer in loading the goods on the latter's collecting vehicle. Although EXW would better reflect this if the seller's obligations were to be extended so as to include loading, it was thought desirable to retain the traditional principle of the seller's minimum obligation under EXW so that it could be used for cases where the seller does not wish to assume any obligation whatsoever with respect to the loading of the goods. If the buyer wants the seller to do more, this should be made clearly in the contract of sale.

2. "F" Term

The "F" term requires the seller to deliver the goods for carriage as instructed by the buyer. The point at which the parties intend delivery to occur in the FCA term has caused difficulty because of the wide variety of circumstances which may surround contracts covered by this term. Thus, the goods may be loaded on a collecting vehicle sent by the buyer to pick them up at the seller's premises; alternatively, the goods may need to be unloaded from a vehicle sent by the seller to deliver the goods at a terminal named by the buyer. INCOTERMS 2000 take account of these alternatives by stipulating that, when the place named in the contract as the place of delivery is the seller's premises, delivery is complete when the goods are loaded on the buyer's collecting vehicle and, in other cases. Delivery is complete when the goods are placed at the disposal of the buyer not unloaded from the seller's vehicle and, in other cases, delivery is complete when the goods are placed at the disposal of the buyer not unloaded from the seller's vehicle. The variations mentioned for different modes of transport in FCA A4 of INCOTERMS 1990 are not repeated in INCOTERMS 2000.

The delivery point under FOB, which is the same under CFR and CIF, has been left unchanged in INCOTERMS 2000 in spite of a considerable debate. Although the notion under FOB to deliver the goods "across the ship's rail" nowadays may seem inappropriate in many cases, it is nevertheless understood by merchants and applied in a manner which takes account of goods and the available loading facilities. It was felt that a change of the FOB-point would create unnecessary confusion, particularly with respect to sale of commodities carried by sea typically under charter parties.

Unfortunately, the word "FOB "is used by some merchants merely to indicate any point of delivery—such as "FOB factory", "FOB plant", "FOB EX seller's words" or other inland points—thereby neglecting what the abbreviation means: Free On Board. It remains the case that such use of "FOB" tends to create confusion and should be avoided.

There is an important change of FAS relating to the obligation to clear the goods for export, since it appears to be the most common practice to put this duty on the seller rather than on the buyer. In order to ensure that this change is duly noted it has been marked with capital letters in the preamble of FAS.

3. "C" Term

The "C" term requires the seller to contract for carriage on usual terms at his own expense. Therefore, a point up to which he would have to pay transport costs must necessarily be indicated after the respective "C" term. Under the CIF and CIP terms the seller also has to take out insurance and bear the insurance cost. Since the point for the division of costs is fixed at a point in the country of destination, the "C" term is frequently mistakenly believed to be arrival contracts, in which the seller would bear all risks and costs until the goods have actually arrived at the agreed point. However, it must be stressed that the "C" term is of the same nature as the "F" term in that the seller fulfils the contract in the country of shipment or dispatch. Thus, the contracts of sale under the "C" term, like the contracts under the "F" term, fall within the category of shipment contracts.

It is in the nature of shipment contracts that, while the seller is bound to pay the normal transport cost for the carriage of the goods by a usual route and in a customary manner to the agreed place, the risk of loss of or damage to the goods, as well as additional costs resulting from events occurring after the goods having been appropriately delivered for carriage, fall upon the buyer. Hence, the "C" term is distinguishable from all other terms in that they contain two "critical" points, one indicating the point to which the seller is bound to arrange and bear the costs of a contract of carriage and another and for the allocation of risk. For this reason, the greatest caution must be observed when adding obligations of the seller to "C" term which seeks to extend the seller's responsibility beyond the aforementioned "critical" point for the allocation of risk. It is of the very essence of the "C" term that the seller is relieved of any further risk and cost after he has duly fulfilled his contract by contracting for carriage and handing over the goods to the carrier and by providing for insurance under the CIF and CIP terms.

The essential nature of the "C" term as shipment contract is also illustrated by the common use of documentary credits as the preferred mode of payment used in such terms. Where it is agreed by the parties to the sale contract that the seller will be paid by presenting the agreed shipping documents to a bank under a documentary credit, it would be quite contrary to the central purpose of the documentary credit for the seller to bear further risks and costs after the moment when payment had been made under documentary credits or otherwise upon shipment and dispatch of the goods. Of course, the seller would have to bear the cost of the contract of carriage irrespective of whether freight is per-paid upon shipment or is payable at destination (freight collect); however, additional costs which may result from events occurring subsequent to shipment and dispatch are necessarily for the account of the buyer.

If the seller has to provide a contract of carriage which involves payment of duties, taxes and other charges, such costs will, of course, fall upon the seller to the extent that they are for his account under that contract. This is now explicitly set forth in the A6 clause of all "C" term.

If it is customary to procure several contracts of carriage involving transshipment of the goods at intermediate places in order to reach the agreed destination, the seller would have to pay all these costs, including any costs incurred when the goods are transshipped from one means of conveyance to the other. If, however, the carrier exercised his rights under a transshipment—or similar clause—in order to avoid unexpected hindrances (such as ice, congestion, labor disturbances, government orders, war or warlike operations) then any additional cost resulting therefore would be for the account of the buyer, since the seller's obligation is limited to procuring the usual contract of carriage.

It happens quite often that the parties to the contract of sale wish to clarify the extent to which the seller should procure a contract of carriage including the costs of discharge. Since such costs are normally covered by the freight when the goods are carried by regular shipping lines, the contract of sale will frequently stipulate that the goods are to be so carried or at least that they are to be carried under "line terms". In other cases, the word "landed" is added after CFR or CIF. However, it is advisable not to use abbreviations added to the "C" term unless, in the relevant trade, the meaning of the abbreviations is clearly understood and accepted by the contracting parties or under any applicable law or custom of the trade.

In particular, the seller should not and indeed could not, (without changing the very nature of the "C" term) undertakes any obligation with respect to the arrival of the goods at destination, since the risk of any delay during the carriage is borne by the buyer. Thus, any obligation with respect to time must necessarily refer to the place of shipment or dispatch, for example, "shipment (dispatch) not later than ...". An agreement for example, "CFR Hamburg not later than ..." is really a misnomer and thus open to different possible interpretations. The parties could be taken to have meant either that the goods must actually arrive at Hamburg at the specified date, in which case the contract is not a shipment contract but an arrival contract or, alternatively, that the seller must ship the goods at such a time that they would normally arrive at Hamburg before the specified date unless the carriage would have been delayed because of unforeseen events.

It happens in commodity trades that goods are bought while they are at sea and that, in such cases, the word "afloat" is added after the trade term. Since the risk of loss of or damage to the goods would then, under the CFR and CIF terms, have passed from the seller to the buyer, difficulties of interpretation might arise. One possibility would be to maintain the ordinary meaning of the CFR and CIF terms with respect to the allocation of risk between seller and buyer, namely that risk passes on shipment. This would mean that the buyer might have to assume the consequences of events having already occurred at the time when the contract of sale enters into force. The other possibility would be to let the passing of the risk coincide with the time when the contract of sale is concluded. The former possibility might well be practical, since it is usually impossible to ascertain the condition of the goods while they are being carried. For this reason the 1980 United Nations Convention on Contracts for the International Sale of Goods article 68 stipulates that "if the circumstances so indicate, the risk is assumed by the buyer from the time the goods were handed over to the carrier who issued the documents embodying the contract of carriage". There is, however, an exception to this rule when "the seller knew or ought to have known that the goods had been lost or damaged and did not disclose this to the buyer". Thus, the interpretation of a CFR or CIF term with the addition of the word "afloat" will depend upon the law applicable to the contract of sale. The parties are advised to ascertain the applicable law and any solution which might follow therefore. In case of doubt, the parties are advised to clarify the matter in their contract.

In practice, the parties frequently continue to use the traditional expression C&F (or C and F, C + F). Nevertheless, in most cases it would appear that they regard these expressions as equivalent to CFR. In order to avoid difficulties of interpreting their contract the parties should use the correct INCOTERMS which is CFR, the only world-wide-accepted standard abbreviation for the term "Cost and Freight (... name port of destination)".

CFR and CIF in A8 of INCOTERMS 1990 obliged the seller to provide a copy of the charter party whenever his transport document (usually the bill of lading) contained a reference to the charter party, for example, by the frequent notation "all other terms and conditions as per charter party". Although, of course, a contracting party should always be able to ascertain all terms of his contract preferably at the time of the conclusion of the contract, it appears that the practice to provide the charter party as aforesaid has created problems particularly in connection with documentary credit transactions. The obligation of the seller under CFR and CIF to provide a copy of the charter party together with other transport documents has been deleted in INCOTERMS 2000.

Although the A8 clauses of INCOTERMS seek to ensure that the seller provides the buyer with "proof of delivery", it should be stressed that the seller fulfils that requirement when he provides the "usual" proof. Under CFR and CIF it would be the "usual transport document" and a bill of lading or a sea waybill. The transport documents must be "clean", meaning that they must not contain clauses or notations expressly declaring a declaring a defective condition of the goods and/or the packaging. Of such clauses or notations appear in the document, it is regarded as "unclean" and would then not be accepted by banks in documentary credit transactions. However, it should be noted that a transport document even without such clauses or notations would usually not provide the buyer with incontrovertible proof as against the carrier that the goods were shipped in conformity with the stipulations of the contract of sale. Usually, the carrier would, in standardized text on the front page of the transport document, refuse to accept responsibility for information with respect to the goods by indicating that the particulars inserted in the transport document constitute the shipper's declarations and therefore that the information is only "said to be" as inserted in the document. Under most applicable laws and principles, the carrier must at least use reasonable means of checking the correctness of the information and his failure to do so may make him liable to the consignee. However, in container trade, the carrier's means of checking the contents in the container would not exist unless he himself was responsible for stowing the container.

There are only two terms which deal with insurance, namely CIF and CIP. Under these terms the seller is obliged to procure insurance for the benefit of the buyer. In other cases it is for the parties themselves to decide whether and to what extent they want to cover themselves by insurance. Since the seller takes out insurance for the benefit of the buyer, he would not know the buyer's precise requirements. Under the *Institute Cargo Clauses* drafted by the Institute of London Underwriters, insurance is available in "minimum cover" under Clause C, "medium cover" under Clause B and "most extended cover" under Clause A. Since in the sale of commodities under the CIF term the buyer may wish to sell the goods again, it is impossible to know the insurance cover suitable to such subsequent buyers and, therefore, the minimum cover under CIF has traditionally been chosen with the possibility for the buyer to require the seller to take out additional insurance. Minimum cover is however unsuitable for sale of manufactured goods where the risk of theft, pilferage or improper handling or custody of the goods would require more than the cover available under Clause C. Since CIP, as distinguished from CIF, would normally not be used for the sale of commodities, it would have been feasible to adopt the most extended cover under CIP rather than minimum cover under CIF. But to vary the seller's insurance obligation under CIF would lead to confusion and both terms therefore limit the seller's insurance obligation to the minimum cover . It is particularly important for the CIP-buyer to observe this: should additional cover be required, he should agree with the seller that the latter could take out additional insurance or, alternatively, arrange for extended insurance cover himself. There are also particular instances where the buyer may wish to obtain even more protection than is available under Institute Clause A, for example, insurance against war, riots, civil commotion, strikes or other labor disturbances. If he wishes the seller to arrange such insurance he must instruct him accordingly, in which case the seller would have to provide such insurance if procurable.

4. "D" Term

The "D" term is different in nature from the "C" terms, since the seller according to the "D" terms is responsible for the arrival of the goods at the agreed place or point of destination at the border or within the county of import. The seller must bear all risks and costs in bringing the goods thereto. Hence, the "D" term signifies arrival contracts, while the "C" terms evidence departure (shipment) contracts.

Under the "D" term except DDP the seller dose not have to deliver the goods cleared for import in the country of destination. Traditionally, the seller had the obligation to clear the goods for import under DEQ, since the goods had to be landed on the quay and thus were brought into the county of import. But owing to changes in customs clearance procedures in most countries, it is now more appropriate that the party domiciled in the country concerned undertakes the clearance and pays the duties and other charges. Thus, a change in DEQ has been made for the sane reason as the change in FAS previously mentioned. As in FAS, in DEQ the change has been marked with capital letter in the preamble.

It appears that in many countries trade terms not included in INCOTERMS are used particularly in railway traffic. However, under such terms it is normally not intended that the seller should assume the risk of or damage to goods circumstances to use CPT indicating the border. If, on the other hand, the parties intend that the seller should bear the risk during the transport DAF indicating the border would be appropriate.

The DDU term was added in the 1990 version of INCOTERMS. The term fulfils an important function whenever the seller is prepared to deliver the goods in the country of destination without clearing the goods for import and paying the duty. In countries where import clearance may be difficult and time consuming, it may be risky for the seller to undertake an obligation to deliver the goods beyond the customs clearance point. Although, according to DDU B5 and B6, the buyer would have to bear the additional risks and costs which might follow from his failure to fulfill his obligations to clear the goods for import, the seller is advised not to use the DDU term in countries where difficulties might be expected in clearing the goods for import.

1.2.10 Expression "No Obligation"

As appears from the expressions "the seller must" and "the buyer must" INCOTERMS are only concerned with the obligations which the parties owe to each other. The words "no obligation" have therefore been inserted whenever one party does not owe an obligation to the other party. Thus, if for instance according to A3 of the respective term the seller has to arrange and pay for the contract of carriage we find the words "no obligation" under the heading "contract of carriage" in B3 setting forth the buyer's position. Again, where neither party owes the other an obligation, the words "no obligation" will appear with respect to both parties, for example, with respect to insurance.

In either case, it is important to point out that even though one party may be under "no obligation" towards the other to perform a certain task, this does not mean that it is not in his interest to perform that task. Thus, for example, just because a CFR buyer owes his seller no duty to make a contract of insurance under B4, it is clearly in his interest to make such a contract, the seller being under no such obligation to procure insurance cover under A4.

1.2.11 Variants of INCOTERMS

In practice, it frequently happens that the parties themselves by adding words to an INCOTERMS seek further precision than the term could offer. It should be underlined that INCOTERMS give no guidance whatsoever for such additions. Thus, if the parties cannot rely on a well-established custom of the trade for the interpretation of such additions they may encounter serious problems when no consistent understanding of the additions could be proven.

If for instance the common expressions "FOB stowed" or "EXW loaded" are used, it is impossible to establish a world-wide understanding to the effect that the seller's obligations are extended not only with respect to the cost of actually loading the goods in the ship or on the vehicle respectively but also include the risk of fortuitous loss of or damage to the goods in the process of stowage and loading. For these reasons, the parties are strongly advised to clarify whether they only mean that the function or the cost of the stowage and loading operations should fall upon the seller or whether he should also bear the risk until the stowage and loading has actually been completed. These are questions to which INCOTERMS do not provide an answer. Consequently, if the contract too fails expressly to describe the parties' intentions, the parties may be put into much unnecessary trouble and cost.

Although INCOTERMS 2000 do not provide for many of these commonly used variants, the preambles to certain trade terms do alert the parties to the need for special contractual terms if the parties wish to go beyond the stipulations of INCOTERMS.

EXW	the added obligation for the seller to load the goods no the buyer's collecting vehicle.
CIF/CIP	the buyer's need for additional insurance.
DEQ	the added obligation for the seller to pay for costs after discharge.

In some cases sellers and buyers refer to commercial practice in liner and charter party trade. In these circumstances, it is necessary to clearly distinguish between the obligations of the parties under the contract of carriage and their obligations to each other under the contract of sale. Unfortunately, there are no authoritative definitions of expressions such as "liner terms" and "terminal handling charges". Distribution of costs under such terms may differ in different places and change from time to time. The parties are recommended to clarify in the contract of sale how such costs should be distributed between themselves.

Expressions frequently used in charter parties, such as "FOB stowed", "FOB stowed and trimmed", are sometimes used in contracts of sale in order to clarify to what extent the seller under FOB has to perform stowage and trimming of the goods onboard the ship. Where such words are added, it is necessary to clarify in the contract of sale whether the added obligations only relate to costs or to both costs and risks.

As has been said, every effort has been made to ensure that INCOTERMS reflect the most common commercial practice. However in some cases particularly where INCOTERMS 2000 differ from INCOTERMS 1990, the parties may wish the trade terms to operate differently. They are reminded of such options in the preamble of the terms signaled by the word "However".

1.2.12 Customs of the Port or Particular Trade

Since INCOTERMS provide a set of terms for use in different trades and regions, it is impossible always to set forth the obligations of the parties with precision. To some extent it is therefore necessary to refer to the custom of the port or of the particular trade or to the practices which the parties themselves may have established in their previous dealings (c. g. article 9 of the 1980 United Nations Convention on Contracts for the International Sale of Goods). It is of course desirable that sellers and buyers keep themselves duly informed of such customs when they negotiate their contract and that, whenever uncertainty arises, they clarify their legal position by appropriate clauses in their contract of sale. Such special provisions in the individual contract would supersede or vary anything that is set forth as a rule of interpretation in the various INCOTERMS.

1.2.13 The Buyer's Options as to the Place of Shipment

In some situations, it may not be possible at the time when the contract of sale is entered into to decide precisely on the exact point or even the place where the goods should be delivered by the seller for carriage. For instance, reference might have been made at this stage merely to a "range" or to a rather large place, for example, seaport, and it is then usually stipulate that the buyer has the right or duty to name later on the more precise point within the range or the place. If the buyer has a duty to name the precise point as aforesaid his failure to do so might result in liability to bear the risks and additional costs resulting from such failure (B5/B7 of all terms). In addition, the buyer's failure to use his right to indicate the point may give the seller the right to select the point which best suits his purpose (FCA A4).

1.2.14 Customs Clearance

The term "customs clearance" has given rise to misunderstandings. Thus, whenever reference is made to an obligation of the seller or the buyer to undertake obligations in connection with passing the goods through customs of the country of export or import it is now made clear that this obligation does not only include the payment of duty and other charges but also the performance and payment of whatever administrative matters are connected with the passing of the goods through customs and the information to the authorities in this connection. Further, it has although quite wrongfully been considered in some quarters inappropriate to use terms dealing with the obligation to clear the goods through customs when, as in intra European Union trade or other free trade areas, there is no longer any obligation to pay duty and no restrictions relating to import or export. In order to clarify the situation, the words "where applicable" have been added in the A2 and B2, A6 and B6 clauses of the relevant INCOTERMS in order for them to be used without any ambiguity where no customs procedures are required.

It is normally desirable that customs clearance is arranged by the party domiciled in the country where such clearance should take place or at least by somebody acting there on his behalf. Thus, the exporter should normally clear the goods for export, while the importer should clear the goods for import.

INCOTERMS 1990 departed from this under the trade terms EXW and FAS (export clearance duty on the buyer) and DEQ (import clearance duty on the seller) but in INCOTERMS 2000 FAS and DEQ place the duty of clearing the goods for export on the seller and to clear them for import on the buyer respectively, while EXW representing the seller's minimum obligation has been left unchanged (export clearance duty on the buyer). Under DDP the seller specifically agrees to do what follows from the very name of the term Delivered Duty Paid namely to clear the goods for import and pay any duty as a consequence thereof.

1.2.15 Packing

In most cases, the parties would know beforehand which packaging is required for the safe carriage of the goods to destination. However, since the seller's obligation to pack the goods may well vary according to the type and duration of the transport envisaged, it has been felt necessary to stipulate that the seller is obliged to pack the goods in such a manner as is required for the transport, but only to the extent that the circumstances relating to the transport are made known to him before the contract of sale is concluded (c. g. articles 35. 1. and 35. 2. b. of the 1980 United Nations Contracts for the International Sale of Goods where the goods ,including packaging, must be "fit for any particular purpose expressly or impliedly made known to the seller at the time of the conclusion of the contract ,except where the circumstances show that the buyer did not rely , or that it was unreasonable for him to rely ,on the seller' skill and judgment").

1.2.16 Inspection of Goods

In many cases ,the buyer may be well advised to arrange for inspection of the goods before or at the time they are handed over by the seller for carriage (so-called pre-shipment inspection or PSI). Unless the contract stipulates, otherwise the buyer would himself have to pay the cost for such inspection that is arranged in his own interest. However, if the inspection has been made in order to enable the seller to comply with any mandatory rules applicable to the export of the goods in his own country, the seller would have to pay for that inspection, unless the EXW term is used, in which case the costs of such inspection are for the account of the buyer.

1.2.17 Mode of Transport and the Appropriate INCOTERMS 2000

Table 1.2 Mode of Transport and the Appropriate INCOTERMS 2000

(1) Any Mode of Transport

Group E		
	EXM	Ex Works (... named place)
Group F		
	FCA	Free Carrier (... named place)
Group C		
	CPT	Carriage Paid To (... named place of destination)
	CIP	Carriage and Insurance Paid To (... named place of destination)

Group D		
	DAF	Delivered At Frontier (... named place)
	DDU	Delivered Duty Unpaid (... named place of destination)
	DDP	Delivered Duty Paid (... named place of destination)
		(2) Maritime and Inland Waterway Transport Only
Group F		
	FAS	Free Alongside Ship (... named port of shipment)
	FOB	Free On Board (... named port of shipment)
Group C		
	CFR	Cost and Freight (... named port of destination)
	CIF	Cost, Insurance and Freight (... named port of destination)
Group D		
	DES	Delivered Ex Ship (... named port of destination)
	DEQ	Delivered Ex Quay (... named port of destination)

1.2.18 The Recommended Use

In some cases the preamble recommends the use or non-use of a particular term, this is particularly important with respect to the choice between FCA and FOB. Regrettably, merchants continue to use FOB when it is totally out of place thereby causing the seller to incur risks subsequent to the handing over of the goods to the carrier named by the buyer. FOB is only appropriate to use where the goods are intended to be delivered "across the ship's rail" or, in any event, to the ship and not where the goods are handed over to the carrier for subsequent entry into the ship, for example stowed in containers or loaded on lorries or wagons in so called roll on roll off traffic. Thus, a strong warning has been made in the preamble of FOB that the term should not be used when the parties do not intend delivery across the ship's rail.

It happens that the parties by mistake use terms intended for carriage of goods by sea also when another mode of transport is contemplated. This may put the seller in the unfortunate position that he cannot fulfill his obligation to tender the proper document to the buyer (such as a bill of lading, sea waybill or the electronic equivalent). The chart printed above makes clear which trade term in INCOTERMS 2000 it is appropriate to use for which mode of transport. Also, it is indicated in the preamble of each term whether it can be used for all modes of transport or only for carriage of foods by sea.

1.2.19 Bill of Lading and Electronic Commerce

Traditionally, the on board bill of lading has been the only acceptable document to be presented by the seller under the CFR and CIF term. The bill of lading fulfils three important functions, namely:

(1) proof of delivery of the foods on board the vessel;

(2) evidence of the contract of carriage;

(3) means of transferring rights to the goods in transit to another party the transfer of the paper document to him.

Transport documents other than the bill of lading would fulfill the two first mentioned functions, but would not control the delivery of the goods at destination or enable a buyer to sell the goods in transit by surrendering the paper document to his buyer. Instead, other transport documents would name the party entitled to receive the goods at destination. The fact that the possession of the bill of lading is required in order to obtain the foods from the carrier at destination makes it particularly difficult to replace by electronic means of communication.

Further, it is customary to issue bills of lading in several originals but it is, of course, of vital importance for a buyer or a bank acting upon his instructions in paying the seller to ensures that all originals are surrendered by the seller (so-called "full set"). This is also a requirement under the ICC Rules for Documentary Credits (the so-called ICC Uniform Customs and Practice, "UCP"; current version at date of publication of INCOTERMS 2000: ICC publication 500).

The transport document must evidence not only delivery of the goods to the carrier but also that the goods, as far as could be ascertained by the carrier, were received in good order and condition. Any notation on the transport document which would indicate that the goods had not been in such condition would make the document "unclean" and would thus make it unacceptable under the UCP.

In spite of the particular legal nature of the bill of lading it is expected that it will be replaced by electronic means in the near future. The 1990 version of INCOTERMS had already taken this expected development into proper account. According to the A8 clauses, paper documents may be replaced by electronic messages provided the parties have agreed to communicate electronically. Such messages could be transmitted directly to the parties concerned or though a third party providing added-value services. One such service that can be usefully provided by a third party is registration of successive holders of a bill of lading. Systems providing such service, such as the so-called BOLERO service, may require further support by appropriate legal norms and principles as evidenced by the CMI 1990 Rules for Electronic Bills of Lading and articles 16—17 of the 1996 UNCITRAL Model Law on Electronic Commerce.

1.2.20 Non-negotiable Transport Documents Instead of Bills of Lading

In recent years, a considerable simplification of documentary practices has been achieved. Bills of lading are frequently replaced by non-negotiable documents similar to those which are used for other modes of transport than carriage by sea. These documents are called "sea waybills", "liner waybills", "freight receipts", or variants of such expressions. Non-negotiable documents are quite satisfactory to use except where the buyer wishes to sell the goods in transit by surrendering a paper document to the new buyer. In order to make this possible, the obligation of the seller to provide a bill of lading under CFR and CIF must necessarily be retained. However, when the contracting parties known that the buyer does not contemplate selling the goods in transit, they may specifically agree to relieve the seller from the obligation to provide a bill of lading, or, alternatively, they may use CPT and CIP where there is no requirement to provide a bill of lading.

1.2.21 Right to Give Instruction to the Carrier

A buyer paying for the goods under a "C" term should ensure that the seller upon payment is prevented from disposing of the goods by giving new instructions to the carrier. Some transport documents used for particular modes of transport (air, road or rail) offer the contracting parties a possibility to bar the seller from giving such new instructions to the carrier by providing the buyer with a particular original or duplicate of the waybill. However, the documents used instead of bills of lading for maritime carriage do not normally contain such a barring function. The Comity International has remedied this shortcoming of the above-mentioned documents by introducing the 1990 "*Uniform Rules for Sea Waybills*" enabling the parties to insert a "no-disposal" clause whereby the seller surrenders the right to dispose of the goods by instructions to the carrier to deliver the goods to somebody else or at another place than stipulated in the waybill.

1.2.22 ICC Arbitration

Contracting parties who wish to have the possibility of resorting to ICC Arbitration in the event of a dispute with their contract or, in the event that no single contractual document between them. The fact of incorporating one or more INCOTERMS in a contract or the related correspondence does NOT by itself constitute an agreement to have resort to ICC Arbitration.

The following standard arbitration clause is recommended by ICC.

"All disputes arising out of or in connection with the present contract shall be finally settled under the rules of Arbitration of the International Chamber of Commerce by one or more arbitrators appointed in accordance with the said Rules."

1.3 INCOTERMS 2010

RULES FOR ANY MODE OR MODES OF TRANSPORT

1.3.1 EX WORKS

EXW (... named place of delivery)

This rule may be used irrespective of the mode of transport selected and may also be used where more than one mode of transport is employed. It is suitable for domestic trade, while FCA is usually more appropriate for international trade.

"Ex Works" means that the seller delivers when it places the goods at the disposal of the buyer at the seller's premises or at another named place (i. e., works, factory, warehouse, etc.). The seller does not need to load the goods on any collecting vehicle, nor does it need to clear the goods for export, where such clearance is applicable.

The parties are well advised to specify as clearly as possible the point within the named place of delivery, as the costs and risks to that point are for the account of the seller. The buyer bears all costs and risks involved in taking the goods from the agreed point, if any, at the named place of delivery.

EXW represents the minimum obligation for the seller. The rule should be used with care as:

(1) The seller has no obligation to the buyer to load the goods, even though in practice the seller may be in a better position to do so. If the seller does load the goods, it does so at the buyer's risk and expense. In cases where the seller is in a better position to load the goods, FCA, which obliges the seller to do so at its own risk and expense, is usually more appropriate.

(2) A buyer who buys from a seller on an EXW basis for export needs to be aware that the seller has an obligation to provide only such assistance as the buyer may require to effect that export: the seller is not bound to organize the export clearance. Buyers are therefore well advised not to use EXW if they cannot directly or indirectly obtain export clearance.

A THE SELLER'S OBLIGATIONS

A1 General obligations of the seller

The seller must provide the goods and the commercial invoice in conformity with the contract of sale and any other evidence of conformity that may be required by the contract.

A2 Licences and other formalities

Where applicable, the seller must provide the buyer, at the buyer's request, risk and expense, assistance in obtaining any export licence, or other official authorization necessary for the export of the goods.

A3 Contracts of carriage and insurance

(1) Contract of carriage

The seller has no obligation to make a contract of carriage.

(2) Contract of insurance

The seller has no obligation to make a contract of insurance. However, the seller must provide the buyer, at the buyer's request, risk and expense, with information that the buyer needs for obtaining insurance.

A4 Delivery

The seller must deliver the goods by placing them at the disposal of the buyer at the agreed point, if any, at the named place of delivery, not loaded on any collecting vehicle. If no specific point has been agreed within the named place of delivery, and if there are several points available, the seller may select the point that best suits its purpose. The seller must deliver the goods on the agreed date or within the agreed period.

A5 Transfer of risks

The seller bears all risks of loss of or damage to the goods until they have been delivered in accordance with A4 with the exception of loss or damage in the circumstances described in B5.

A6 Allocation of costs

The seller must pay all costs relating to the goods until they have been delivered in accordance with A4, other than those payable by the buyer as envisaged in B6.

A7 Notices to the buyer

The seller must give the buyer any notice needed to enable the buyer to take delivery of the goods.

A8 Delivery document

The seller has no obligation to the buyer.

A9 Checking-packaging-marking

The seller must pay the costs of those checking operations (such as checking quality, measuring, weighing, counting).

The seller must, at its own expense, package the goods, unless it is usual for the particular trade to transport the type of goods sold unpackaged. Packaging is to be marked appropriately.

A10 Other Obligations

The seller must, where applicable, in a timely manner, provide to or render assistance in obtaining for the buyer, at the buyer's request, risk and expense, any documents and information, including security-related information, that the buyer needs for the export and/or import of the goods and/or for their transport to the final destination.

B THE BUYER'S OBLIGATIONS

B1 General obligations of the buyer

The buyer must pay the price of the goods as provided in the contract of sale.

B2 Licences and other formalities

Where applicable, it is up to the buyer to obtain, at its own risk and expense, any export and import licence or other official authorization and carry out all customs formalities for the export of the goods.

B3 Contracts of carriage and insurance

(1) Contract of carriage

The buyer has obligation to make a contract of carriage.

(2) Contract of insurance

The buyer has obligation to make a contract of insurance.

B4 Taking delivery

The buyer must take delivery of the goods when A4 and A7 have been complied with.

B5 Transfer of risks

The buyer bears all risks of loss of or damage to the goods from the time they have been delivered as envisaged in A4. If the buyer fails to give notice in accordance with B7, then the buyer bears all risks of loss of or damage to the goods from the agreed date or the expiry date of the agreed period for delivery, provided that the goods have been clearly identified as the contract goods.

B6 Allocation of costs

The buyer must:

(1) Pay all costs relating to the goods from the time they have been delivered as envisaged in A4;

(2) Pay any additional costs incurred by failing either to take delivery of the goods when they have been placed at its disposal or to give appropriate notice in accordance with B7, provided that

the goods have been clearly identified as the contract goods;

(3) Pay, where applicable, all duties, taxes and other charges, as well as the costs of carrying out customs formalities payable upon export;

(4) Reimburse all costs and charges incurred by the seller in providing assistance as envisaged in A2.

B7 Notices to the seller

The buyer must, whenever it is entitled to determine the time within an agreed period and/or the point of taking delivery within the named place, give the seller sufficient notice thereof.

B8 Proof of delivery

The buyer must provide the seller with appropriate evidence of having taken delivery.

B9 Inspection of goods

The buyer must pay the costs of any mandatory pre-shipment inspection, including inspection mandated by the authorities of the country of export.

B10 Other Obligations

The buyer must reimburse the seller for all costs and charges incurred by the seller in providing or rendering assistance in obtaining documents and information as envisaged in A10.

1.3.2 Free Carrier

FCA (... named place of delivery)

This rule may be used irrespective of the mode of transport selected and may also be used where more than one mode of transport is employed.

"Free Carrier" means that the seller delivers the goods to the carrier or another person nominated by the buyer at the seller's premises or another named place. The parties are well advised to specify as clearly as possible the point within the named place of delivery, as the risk passes to the buyer at that point. FCA requires the seller to clear the goods for export, where applicable. However, the seller has no obligation to clear the goods for import, pay any import duty or carry out any import customs formalities.

A THE SELLER'S OBLIGATIONS

A1 General obligations of the seller

The seller must provide the goods and the commercial invoice in conformity with the contract of sale and any other evidence of conformity that may be required by the contract.

A2 Licences and other formalities

Where applicable, the seller must obtain, at its own risk and expense, any export licence or other official authorization and carry out all customs formalities necessary for the export of the goods.

A3 Contracts of carriage and insurance

(1) Contract of carriage

The seller has no obligation to make a contract of carriage. However, if requested by the buyer or if it is commercial practice and the buyer does not give an instruction to the contrary in due time, the seller may contract for carriage on usual terms at the buyer's risk and expense. In either case, the seller may decline to make the contract of carriage and, if it does, shall promptly notify the buyer.

(2) Contract of insurance

The seller has no obligation to make a contract of insurance. However, the seller must provide the buyer, at the buyer's request, risk, and expense, with information that the buyer needs for obtaining insurance.

A4 Delivery

The seller must deliver the goods to the carrier or another person nominated by the buyer at the agreed point, if any, at the named place on the agreed date or within the agreed period.

Delivery is completed:

(1) If the named place is the seller's premises, when the goods have been loaded on the means of transport provided by the buyer.

(2) In any other case, when the goods are placed at the disposal of the carrier or another person nominated by the buyer on the seller's means of transport ready for unloading.

If no specific point has been notified by the buyer within the named place of delivery, and if there are several points available, the seller may select the point that best suits its purpose.

A5 Transfer of risks

The seller bears all risks of loss of or damage to the goods until they have been delivered in accordance with A4, with the exception of loss or damage in the circumstances described in B5.

A6 Allocation of costs

The seller must pay:

(1) All costs relating to the goods until they have been delivered in accordance with A4, other than those payable by the buyer as envisaged in B6.

(2) Where applicable, the costs of customs formalities necessary for export, as well as all duties, taxes, and other charges payable upon export.

A7 Notices to the buyer

The seller must, at the buyer's risk and expense, give the buyer sufficient notice either that the goods have been delivered in accordance with A4 or that the carrier or another person nominated by the buyer has failed to take the goods within the time agreed.

A8 Delivery document

The seller must provide the buyer, at the seller's expense, with the usual proof that the goods have been delivered in accordance with A4.

The seller must provide assistance to the buyer, at the buyer's request, risk and expense, in obtaining a transport document.

A9 Checking-packaging-marking

The seller must pay the costs of those checking operations (such as checking quality, measuring, weighing, counting) that are necessary for the purpose of delivering the goods in accordance with A4, as well as the costs of any pre-shipment inspection mandated by the authority of the country of export.

The seller must, at its own expense, package the goods, unless it is usual for the particular trade to transport the type of goods sold unpackaged. The seller may package the goods in the manner appropriate for their transport, unless the buyer has notified the seller of specific packaging requirements before the contract of sale is concluded. Packaging is to be marked appropriately.

A10 Other Obligations

The seller must, where applicable, in a timely manner, provide to or render assistance in obtaining for the buyer, at the buyer's request, risk and expense, any documents and information, including security-related information, that the buyer needs for the import of the goods and/or for their transport to the final destination.

B THE BUYER'S OBLIGATIONS

B1 General obligations of the buyer

The buyer must pay the price of the goods as provided in the contract of sale.

B2 Licences and other formalities

Where applicable, it is up to the buyer to obtain, at its own risk and expense, any import licence or other official authorization and carry out all customs formalities for the import of the goods and for their transport through any country.

B3 Contracts of carriage and insurance

(1) Contract of carriage

The buyer must contract at its own expense for the carriage of the goods from the named place of delivery, except when the contract of carriage is made by the seller as provided for in A3 a).

(2) Contract of insurance

The buyer has obligation to make a contract of insurance.

B4 Taking delivery

The buyer must take delivery of the goods when they have been delivered as envisaged in A4.

B5 Transfer of risks

The buyer bears all risks of loss of or damage to the goods from the time they have been delivered as envisaged in A4. If the buyer fails in accordance with B7 to notify the nomination of a carrier or another person as envisaged in A4 or to give notice; or the carrier or person nominated by the buyer as envisaged in A4 fails to take the goods into its charge, then, the buyer bears all risks of loss of or damage to the goods.

B6 Allocation of costs

The buyer must pay:

(1) All costs relating to the goods from the time they have been delivered as envisaged in A4.

(2) Any additional costs incurred, either because: the buyer fails to nominate a carrier or another person, or the carrier or person nominated by the buyer as envisaged in A4 fails to take the goods into its charge, or the buyer has failed to give appropriate notice in accordance with B7, provided that the goods have been clearly identified as the contract goods.

(3) Where applicable, all duties, taxes and other charges as well as the costs of carrying out customs formalities payable upon import of the goods and the costs for their transport through any country.

B7 Notices to the seller

The buyer must notify the seller of the name of the carrier or another person nominated within sufficient time as to enable the seller to deliver the goods in accordance with that article; where necessary, the selected time within the period agreed for delivery when the carrier or person nominated will take the goods; the mode of transport to be used by the person nominated; and the point of taking delivery within the named place.

B8 Proof of delivery

The buyer must accept the proof of delivery provided as envisaged in A8.

B9 Inspection of goods

The buyer must pay the costs of any mandatory pre-shipment inspection, except when such an inspection is mandated by the authorities of the country of export.

B10 Other Obligations

The buyer must reimburse the seller for all costs and charges incurred by the seller in providing or rendering assistance in obtaining documents and information as envisaged in A10.

1.3.3 CARRIAGE PAID TO

CPT (... named place of destination)

This rule may be used irrespective of the mode of transport selected and may also be used where more than one mode of transport is employed.

"Carriage Paid To" means that the seller delivers the goods to the carrier or another person nominated by the seller at an agreed place and that the seller must contract for and pay the costs of carriage necessary to bring the goods to the named place of destination.

This rule has two critical points, because risk passes and costs are transferred at different places. The parties are well advised to identify as precisely as possible in the contract both the place of delivery, where the risk passes to the buyer, and the named place of destination to which the seller must contract for the carriage. If several carriers are used for the carriage to the agreed destination and the parties do not agree on a specific point of delivery, the default position is that risk passes when the goods have been delivered to the first carrier at a point entirely of the seller's choosing and over which the buyer has no control. Should the parties wish the risk to pass at a later stage (e. g. , at an ocean port or an airport), they need to specify this in their contract of sale. The parties are also well advised to identify as precisely as possible the point within the agreed place of destination, as the costs to that point are for the account of the seller. The seller is advised to procure contracts of carriage that match this choice precisely. If the seller incurs costs under its contract of carriage related to unloading at the named place of destination, the seller is not entitled to recover such costs from the buyer unless otherwise agreed between the parties.

CPT requires the seller to clear the goods for export, where applicable. However, the seller has no obligation to clear the goods for import, pay any import duty or carry out any import customs formalities.

A THE SELLER'S OBLIGATIONS

A1 General obligations of the seller

The seller must provide the goods and the commercial invoice in conformity with the contract of sale and any other evidence of conformity that may be required by the contract.

A2 Licences and other formalities

Where applicable, the seller must obtain, at its own risk and expense, any export licence or other official authorization and carry out all customs formalities necessary for the export of the goods, and for their transport through any country prior to delivery.

A3 Contracts of carriage and insurance

(1) Contract of carriage

The seller must contract or procure a contract for the carriage of the goods from the agreed point of delivery, if any, at the place of delivery to the named place of destination or, if agreed, any point at that place. The contract of carriage must be made on usual terms at the seller's expense and provide for carriage by the usual route and in a customary manner. If a specific point is not agreed or is not determined by practice, the seller may select the point of delivery and the point at the named place of destination that best suit its purpose.

(2) Contract of insurance

The seller has no obligation to make a contract of insurance. However, the seller must provide the buyer, at the buyer's request, with information that the buyer needs for obtaining insurance.

A4 Delivery

The seller must deliver the goods by handing them over to the carrier contracted in accordance with A3 on the agreed date or within the agreed period.

A5 Transfer of risks

The seller bears all risks of loss of or damage to the goods until they have been delivered in accordance with A4, with the exception of loss or damage in the circumstances described in B5.

A6 Allocation of costs

The seller must pay:

(1) All costs relating to the goods until they have been delivered in accordance with A4.

(2) The freight and all other costs resulting from A3 a), including the costs of loading the goods and any charges for unloading at the place of destination that were for the seller's account under the contract of carriage.

(3) Where applicable, the costs of customs formalities necessary for export, as well as all duties, taxes and other charges payable upon export, and the costs for their transport through any country that were for the seller's account under the contract of carriage.

A7 Notices to the buyer

The seller must notify the buyer that the goods have been delivered in accordance with A4.

The seller must give the buyer any notice needed in order to allow the buyer to take measures that are normally necessary to enable the buyer to take the goods.

A8 Delivery document

The seller must provide the buyer, at the seller's expense, with the usual proof that the goods have been delivered in accordance with A4.

The seller must provide assistance to the buyer, at the buyer's request, risk and expense, in obtaining a transport document.

A9 Checking-packaging-marking

The seller must pay the costs of those checking operations (such as checking quality, measuring, weighing, counting) that are necessary for the purpose of delivering the goods in accordance with A4, as well as the costs of any pre-shipment inspection mandated by the authority of the country of export. The seller must, at its own expense, package the goods, unless it is usual for the particular trade to transport the type of goods sold unpackaged. The seller may package the goods in the manner appropriate for their transport, unless the buyer has notified the seller of specific packaging requirements before the contract of sale is concluded. Packaging is to be marked appropriately.

A10 Other Obligations

The seller must, where applicable, in a timely manner, provide to or render assistance in obtaining for the buyer, at the buyer's request, any documents and information, including security-related information, that the buyer needs for the import of the goods and/or for their transport to the final destination.

B THE BUYER'S OBLIGATIONS

B1 General obligations of the buyer

The buyer must pay the price of the goods as provided in the contract of sale.

B2 Licences and other formalities

Where applicable, it is up to the buyer to obtain, at its own risk and expense, any import licence or other official authorization and carry out all customs formalities for the import of the goods and for their transport through any country.

B3 Contracts of carriage and insurance

(1) Contract of carriage

The buyer has no obligation to make a contract of carriage.

(2) Contract of insurance

The buyer has obligation to make a contract of insurance.

B4 Taking delivery

The buyer must take delivery of the goods when they have been delivered as envisaged in A4 and receive them from the carrier at the named place of destination.

B5 Transfer of risks

The buyer bears all risks of loss of or damage to the goods from the time they have been delivered as envisaged in A4. If the buyer fails to give notice in accordance with B7, it must bear all risks of loss of or damage to the goods from the agreed date or the expiry date of the agreed period for delivery, provided that the goods have been clearly identified as the contract goods.

B6 Allocation of costs

The buyer must pay:

(1) All costs relating to the goods from the time they have been delivered as envisaged in A4.

(2) All costs and charges relating to the goods while in transit until their arrival at the agreed place of destination, unless such costs and charges were for the seller's account under the contract of carriage.

(3) Unloading costs, unless such costs were for the seller's account under the contract of carriage.

(4) Any additional costs incurred if the buyer fails to give notice in accordance with B7, from the agreed date or the expiry date of the agreed period for dispatch, provided that the goods have been clearly identified as the contract goods.

(5) Where applicable, all duties, taxes and other charges, as well as the costs of carrying out customs formalities payable upon import of the goods and the costs for their transport through any country, unless included within the cost of the contract of carriage.

B7 Notices to the seller

The buyer must, whenever it is entitled to determine the time for dispatching the goods and/or the named place of destination or the point of receiving the goods within that place, give the seller sufficient notice thereof.

B8 Proof of delivery

The buyer must accept the transport document provided as envisaged in A8 if it is in conformity with the contract.

B9 Inspection of goods

The buyer must pay the costs of any mandatory pre-shipment inspection, except when such inspection is mandated by the authorities of the country of export.

B10 Other Obligations

The buyer must reimburse the seller for all costs and charges incurred by the seller in providing or rendering assistance in obtaining documents and information as envisaged in A10.

1.3.4 CARRIAGE AND INSURANCE PAID TO

CIP (... named place of destination)

This rule may be used irrespective of the mode of transport selected and may also be used where more than one mode of transport is employed.

"Carriage and Insurance Paid to" means that the seller delivers the goods to the carrier or another person nominated by the seller at an agreed place and that the seller must contract for and pay the costs of carriage necessary to bring the goods to the named place of destination.

The seller also contracts for insurance cover against the buyer's risk of loss of or damage to the goods during the carriage. The buyer should note that under CIP the seller is required to obtain insurance only on minimum cover. Should the buyer wish to have more insurance protection, it will need either to agree as much expressly with the seller or to make its own extra insurance arrangements.

This rule has two critical points, because risk passes and costs are transferred at different places. The parties are well advised to identify as precisely as possible in the contract both the place of delivery, where the risk passes to the buyer, and the named place of destination to which the seller must contract for carriage. If several carriers are used for the carriage to the agreed destination and the parties do not agree on a specific point of delivery, the default position is that risk passes when the goods have been delivered to the first carrier at a point entirely of the seller's choosing and over which the buyer has no control. Should the parties wish the risk to pass at a later stage (e. g. , at an ocean port or an airport), they need to specify this in their contract of sale. The parties are also well advised to identify as precisely as possible the point within the agreed place of destination, as the costs to that point are for the account of the seller. The seller is advised to procure contracts of carriage that match this choice precisely. If the seller incurs costs under its contract of carriage related to unloading at the named place of destination, the seller is not entitled to recover such costs from the buyer unless agreed between the parties.

CIP requires the seller to clear the goods for export, where applicable. However, the seller has no obligation to clear the goods for import, pay any import duty or carry out any import customs formalities.

A THE SELLER'S OBLIGATIONS

A1 General obligations of the seller

The seller must provide the goods and the commercial invoice in conformity with the contract of sale and any other evidence of conformity that may be required by the contract.

A2 Licences and other formalities

Where applicable, the seller must obtain, at its own risk and expense, any export licence or other official authorization and carry out all customs formalities necessary for the export of the goods and for their transport through any country prior to delivery.

A3 Contracts of carriage and insurance

(1) Contract of carriage

The seller must contract or procure a contract for the carriage of the goods from the agreed point of delivery, if any, at the place of delivery to the named place of destination or, if agreed, any point at that place. The contract of carriage must be made on usual terms at the seller's expense and provide for carriage by the usual route and in a customary manner. If a specific point is not agreed or is not determined by practice, the seller may select the point of delivery and the point at the named place of destination that best suit its purpose.

(2) Contract of insurance

The seller must obtain at its own expense cargo insurance and must provide the buyer with the insurance policy or other evidence of insurance cover. The insurance shall be contracted with underwriters or an insurance company of good repute and entitle the buyer, or any other person having an insurable interest in the goods, to claim directly from the insurer. The insurance shall cover, at a minimum, the price provided in the contract plus 10% (i. e., 110%) and shall be in the currency of the contract.

A4 Delivery

The seller must deliver the goods by handing them over to the carrier contracted in accordance with A3 on the agreed date or within the agreed period.

A5 Transfer of risks

The seller bears all risks of loss of or damage to the goods until they have been delivered in accordance with A4, with the exception of loss or damage in the circumstances described in B5.

A6 Allocation of costs

The seller must pay:

(1) All costs relating to the goods until they have been delivered in accordance with A4.

(2) The freight and all other costs resulting from A3 a), including the costs of loading the goods and any charges for unloading at the place of destination that were for the seller's account under the contract of carriage.

(3) The costs of insurance resulting from A3 b); where applicable, the costs of customs formalities necessary for export, as well as all duties, taxes and other charges payable upon export, and the costs for their transport through any country that were for the seller's account under the contract of carriage.

A7 Notices to the buyer

The seller must notify the buyer that the goods have been delivered in accordance with A4. The seller must give the buyer any notice needed in order to allow the buyer to take measures that are normally necessary to enable the buyer to take the goods.

A8 Delivery document

If customary or at the buyer's request, the seller must provide the buyer, at the seller's expense, with the usual transport document for the transport contracted in accordance with A3.

A9 Checking-packaging-marking

The seller must pay the costs of those checking operations (such as checking quality, measuring, weighing, counting) that are necessary for the purpose of delivering the goods in accordance with A4 as well as the costs of any pre-shipment inspection mandated by the authority of the country of export.

The seller must, at its own expense, package the goods, unless it is usual for the particular trade to transport the type of goods sold unpackaged. The seller may package the goods in the manner appropriate for their transport, unless the buyer has notified the seller of specific packaging requirements before the contract of sale is concluded. Packaging is to be marked appropriately.

A10 Other Obligations

The seller must, where applicable, in a timely manner, provide to or render assistance in obtaining for the buyer, at the buyer's request, risk and expense, any documents and information, including security-related information, that the buyer needs for the import of the goods and/or for their transport to the final destination.

B THE BUYER'S OBLIGATIONS

B1 General obligations of the buyer

The buyer must pay the price of the goods as provided in the contract of sale.

B2 Licences and other Formalities

Where applicable, it is up to the buyer to obtain, at its own risk and expense, any import licence or other official authorization and carry out all customs formalities for the import of the goods and for their transport through any country.

B3 Contracts of carriage and insurance

(1) Contract of carriage

The buyer has no obligation to make a contract of carriage.

(2) Contract of insurance

The buyer has no obligation to make a contract of insurance.

B4 Taking delivery

The buyer must take delivery of the goods when they have been delivered as envisaged in A4 and receive them from the carrier at the named place of destination.

B5 Transfer of risks

The buyer bears all risks of loss of or damage to the goods from the time they have been delivered as envisaged in A4. If the buyer fails to give notice in accordance with B7, it must bear all risks of loss of or damage to the goods from the agreed date or the expiry date of the agreed period for delivery, provided that the goods have been clearly identified as the contract goods.

B6 Allocation of costs

The buyer must, subject to the provisions of A3, pay:

(1) All costs relating to the goods from the time they have been delivered as envisaged in A4.

(2) All costs and charges relating to the goods while in transit until their arrival at the agreed place of destination, unless such costs and charges were for the seller's account under the contract of carriage.

(3) Unloading costs, unless such costs were for the seller's account under the contract of carriage.

(4) Any additional costs incurred if it fails to give notice in accordance with B7, from the agreed date or the expiry date of the agreed period for dispatch, provided that the goods have been clearly identified as the contract goods.

(5) Where applicable, all duties, taxes and other charges as well as the costs of carrying out customs formalities payable upon import of the goods and the costs for their transport through any country, unless included within the cost of the contract of carriage.

B7 Notices to the seller

The buyer must, whenever it is entitled to determine the time for dispatching the goods and/or the named place of destination or the point of receiving the goods within that place, give the seller sufficient notice thereof.

B8 Proof of delivery

The buyer must accept the transport document provided as envisaged in A8 if it is in conformity with the contract.

B9 Inspection of goods

The buyer must pay the costs of any mandatory pre-shipment inspection, except when such inspection is mandated by the authorities of the country of export.

B10 Other Obligations

The buyer must reimburse the seller for all costs and charges incurred by the seller in providing or rendering assistance in obtaining documents and information as envisaged in A10.

1.3.5 DAT

DELIVERED AT TERMINAL

DAT (... named terminal at port or place of destination)

This rule may be used irrespective of the mode of transport selected and may also be used where more than one mode of transport is employed.

"Delivered at Terminal" means that the seller delivers when the goods, once unloaded from the arriving means of transport, are placed at the disposal of the buyer at a named terminal at the named port or place of destination. "Terminal" includes any place, whether covered or not, such as a quay, warehouse, container yard or road, rail or air cargo terminal.

The seller bears all risks involved in bringing the goods to and unloading them at the terminal at the named port or place of destination. The parties are well advised to specify as clearly as possible the terminal and, if possible, a specific point within the terminal at the agreed port or place of destination, as the risks to that point are for the account of the seller. The seller is advised to procure a contract of carriage that matches this choice precisely.

Moreover, if the parties intend the seller to bear the risks and costs involved in transporting and handling the goods from the terminal to another place, then the DAP or DDP rules should be used.

DAT requires the seller to clear the goods for export, where applicable. However, the seller has no obligation to clear the goods for import, pay any import duty or carry out any import customs formalities.

A THE SELLER'S OBLIGATIONS

A1 General obligations of the seller

The seller must provide the goods and the commercial invoice in conformity with the contract of sale and any other evidence of conformity that may be required by the contract.

A2 Licences and other formalities

Where applicable, the seller must obtain, at its own risk and expense, any export licence and other official authorization and carry out all customs formalities necessary for the export of the goods and for their transport through any country prior to delivery.

A3 Contracts of carriage and insurance

(1) Contract of carriage

The seller must contract at its own expense for the carriage of the goods to the named terminal at the agreed port or place of destination. If a specific terminal is not agreed or is not determined by practice, the seller may select the terminal at the agreed port or place of destination that best suits its purpose.

(2) Contract of insurance

The seller has no obligation to make a contract of insurance. However, the seller must provide the buyer, at the buyer's request, with information that the buyer needs for obtaining insurance.

A4 Delivery

The seller must unload the goods from the arriving means of transport and must then deliver them by placing them at the disposal of the buyer at the named terminal referred to at the port or place of destination on the agreed date or within the agreed period.

A5 Transfer of risks

The seller bears all risks of loss of or damage to the goods until they have been delivered in accordance with A4 with the exception of loss or damage in the circumstances described in B5.

A6 Allocation of costs

The seller must pay:

(1) In addition to costs resulting from A3 a), all costs relating to the goods until they have been delivered in accordance with A4, other than those payable by the buyer as envisaged in B6.

(2) Where applicable, the costs of customs formalities necessary for export as well as all duties, taxes and other charges payable upon export and the costs for their transport through any country, prior to delivery in accordance with A4.

A7 Notices to the buyer

The seller must give the buyer any notice needed in order to allow the buyer to take measures that are normally necessary to enable the buyer to take delivery of the goods.

A8 Delivery document

The seller must provide the buyer, at the seller's expense, with a document enabling the buyer to take delivery of the goods.

A9 Checking-packaging-marking

The seller must pay the costs of those checking operations (such as checking quality, measuring, weighing, counting) that are necessary for the purpose of delivering the goods in accordance with A4, as well as the costs of any pre-shipment inspection mandated by the authority of the country of export. The seller must, at its own expense, package the goods, unless it is usual for the particular trade to transport the type of goods sold unpackaged. The seller may package the goods in the manner appropriate for their transport, unless the buyer has notified the seller of specific packaging requirements before the contract of sale is concluded. Packaging is to be marked appropriately.

A10 Other Obligations

The seller must, where applicable, in a timely manner, provide to or render assistance in obtaining for the buyer, at the buyer's request, risk and expense, any documents and information, including security-related information, that the buyer needs for the import of the goods and/or for their transport to the final destination.

B THE BUYER'S OBLIGATIONS

B1 General obligations of the buyer

The buyer must pay the price of the goods as provided in the contract of sale.

B2 Licences and other formalities

Where applicable, the buyer must obtain, at its own risk and expense, any import licence or other official authorization and carry out all customs formalities for the import of the goods.

B3 Contracts of carriage and insurance

(1) Contract of carriage

The buyer has no obligation to make a contract of carriage.

(2) Contract of insurance

The buyer has obligation to make a contract of insurance.

B4 Taking delivery

The buyer must take delivery of the goods when they have been delivered as envisaged in A4.

B5 Transfer of risks

The buyer bears all risks of loss of or damage to the goods from the time they have been delivered as envisaged in A4. If the buyer fails to fulfil its obligations in accordance with B7, then it bears all resulting risks of loss of or damage to the goods; or the buyer fails to give notice in accordance with B7, then it bears all risks of loss of or damage to the goods from the agreed date or the expiry date of the agreed period for delivery, provided that the goods have been clearly identified as the contract goods.

B6 Allocation of costs

The buyer must pay:

(1) All costs relating to the goods from the time they have been delivered as envisaged in A4.

(2) Any additional costs incurred by the seller if the buyer fails to fulfil its obligations in accordance with B2, provided that the goods have been clearly identified as the contract goods.

(3) Where applicable, the costs of customs formalities as well as all duties, taxes and other charges payable upon import of the goods.

B7 Notices to the seller

The buyer must, whenever it is entitled to determine the time within an agreed period and/or the point of taking delivery at the named terminal, give the seller sufficient notice thereof.

B8 Proof of delivery

The buyer must accept the delivery document provided as envisaged in A8.

B9 Inspection of goods

The buyer must pay the costs of any mandatory pre-shipment inspection, except when such inspection is mandated by the authorities of the country of export.

B10 Other Obligations

The buyer must, in a timely manner, advise the seller of any security information requirements so that the seller may comply with A10. The buyer must reimburse the seller for all costs and charges incurred by the seller in providing or rendering assistance in obtaining documents and information as envisaged in A10. The buyer must, where applicable, in a timely manner, provide to or render assistance in obtaining for the seller, at the seller's request, risk and expense, any documents and information, including security-related information, that the seller needs for the transport and export of the goods and for their transport through any country.

1.3.6 DELIVERED AT PLACE

DAP (... named place of destination)

This rule may be used irrespective of the mode of transport selected and may also be used where more than one mode of transport is employed.

"Delivered at Place" means that the seller delivers when the goods are placed at the disposal of the buyer on the arriving means of transport ready for unloading at the named place of destination. The seller bears all risks involved in bringing the goods to the named place.

The parties are well advised to specify as clearly as possible the point within the agreed place of destination, as the risks to that point are for the account of the seller. The seller is advised to procure contracts of carriage that match this choice precisely. If the seller incurs costs under its contract of carriage related to unloading at the place of destination, the seller is not entitled to recover such costs from the buyer unless otherwise agreed between the parties.

DAP requires the seller to clear the goods for export, where applicable. However, the seller has no obligation to clear the goods for import, pay any import duty or carry out any import customs formalities. If the parties wish the seller to clear the goods for import, pay any import duty and carry out any import customs formalities, the DDP term should be used.

A THE SELLER'S OBLIGATIONS

A1 General obligations of the seller

The seller must provide the goods and the commercial invoice in conformity with the contract of sale and any other evidence of conformity that may be required by the contract.

A2 Licences and other formalities

Where applicable, the seller must obtain, at its own risk and expense, any export licence and other official authorization and carry out all customs formalities necessary for the export of the goods and for their transport through any country prior to delivery.

A3 Contracts of carriage and insurance

(1) Contract of carriage

The seller must contract at its own expense for the carriage of the goods to the named place of destination or to the agreed point, if any, at the named place of destination. If a specific point is not agreed or is not determined by practice, the seller may select the point at the named place of destination that best suits its purpose.

(2) Contract of insurance

The seller has no obligation to the buyer to make a contract of insurance. However, the seller must provide the buyer, at the buyer's request, risk, and expense, with information that the buyer needs for obtaining insurance.

A4 Delivery

The seller must deliver the goods by placing them at the disposal of the buyer on the arriving means of transport ready for unloading at the agreed point, if any, at the named place of destination on the agreed date or within the agreed period.

A5 Transfer of risks

The seller bears all risks of loss of or damage to the goods until they have been delivered in accordance with A4, with the exception of loss or damage in the circumstances described in B5.

A6 Allocation of costs

The seller must pay:

(1) In addition to costs resulting from A3 a), all costs relating to the goods until they have been delivered in accordance with A4.

(2) Where applicable, the costs of customs formalities necessary for export as well as all duties, taxes and other charges payable upon export and the costs for their transport through any country, prior to delivery in accordance with A4.

A7 Notices to the buyer

The seller must give the buyer any notice needed in order to allow the buyer to take measures that are normally necessary to enable the buyer to take delivery of the goods.

A8 Delivery document

The seller must provide the buyer, at the seller's expense, with a document enabling the buyer to take delivery of the goods.

A9 Checking-packaging-marking

The seller must pay the costs of those checking operations (such as checking quality, measuring, weighing, counting) that are necessary for the purpose of delivering the goods in accordance with A4, as well as the costs of any pre-shipment inspection mandated by the authority of the country of export. The seller must, at its own expense, package the goods, unless it is usual for the particular trade to transport the type of goods sold unpackaged. The seller may package the goods in the manner appropriate for their transport, unless the buyer has notified the seller of specific packaging requirements before the contract of sale is concluded. Packaging is to be marked appropriately.

A10 Other Obligations

The seller must, where applicable, in a timely manner, provide to or render assistance in obtaining for the buyer, at the buyer's request, risk and expense, any documents and information, including security-related information, that the buyer needs for the import of the goods and/or for their transport to the final destination. The seller must reimburse the buyer for all costs and charges incurred by the buyer in providing or rendering assistance in obtaining documents and information as envisaged in B10.

B THE BUYER'S OBLIGATIONS

B1 General obligations of the buyer

The buyer must pay the price of the goods as provided in the contract of sale.

B2 Licences and other formalities

Where applicable, the buyer must obtain, at its own risk and expense, any import licence or other official authorization and carry out all customs formalities for the import of the goods.

B3 Contracts of carriage and insurance

(1) Contract of carriage

The buyer has no obligation to make a contract of carriage.

(2) Contract of insurance

The buyer has obligation to make a contract of insurance.

B4 Taking delivery

The buyer must take delivery of the goods when they have been delivered as envisaged in A4.

B5 Transfer of risks

The buyer bears all risks of loss of or damage to the goods from the time they have been delivered as envisaged in A4. If the buyer fails to give notice in accordance with B7, then it bears all risks of loss of or damage to the goods from the agreed date or the expiry date of the agreed period for delivery, provided that the goods have been clearly identified as the contract goods.

B6 Allocation of costs

The buyer must pay:

(1) All costs relating to the goods from the time they have been delivered as envisaged in A4.

(2) Any additional costs incurred by the seller if the buyer fails to fulfill its obligations in accordance with B2, provided that the goods have been clearly identified as the contract goods.

(3) Where applicable, the costs of customs formalities, as well as all duties, taxes and other charges payable upon import of the goods.

B7 Notices to the seller

The buyer must, whenever it is entitled to determine the time within an agreed period and/or the point of taking delivery within the named place of destination, give the seller sufficient notice thereof.

B8 Proof of delivery

The buyer must accept the delivery document provided as envisaged in A8.

B9 Inspection of goods

The buyer must pay the costs of any mandatory pre-shipment inspection, except when such inspection is mandated by the authorities of the country of export.

B10 Other Obligations

The buyer must, in a timely manner, advise the seller of any security information requirements so that the seller may comply with A10. The buyer must reimburse the seller for all costs and charges incurred by the seller in providing or rendering assistance in obtaining documents and information as envisaged in A10. The buyer must, where applicable, in a timely manner, provide to or render assistance in obtaining for the seller, at the seller's request, risk and expense, any documents and information, including security-related information, that the seller needs for the transport and export of the goods and for their transport through any country.

1.3.7 DELIVERED DUTY PAID

DDP (... named place of destination)

This rule may be used irrespective of the mode of transport selected and may also be used where more than one mode of transport is employed.

"Delivered Duty Paid" means that the seller delivers the goods when the goods are placed at the disposal of the buyer, cleared for import on the arriving means of transport ready for unloading at the named place of destination. The seller bears all the costs and risks involved in bringing the goods to the place of destination and has an obligation to clear the goods not only for export but also for import, to pay any duty for both export and import and to carry out all customs formalities.

DDP represents the maximum obligation for the seller. The parties are well advised to specify as clearly as possible the point within the agreed place of destination, as the costs and risks to that point are for the account of the seller. The seller is advised to procure contracts of carriage that match this choice precisely. If the seller incurs costs under its contract of carriage related to unloading at the place of destination, the seller is not entitled to recover such costs from the buyer unless otherwise agreed between the parties.

The parties are well advised not to use DDP if the seller is unable directly or indirectly to obtain import clearance.

If the parties wish the buyer to bear all risks and costs of import clearance, the DAP rule should be used.

Any VAT or other taxes payable upon import are for the seller's account unless expressly agreed otherwise in the sales contract.

A THE SELLER'S OBLIGATIONS

A1 General obligations of the seller

The seller must provide the goods and the commercial invoice in conformity with the contract of sale and any other evidence of conformity that may be required by the contract.

A2 Licences and other formalities

Where applicable, the seller must obtain, at its own risk and expense, any export and import licence and other official authorization and carry out all customs formalities necessary for the export of the goods, for their transport through any country and for their import.

A3 Contracts of carriage and insurance

(1) Contract of carriage

The seller must contract at its own expense for the carriage of the goods to the named place of destination or to the agreed point, if any, at the named place of destination. If a specific point is not agreed or is not determined by practice, the seller may select the point at the named place of destination that best suits its purpose.

(2) Contract of insurance

The seller has no obligation to make a contract of insurance. However, the seller must provide the buyer, at the buyer's request, risk, and expense, with information that the buyer needs for obtaining insurance.

A4 Delivery

The seller must deliver the goods by placing them at the disposal of the buyer on the arriving means of transport ready for unloading at the agreed point, if any, at the named place of destination on the agreed date or within the agreed period.

A5 Transfer of risks

The seller bears all risks of loss of or damage to the goods until they have been delivered in accordance with A4, with the exception of loss or damage in the circumstances described in B5.

A6 Allocation of costs

The seller must pay:

(1) In addition to costs resulting from A3 a), all costs relating to the goods until they have been delivered in accordance with A4.

(2) Where applicable, the costs of customs formalities necessary for export and import as well as all duties, taxes and other charges payable upon export and import of the goods, and the costs for their transport through any country prior to delivery in accordance with A4.

A7 Notices to the buyer

The seller must give the buyer any notice needed in order to allow the buyer to take measures that are normally necessary to enable the buyer to take delivery of the goods.

A8 Delivery document

The seller must provide the buyer, at the seller's expense, with a document enabling the buyer to take delivery of the goods as envisaged in A4/B4.

A9 Checking-packaging-marking

The seller must pay the costs of those checking operations (such as checking quality, measuring, weighing, counting) that are necessary for the purpose of delivering the goods in accordance with A4, as well as the costs of any pre-shipment inspection mandated by the authority of the country of export or of import.

The seller must, at its own expense, package the goods, unless it is usual for the particular trade to transport the type of goods sold unpackaged. The seller may package the goods in the manner appropriate for their transport, unless the buyer has notified the seller of specific packaging requirements before the contract of sale is concluded. Packaging is to be marked appropriately.

A10 Other Obligations

The seller must reimburse the buyer for all costs and charges incurred by the buyer in providing or rendering assistance in obtaining documents and information as envisaged in B10.

B THE BUYER'S OBLIGATIONS

B1 General obligations of the buyer

The buyer must pay the price of the goods as provided in the contract of sale.

B2 Licences and other formalities

Where applicable, the buyer must provide assistance to the seller, at the seller's request, risk and expense, in obtaining any import licence or other official authorization for the import of the goods.

B3 Contracts of carriage and insurance

(1) Contract of carriage

The buyer has no obligation to make a contract of carriage.

(2) Contract of insurance

The buyer has obligation to make a contract of insurance.

B4 Taking delivery

The buyer must take delivery of the goods when they have been delivered as envisaged in A4.

B5 Transfer of risks

The buyer bears all risks of loss of or damage to the goods from the time they have been delivered as envisaged in A4. If the buyer fails to fulfill its obligations in accordance with B2, then it bears all resulting risks of loss of or damage to the goods; or the buyer fails to give notice in accordance with B7, then it bears all risks of loss of or damage to the goods from the agreed date or the expiry date of the agreed period for delivery, provided that the goods have been clearly identified as the contract goods.

B6 Allocation of costs

The buyer must pay:

(1) All costs relating to the goods from the time they have been delivered as envisaged in A4.

(2) Any additional costs incurred if it fails to fulfill its obligations in accordance with B2 or to give notice in accordance with B7, provided that the goods have been clearly identified as the contract goods.

B7 Notices to the seller

The buyer must, whenever it is entitled to determine the time within an agreed period and/or the point of taking delivery within the named place of destination, give the seller sufficient notice thereof.

B8 Proof of delivery

The buyer must accept the proof of delivery provided as envisaged in A8.

B9 Inspection of goods

The buyer has no obligation to the seller to pay the costs of any mandatory pre-shipment inspection mandated by the authority of the country of export or of import.

B10 Other Obligations

The buyer must, in a timely manner, advise the seller of any security information requirements. The buyer must reimburse the seller for all costs and charges incurred by the seller in providing or rendering assistance in obtaining documents and information. The buyer must, where applicable, in a timely manner, provide to or render assistance in obtaining for the seller, at the seller's request, risk and expense, any documents and information, including security-related information, that the seller needs for the transport, export and import of the goods and for their transport through any country.

RULES FOR SEA AND IINLAND WATERWAY TRANSPORT

1.3.8 FREE ALONGSIDE SHIP

FAS (... named port of shipment)

This rule is to be used only for sea or inland waterway transport.

"Free Alongside Ship" means that the seller delivers when the goods are placed alongside the vessel (e.g., on a quay or a barge) nominated by the buyer at the named port of shipment. The risk of loss of or damage to the goods passes when the goods are alongside the ship, and the buyer bears all costs from that moment onwards. The parties are well advised to specify as clearly as possible the loading point at the named port of shipment, as the costs and risks to that point are for the account of the seller and these costs and associated handling charges may vary according to the practice of the port.

Where the goods are in containers, it is typical for the seller to hand the goods over to the carrier at a terminal and not alongside the vessel. In such situations, the FAS rule would be inappropriate, and the FCA rule should be used. FAS requires the seller to clear the goods for export, where applicable. However, the seller has no obligation to clear the goods for import, pay any import duty or carry out any import customs formalities.

A THE SELLER'S OBLIGATIONS

A1 General obligations of the seller

The seller must provide the goods and the commercial invoice in conformity with the contract of sale and any other evidence of conformity that may be required by the contract.

A2 Licences and other formalities

Where applicable, the seller must obtain, at its own risk and expense, any export licence or other official authorization and carry out all customs formalities necessary for the export of the goods.

A3 Contracts of carriage and insurance

(1) Contract of carriage

The seller has no obligation to make a contract of carriage.

(2) Contract of insurance

The seller has no obligation to make a contract of insurance. However, the seller must provide the buyer, at the buyer's request, risk, and expense (if any), with information that the buyer needs for obtaining insurance.

A4 Delivery

The seller must deliver the goods either by placing them alongside the ship nominated by the buyer at the loading point, if any, indicated by the buyer at the named port of shipment or by procuring the goods so delivered.

A5 Transfer of risks

The seller bears all risks of loss of or damage to the goods until they have been delivered with the exception of loss or damage in the circumstances described in B5.

A6 Allocation of costs

The seller must pay:

(1) All costs relating to the goods until they have been delivered in accordance with A4.

(2) Where applicable, the costs of customs formalities necessary for export as well as all duties, taxes and other charges payable upon export.

A7 Notices to the buyer

The seller must, at the buyer's risk and expense, give the buyer sufficient notice either that the goods have been delivered in accordance with A4 or that the vessel has failed to take the goods within the time agreed. the time they have been delivered as envisaged in A4. If:

(1) The buyer fails to give notice in accordance with B7.

(2) The vessel nominated by the buyer fails to arrive on time, or fails to take the goods or closes for cargo earlier than the time notified in accordance with B7; then the buyer bears all risks

of loss of or damage to the goods from the agreed date or the expiry date of the agreed period for delivery, provided that the goods have been clearly identified as the contract goods.

A8 Delivery document

The seller must provide the buyer, at the seller's expense, with the usual proof that the goods have been delivered in accordance with A4.

Unless such proof is a transport document, the seller must provide assistance to the buyer, at the buyer's request, risk and expense, in obtaining a transport document.

A9 Checking-packaging-marking

The seller must pay the costs of those checking operations (such as checking quality, measuring, weighing, counting) that are necessary for the purpose of delivering the goods in accordance with A4, as well as the costs of any pre-shipment inspection mandated by the authority of the country of export.

The seller must, at its own expense, package the goods, unless it is usual for the particular trade to transport the type of goods sold unpackaged. The seller may package the goods in the manner appropriate for their transport, unless the buyer has notified the seller of specific packaging requirements before the contract of sale is concluded. Packaging is to be marked appropriately.

A10 Other Obligations

The seller must, where applicable, in a timely manner, provide to or render assistance in obtaining for the buyer, at the buyer's request, risk and expense, any documents and information, including security-related information, that the buyer needs for the import of the goods and/or for their transport to the final destination.

B THE BUYER'S OBLIGATIONS

B1 General obligations of the buyer

The buyer must pay the price of the goods as provided in the contract of sale.

B2 Licences and other formalities

Where applicable, it is up to the buyer to obtain, at its own risk and expense, any import licence or other official authorization and carry out all customs formalities for the import of the goods and for their transport through any country.

B3 Contracts of carriage and insurance

(1) Contract of carriage

The buyer must contract, at its own expense for the carriage of the goods from the named port of shipment, except where the contract of carriage is made by the seller.

(2) Contract of insurance

The buyer has obligation make a contract of insurance.

B4 Taking delivery

The buyer must take delivery of the goods when they have been delivered as envisaged in A4.

B5 Transfer of risks

The buyer bears all risks of loss of or damage to the goods from the time they have been delivered the buyer fails to notify the nomination of a vessel in accordance with B7.

(1) The vessel nominated by the buyer fails to arrive on time to enable the seller to comply with A4, (2) is unable to take the goods, or closes for cargo earlier than the time notified in accordance with B7; then, the buyer bears all risks of loss of or damage to the goods: from the agreed date, or in the absence of an agreed date, from the date notified by the seller under A7 within the agreed period, or, if no such date has been notified, from the expiry date of any agreed period for delivery, provided that the goods have been clearly identified as the contract goods.

B6 Allocation of costs

The buyer must pay:

(1) All costs relating to the goods from the time they have been delivered as envisaged in A4.

(2) Any additional costs incurred, either because: the buyer has failed to give appropriate notice in accordance with B7, or the vessel nominated by the buyer fails to arrive on time, is unable to take the goods, or closes for cargo earlier than the time notified in accordance with B7, provided that the goods have been clearly identified as the contract goods.

(3) Where applicable, all duties, taxes and other charges, as well as the costs of carrying out customs formalities payable upon import of the goods and the costs for their transport through any country.

B7 Notices to the seller

The buyer must give the seller sufficient notice of the vessel name, loading point and, where necessary, the selected delivery time within the agreed period.

B8 Proof of delivery

The buyer must accept the proof of delivery provided as envisaged in A8.

B9 Inspection of goods

The buyer must pay the costs of any mandatory pre-shipment inspection, except when such inspection is mandated by the authorities of the country of export.

B10 Other Obligations

The buyer must reimburse the seller for all costs and charges incurred by the seller in providing or rendering assistance in obtaining documents and information as envisaged in A10.

1.3.9 FOB

FREE ON BOARD (... named port of shipment)

This rule is to be used only for sea or inland waterway transport.

"Free on Board" means that the seller delivers the goods on board the vessel nominated by the buyer at the named port of shipment or procures the goods already so delivered. The risk of loss of or damage to the goods passes when the goods are on board the vessel, and the buyer bears all costs from that moment onwards.

FOB may not be appropriate where goods are handed over to the carrier before they are on board the vessel, for example goods in containers, which are typically delivered at a terminal. In such situations, the FCA rule should be used.

FOB requires the seller to clear the goods for export, where applicable. However, the seller has no obligation to clear the goods for import, pay any import duty or carry out any import customs formalities.

A THE SELLER'S OBLIGATIONS

A1 General obligations of the seller

The seller must provide the goods and the commercial invoice in conformity with the contract of sale and any other evidence of conformity that may be required by the contract.

A2 Licences and other formalities

Where applicable, the seller must obtain, at its own risk and expense, any export licence or other official authorization and carry out all customs formalities necessary for the export of the goods.

A3 Contracts of carriage and insurance

(1) Contract of carriage

The seller has no obligation to make a contract of carriage.

(2) Contract of insurance

The seller has no obligation to make a contract of insurance. However, the seller must provide the buyer, at the buyer's request, risk, and expense, with information that the buyer needs for obtaining insurance.

A4 Delivery

The seller must deliver the goods either by placing them on board the vessel nominated by the buyer at the loading point, if any, indicated by the buyer at the named port of shipment or by procuring the goods so delivered.

A5 Transfer of risks

The seller bears all risks of loss of or damage to the goods until they have been delivered with the exception of loss or damage in the circumstances described in B5.

A6 Allocation of costs

The seller must pay:

(1) All costs relating to the goods until they have been delivered, other than those payable by the buyer.

(2) Where applicable, the costs of customs formalities necessary for export, as well as all duties, taxes and other charges payable upon export.

A7 Notices to the buyer

The seller must, at the buyer's risk and expense, give the buyer sufficient notice either that the goods have been delivered in accordance with A4 or that the vessel has failed to take the goods within the time agreed.

A8 Delivery document

The seller must provide the buyer, at the seller's expense, with the usual proof that the goods have been delivered in accordance with A4.

Unless such proof is a transport document, the seller must provide assistance to the buyer, at the buyer's request, risk and expense, in obtaining a transport document.

A9 Checking-packaging-marking

The seller must pay the costs of those checking operations (such as checking quality, measuring, weighing, counting) that are necessary for the purpose of delivering the goods in accordance withA4, as well as the costs of any pre-shipment inspection mandated by the authority of the country of export.

The seller must, at its own expense, package the goods, unless it s usual for the particular trade to transport the type of goods sold unpackaged. The seller may package the goods in the manner appropriate for their transport, unless the buyer has notified the seller of specific packaging requirements before the contract of sale is concluded. Packaging is to be marked appropriately.

A10 Other Obligations

The seller must, where applicable, in a timely manner, provide to or render assistance in obtaining for the buyer, at the buyer's request, risk and expense, any documents and information, including security-related information, that the buyer needs for the import of the goods and/or for their transport to the final destination.

B THE BUYER'S OBLIGATIONS

B1 General obligations of the buyer

The buyer must pay the price of the goods as provided in the contract of sale.

B2 Licences and other formalities

Where applicable, it is up to the buyer to obtain, at its own risk and expense, any import licence or other official authorization and carry out all customs formalities for the import of the goods and for their transport through any country.

B3 Contracts of carriage and insurance

(1) Contract of carriage

The buyer must contract, at its own expense for the carriage of the goods from the named port of shipment, except where the contract of carriage is made by the seller.

(2) Contract of insurance

The buyer has obligation to make a contract of insurance.

B4 Taking delivery

The buyer must take delivery of the goods when they have been delivered as envisaged in A4.

B5 Transfer of risks

The buyer bears all risks of loss of or damage to the goods from the time they have been delivered the buyer fails to notify the nomination of a vessel in accordance with B7. The vessel nominated by the buyer fails to arrive on time to enable the seller to comply with A4, is unable to take the goods, or closes for cargo earlier than the time notified in accordance withB7; then, the buyer bears all risks of loss of or damage to the goods: fromthe agreed date, or in the absence of an agreed date, fromthe date notified by the seller under A7 within the agreed period, or, if no such date has been notified, fromthe expiry date of any agreed period for delivery, provided that the goods have been clearly identified as the contract goods.

B6 Allocation of costs

The buyer must pay:

(1) All costs relating to the goods from the time they have been delivered.

(2) Any additional costs incurred, either because: he buyer has failed to give appropriate notice in accordance with B7, or he vessel nominated by the buyer fails to arrive on time, is unable to take the goods, or closes for cargo earlier than the time notified in accordance with B7, provided that the goods have been clearly identified as the contract goods; and

(3) Where applicable, all duties, taxes and other charges, as well as the costs of carrying

out customs formalities payable upon import of the goods and the costs for their transport through any country.

B7 Notices to the seller

The buyer must give the seller sufficient notice of the vessel name, loading point and, where necessary, the selected delivery time within the agreed period.

B8 Proof of delivery

The buyer must accept the proof of delivery provided as envisaged in A8.

B9 Inspection of goods

The buyer must pay the costs of any mandatory pre-shipment inspection, except when such an inspection is mandated by the authorities of the country of export.

B10 Other Obligations

The buyer must reimburse the seller for all costs and charges incurred by the seller in providing or rendering assistance in obtaining documents and information as envisaged in A10.

1.3.10 COST AND FREIGHT

CFR (... named port of destination)

This rule is to be used only for sea or inland waterway transport.

"Cost and Freight" means that the seller delivers the goods on board the vessel or procures the goods already so delivered. The risk of loss of or damage to the goods passes when the goods are on board the vessel.

CFR may not be appropriate where goods are handed over to the carrier before they are on board the vessel, for example goods in containers, which are typically delivered at a terminal. In such circumstances, the CPT rule should be used.

CFR requires the seller to clear the goods for export, where applicable. However, the seller has no obligation to clear the goods for import, pay any import duty or carry out any import customs formalities.

A THE SELLER'S OBLIGATIONS

A1 General obligations of the seller

The seller must provide the goods and the commercial invoice in conformity with the contract of sale and any other evidence of conformity that may be required by the contract.

A2 Licences and other formalities

Where applicable, the seller must obtain, at its own risk and expense, any export licence or other official authorization and carry out all customs formalities necessary for the export of the goods.

A3 Contracts of carriage and insurance

(1) Contract of carriage

The seller must contract or procure a contract for the carriage of the goods from the agreed point of delivery, if any, at the place of delivery to the named port of destination or, if agreed, any point at that port. The contract of carriage must be made on usual terms at the seller's expense and provide for carriage by the usual route in a vessel of the type normally used for the transport of the type of goods sold.

(2) Contract of insurance

The seller has no obligation to make a contract of insurance. However, the seller must provide the buyer, at the buyer's request, risk, and expense, with information that the buyer needs for obtaining insurance.

A4 Delivery

The seller must deliver the goods either by placing them on board the vessel or by procuring the goods so delivered. In either case, the seller must deliver the goods on the agreed date or within the agreed period and in the manner customary at the port.

A5 Transfer of risks

The seller bears all risks of loss of or damage to the goods until they have been delivered, with the exception of loss or damage in the circumstances described inB5.

A6 Allocation of costs

The seller must pay:

(1) All costs relating to the goods until they have been delivered in accordance with A4.

(2) The freight and all other costs resulting from A3 a), including the costs of loading the goods on board and any charges for unloading at the agreed port of discharge that were for the seller's account under the contract of carriage.

(3) Where applicable, the costs of customs formalities necessary for export as well as all duties, taxes and other charges payable upon export, and the costs for their transport through anycountry that were for the seller's account under the contract of carriage.

A7 Notices to the buyer

The seller must give the buyer any notice needed in order to allow the buyer to take measures that are normally necessary to enable the buyer to take the goods.

A8 Delivery document

The seller must, at its own expense, provide the buyer without delay with the usual transport document for the agreed port of destination. This transport document must cover the contract goods, be dated within the period agreed for shipment, enable the buyer to claim the goods from the carrier at the port of destination and, unless otherwise agreed, enable the buyer to sell the goods in transit by the transfer of the document to a subsequent buyer or by notification to the carrier.

When such a transport document is issued in negotiable forms and in several originals, a full set of originals must be presented to the buyer.

A9 Checking-packaging-marking

The seller must pay the costs of those checking operations (such as checking quality, measuring, weighing, counting) that are necessary for the purpose of delivering the goods in accordance with A4, as well as the costs of any pre-shipment inspection mandated by the authority of the country of export. The seller must, at its own expense, package the goods, unless it is usual for the particular trade to transport the type of goods sold unpackaged. The seller may package the goods in the manner appropriate for their transport, unless the buyer has notified the seller of specific packaging requirements before the contract of sale is concluded. Packaging is to be marked appropriately.

A10 Other Obligations

The seller must, where applicable, in a timely manner, provide to or render assistance in obtaining for the buyer, at the buyer's request, risk and expense, any documents and information, including security-related information, that the buyer needs for the import of the goods and/or for their transport to the final destination.

The seller must reimburse the buyer for all costs and charges incurred by the buyer in providing or rendering assistance in obtaining documents and information as envisaged in B10.

B THE BUYER'S OBLIGATIONS

B1 General obligations of the buyer

The buyer must pay the price of the goods as provided in the contract of sale.

B2 Licences and other formalities

Where applicable, it is up to the buyer to obtain, at its own risk and expense, any import licence or other official authorization and carry out all customs formalities for the import of the goods and for their transport through any country.

B3 Contracts of carriage and insurance

(1) Contract of carriage

The buyer has no obligation to make a contract of carriage.

(2) Contract of insurance

The buyer has obligation to make a contract of insurance.

B4 Taking delivery

The buyer must take delivery of the goods when they have been delivered as envisaged in A4 and receive them from the carrier at the named port of destination.

B5 Transfer of risks

The buyer bears all risks of loss of or damage to the goods from the time they have been delivered. If the buyer fails to give notice in accordance with B7, then it bears all risks of loss of or damage to the goods from the agreed date or the expiry date of the agreed period for shipment, provided that the goods have been clearly identified as the contract goods.

B6 Allocation of costs

The buyer must, subject to the provisions of A3 a), pay:

(1) All costs relating to the goods from the time they have been delivered as envisaged in A4.

(2) All costs and charges relating to the goods while in transit until their arrival at the port of destination, unless such costs and charges were for the seller's account under the contract of carriage.

(3) Unloading costs including lighterage and wharfage charges, unless such costs and charges were for the seller's account under the contract of carriage.

(4) Any additional costs incurred if it fails to give notice in accordance with B7, from the agreed date or the expiry date of the agreed period for shipment, provided that the goods have been clearly identified as the contract goods.

(5) Where applicable, all duties, taxes and other charges, as well as the costs of carrying out customs formalities payable upon import of the goods and the costs for their transport through any country unless included within the cost of the contract of carriage.

B7 Notices to the seller

The buyer must, whenever it is entitled to determine the time for shipping the goods and/or the point of receiving the goods within the named port of destination, give the seller sufficient notice thereof.

B8 Proof of delivery

The buyer must accept the transport document provided as envisaged in A8 if it is in conformity with the contract.

B9 Inspection of goods

The buyer must pay the costs of any mandatory pre-shipment inspection, except when such inspection is mandated by the authorities of the country of export.

B10 Other Obligations

The buyer must reimburse the seller for all costs and charges incurred by the seller in providing or rendering assistance in obtaining documents and information as envisaged in A10.

1.3.11 INSURANCE AND FREIGHT

CIF (... named port of destination)

This rule is to be used only for sea or inland waterway transport.

"Cost, Insurance and Freight" means that the seller delivers the goods on board the vessel or procures the goods already so delivered. The risk of loss of or damage to the goods passes when the goods are on board the vessel. The seller must contract for and pay the costs and freight necessary to bring the goods to the named port of destination. The seller also contracts for insurance cover against the buyer's risk of loss of or damage to the goods during the carriage. The buyer should note that under CIF the seller is required to obtain insurance only on minimum cover. Should the buyer wish to have more insurance protection, it will need either to agree as much expressly with the seller or to make its own extra insurance arrangements.

CIF may not be appropriate where goods are handed over to the carrier before they are on board the vessel, for example goods in containers, which are typically delivered at a terminal. In such circumstances, the CIP rule should be used. CIF requires the seller to clear the goods for export, where applicable. However, the seller has no obligation to clear the goods for import, pay any import duty or carry out any import customs formalities.

A THE SELLER'S OBLIGATIONS

A1 General obligations of the seller

The seller must provide the goods and the commercial invoice in conformity with the contract of sale and any other evidence of conformity that may be required by the contract.

A2 Licencesand other formalities

Where applicable, the seller must obtain, at its own risk and expense, any export licence or other official authorization and carry out all customs formalities necessary for the export of the goods.

A3 Contracts of carriage and insurance

(1) Contract of carriage

The seller must contract or procure a contract for the carriage of the goods from the agreed point of delivery, if any, at the place of delivery to the named port of destination or, if agreed, any point at that port. The contract of carriage must be made on usualterms at the seller's expense and provide for carriage by the usual route in a vessel of the type normally used for the transport of the type of goods sold.

(2) Contract of insurance

The seller must obtain, at its own expense, cargo insurance complying at least with the minimum cover provided by Clauses When required by the buyer, the seller shall, subject to the buyer providing any necessary information requested by the seller, provide at the buyer's expense any additional cover, The insurance shall cover, at a minimum, the price provided in the contract plus 10% (i. e., 110%) and shall be in the currency of the contract. The insurance shall cover the goods from the point of delivery set out in A4 and A5 to at least the named port of destination. The seller must provide the buyer with the insurance policy or other evidence of insurance cover. Moreover, the seller must provide the buyer, at the buyer's request, risk, and expense, with information that the buyer needs to procure any additional insurance.

A4 Delivery

The seller must deliver the goods either by placing them on board the vessel or by procuring the goods so delivered. In either case, the seller must deliver the goods on the agreed date or within the agreed period and in the manner customary at the port.

A5 Transfer of risks

The seller bears all risks of loss of or damage to the goods until they have been delivered with the exception of loss or damage in the circumstances described in B5.

A6 Allocation of costs

The seller must pay:

(1) All costs relating to the goods until they have been delivered in accordance with A4.

(2) The freight and all other costs resulting from A3 a), including the costs of loading the goods on board and any charges for unloading at the agreed port of discharge that were for the seller's account under the contract of carriage.

(3) The costs of insurance resulting from A3 b).

(4) Where applicable, the costs of customs formalities necessary for export, as well as all duties, taxes and other charges payable upon export, and the costs for their transport through any country that were for the seller's account under the contract of carriage.

A7 Notices to the buyer

The seller must give the buyer any notice needed in order to allow the buyer to take measures that are normally necessary to enable the buyer to take the goods.

A8 Delivery document

The seller must, at its own expense provide the buyer without delay with the usual transport document for the agreed port of destination.

This transport document must cover the contract goods, be dated within the period agreed for shipment, enable the buyer to claim the goods from the carrier at the port of destination and, unless otherwise agreed, enable the buyer to sell the goods in transit by the transfer of the document to a subsequent buyer or by notification to the carrier. When such a transport document is issued in negotiable form and in several originals, a full set of originals must be presented to the buyer.

A9 Checking-packaging-marking

The seller must pay the costs of those checking operations (such as checking quality, measuring, weighing, counting) that are necessary for the purpose of delivering the goods in accordance with A4, as well as the costs of any pre-shipment inspection mandated by the authority of the country of export.

The seller must, at its own expense, package the goods, unless it is usual for the particular trade to transport the type of goods sold unpackaged. The seller may package the goods in the manner appropriate for their transport, unless the buyer has notified the seller of specific packaging requirements before the contract of sale is concluded. Packaging is to be marked appropriately.

A10 Other Obligations

The seller must, where applicable, in a timely manner, provide to or render assistance in obtaining for the buyer, at the buyer's request, risk and expense, any documents and information, including security-related information, that the buyer needs for the import of the goods and/or for their transport to the final destination.

B THE BUYER'S OBLIGATIONS

B1 General obligations of the buyer

The buyer must pay the price of the goods as provided in the contract of sale.

B2 Licences and other formalities

Where applicable, it is up to the buyer to obtain, at its own risk and expense, any import licence or other official authorization and carry out all customs formalities for the import of the goods and for their transport through any country.

B3 Contracts of carriage and insurance

(1) Contract of carriage

The buyer has no obligations to make a contract of carriage.

(2) Contract of insurance

The buyer has no obligations to make a contract of insurance.

B4 Taking delivery

The buyer must take delivery of the goods when they have been delivered as envisaged in A4 and receive them from the carrier at the named port of destination.

B5 Transfer of risks

The buyer bears all risks of loss of or damage to the goods from the time they have been delivered.

If the buyer fails to give notice in accordance with B7, then it bears all risks of loss of or damage to the goods from the agreed date or the expiry date of the agreed period for shipment, provided that the goods have been clearly identified as the contract goods.

B6 Allocation of costs

The buyer must, subject to the provisions of A3, pay:

(1) All costs relating to the goods from the time they have been delivered as envisaged in A4.

(2) All costs and charges relating to the goods while in transit until their arrival at the port of destination, unless such costs and charges were for the seller's account under the contract of carriage.

(3) Unloading costs including lighterage and wharfage charges, unless such costs and charges were for the seller's account under the contract of carriage.

(4) Any additional costs incurred if it fails to give notice in accordance with B7, from the agreed date or the expiry date of the agreed period for shipment, provided that the goods have been clearly identified as the contract goods.

(5) Where applicable, all duties, taxes and other charges, as well as the costs of carrying out customs formalities payable upon import of the goods and the costs for their transport through any country, unless included within the cost of the contract of carriage.

B7 Notices to the seller

The buyer must, whenever it is entitled to determine the time for shipping the goods and/or the point of receiving the goods within the named port of destination, give the seller sufficient notice thereof.

B8 Proof of delivery

The buyer must accept the transport document provided as envisaged in A8 if it is in conformity with the contract.

B9 Inspection of goods

The buyer must pay the costs of any mandatory pre-shipment inspection, except when such inspection is mandated by the authorities of the country of export.

B10 Other Obligations

The buyer must reimburse the seller for all costs and charges incurred by the seller in providing or rendering assistance in obtaining documents and information as envisaged in A10.

1.4 Use of INCOTERMS 2010

The INCOTERMS rules explain a set of three-letter trade terms reflecting business-to-business practice in contracts for the sale of goods. The INCOTERMS rules describe mainly the tasks, costs and risks involved in the delivery of goods from sellers to buyers.

1.4.1 Incorporate the INCOTERMS 2010 rules into your contract of sale

If you want the INCOTERMS 2010 rules to apply to your contract, you should make this clear in the contract, through such words as "the chosen INCOTERMS rule including the named place, followed by INCOTERMS 2010".

1.4.2 Choose the appropriate INCOTERMS rule

The chosen INCOTERMS rule needs to be appropriate to the goods, to the means of their transport, and above all to whether the parties intend to put additional obligations, for example, the obligation to organize carriage or insurance, on the seller or on the buyer. The Guidance Note to each INCOTERMS rule contains information that is particularly helpful when making this choice. Whichever INCOTERMS rule is chosen, the parties should be aware the interpretation of their contract may well be influenced by customs particular to the port or place being used.

1.4.3 Specify your place or port as precisely as possible

The chosen INCOTERMS rule can work only if the parties name a place or port, and will work best if the parties specify the place or port as precisely as possible. A good example of such precision would be:

"FCA 38 Cours Albert 1er, Paris, France INCOTERMS 2010".

Under the INCOTERMS rule:

EXW   Ex Works

FCA   Free Carrier

DAT   Delivered at Terminal

DAP   Delivered at Place

DDP   Delivered Duty Paid

FAS   Free Alongside Ship

FOB Free on Board

The named place is the place where delivery takes place and where risk passes from the seller to the buyer.

Under the INCOTERMS rule:

CPT Carriage Paid to

CIP Carriage and Insurance Paid to

CFR Cost and Freight

CIF Cost, Insurance and Freight

The named place differs from the place of delivery. Under these four INCOTERMS rules, the named place is the place of destination to which carriage is paid. Indications as to place or destination can helpfully be further specified by stating a precise point in that place or destination in order to avoid doubt or argument.

1.4.4 Remember that INCOTERMS rules do not give you a complete contract of sale

INCOTERMS rules do say which party to the sale contract has the obligation to make carriage or insurance arrangements, when the seller delivers the goods to the buyer, and which costs each party is responsible for.

INCOTERMS rules, however, say nothing about the price to be paid or the method of its payment. Neither do they deal with the transfer of ownership of the goods, or the consequences of a breach of contract. These matters are normally dealt with through express terms in the contract of sale or in the law governing that contract. The parties should be aware that mandatory local law may override any aspect of the sale contract, including the chosen INCOTERMS rules.

1.4.5 Main features of the Incoterm 2010 rules

1. Two new INCOTERMS rules—DAT and DAP—have replaced the INCOTERMS 2000 rules DAF, DES, DEQ and DDU

The number of INCOTERMS rules has been reduced from 13 to 11. This has been achieved by substituting two rules that may be used irrespective of the agreed mode of transport—DAT, Delivered at Terminal, and DAP, Delivered at Place — for the INCOTERMS 2000 rules DAF, DES, DEQ and DDU.

Under both new rules, delivery occurs at a named destination: in DAT, at the buyer's disposal unloaded from the arriving vehicle (as under the former DEQ rule); in DAP, likewise at the buyer's disposal, but ready for unloading (as under the former DAF, DES and DDU rules).

The new rules make the INCOTERMS 2000 rules DES and DEQ superfluous. The named terminal in DAT may well be in a port, and DAT can therefore safely be used in cases where the INCOTERMS 2000 rule DEQ once was. Likewise, the arriving "vehicle" under DAP may well be a ship and the named place of destination may well be a port: consequently, DAP can safely be used in cases where the INCOTERMS 2000 rule DES once was. These new rules, like their predecessors, are "delivered", with the seller bearing all the costs (other than those related to import clearance, where applicable) and risks involved in bringing the goods to the named place of destination.

2. Classification of the 11 INCOTERMS 2010 rules

The 11 INCOTERMS 2010 rules are presented in two distinct classes.

Table 1.3 INCOTERMS 2010

RULES FOR ANY MODE OR MODES OF TRANSPOTR	
EXW	EX WORKS
FCA	FREE CARRIER
CPT	CARRIAGE PAID TO
CIP	CARRIAGE AND INSURANCE PAID TO
DAT	DELIVERED AT TERMINAL
DAP	DELIVERED AT PLACE
DDP	DELIVERED DUTY PAID
RULES FOR SEA AND INLAND WATERWAY TRANSPORT	
FAS	FREE ALONGSIDE SHIP
FOB	FREE ON BOARD
CFR	COST AND FREIGHT
CIF	COST INSURANCE AND FREIGHT

The first class includes the seven INCOTERMS 2010 rules that can be used irrespective of the mode of transport selected and irrespective of whether one or more than one mode of transport is employed. EXW, FCA, CPT, CIP, DAT, DAP and DDP belong to this class. They can be used even when there is no maritime transport at all. It is important to remember, however, that these rules can be used in cases where a ship is used for part of the carriage.

In the second class of INCOTERMS 2010 rules, the point of delivery and the place to which the goods are carried to the buyer are both ports, hence the label "sea and inland waterway" rules. FAS, FOB, CFR and CIF belong to this class. Under the last three INCOTERMS rules, all mention of the ship's rail as the point of delivery has been omitted in preference for the goods being delivered when they are "on board" the vessel. This more closely reflects modern commercial reality and avoids the rather dated image of the risk swinging to and fro across an imaginary perpendicular line.

3. Rules for domestic and international trade

INCOTERMS rules have traditionally been used in international sale contracts where goods pass across national boarders. In various areas of the world, however, trade blocs, like the European Union, have made border formalities between different countries less significant. Consequently, the subtitle of the INCOTERMS 2010 rules formally recognize that they are available for application to both international and domestic sale contracts. As a result, the INCOTERMS 2010 rules clearly state in a number of places that the obligation to comply with export/import formalities exists only where applicable.

Two developments have persuaded ICC that a movement in this direction is timely. Firstly, traders commonly use INCOTERMS rules for purely domestic sale contract. The second reason is the greater willingness in the Unites States to use INCOTERMS rules in domestic trade rather than the former Uniform Commercial Code shipment and delivery terms.

4. Guidance Notes

Before each INCOTERMS 2010 rule you will find a Guidance Note. The Guidance Notes explain the fundamentals of each INCOTERMS rule, such as when it should be used, when risk passes, and how costs are allocated between seller and buyer. The Guidance Notes are not part of the actual INCOTERMS 2010 rules, but are intended to help the user accurately and efficiently steer towards the appropriate INCOTERMS rule for a particular transaction.

5. Electronic communication

Previous versions of INCOTERMS rules have specified those documents that could be replaced by EDI messages. Articles A1/B1 of the INCOTERMS 2010 rules, however, now give electronic means of communication the same effect as paper communication, as long as the parties so agree or where customary. This formulation facilitates the evolution of new electronic procedures throughout the lifetime of the INCOTERMS 2010 rules.

6. Insurance cover

The INCOTERMS 2010 rules are the first version of the INCOTERMS rules since the version of the Institute Cargo Clauses and take account of alterations made to those clauses. The INCOTERMS 2010 rules place information duties relating to insurance in articles A3/B3, which deal with contracts of carriage and insurance. These provisions have been moved from the more generic found in article A10/B10 of the INCOTERMS 2010 rules. The language in articles A2/B3 relating to insurance has also been altered with a view to clarifying the parties' obligations in this regard.

7. Security-related Clearances and information required for such clearances

There is heightened concern nowadays about security in the movement of goods, requiring verification that the goods do not pose a threat to life or property for reasons other than their inherent nature.

Therefore, the INCOTERMS 2010 rules have allocated obligations between the buyer and seller to obtain or to render assistance in obtaining security-related clearances, such as chain-of-custody information, in articles A2/B2 and A10/B10 of various INCOTERMS rules.

8. Terminal handling charges

Under INCOTERMS rules CPT, CIP, CFR, CIF, DAT, DAP, and DDP, the seller must make arrangements for the carriage of the goods to the agreed destination. While the freight is paid by the seller, it is actually paid for by the buyer as freight costs are normally included by the seller in the total selling price. The carriage costs will sometimes include the costs of handling and moving the goods within port or container terminal facilities and the carrier or terminal operator may well charge these costs to the buyer who receives the goods. In these circumstances, the buyer will want to avoid paying for the same service twice: once to the seller as part of the total selling price and once independently to the carrier or the terminal operator. The INCOTERMS 2010 rules seek to avoid this happening by clearly allocating such costs in articles A6/B6 of the relevant INCOTERMS rules.

9. String sales

In the sale of commodities, as opposed to the sale of manufactured goods, cargo is frequently sold several times during transit "down a string" when this happens, a seller in the middle of the string don't have to ship the goods because these have already been shipped by the first seller in the string. The seller in the middle of the string therefore performs its obligations towards its buyer not by shipping the goods, but by "procuring" goods that have been shipped. For clarification purposes, INCOTERMS 2010 rules include the obligation to "procure goods shipped" as an alternative to the obligation to ship goods in the relevant INCOTERMS rules.

1.4.6 RULES FOR ANY MODE OR MODES OF TRANSPORT

1. Variants of INCOTERMS rules

Sometimes the parties want to alter an INCOTERMS rules. The INCOTERMS 2010 rules do not prohibit such alteration, but there are dangers in so doing. In order to avoid any unwelcome surprises, the parties would need to make the intended effect of such alterations extremely clear in their contract. Thus, for example, if the allocation of costs in the INCOTERMS 2010 rules are altered in the contract, the parties should also clearly state whether they intend to vary the point at which the risk passes from seller to buyer.

2. Status of this introduction

This introduction gives general information on the use and interpretation of the INCOTERMS 2010 rules, but does not form part of those rules.

3. Explanation of terms used in the INCOTERMS 2010 rules

As in the INCOTERMS rules, the seller's and buyer's obligations are presented in mirror fashion, reflecting under column A the seller's obligations and under column B the buyer's obligations. These obligations can be carried out personally by the seller or the buyer or sometimes, subject to terms in the contract or the applicable law, through intermediaries such as carriers, freight forwarders or other persons nominated by the seller or the buyer for a specific purpose.

The text of the INCOTERMS 2010 rules is meant to be self-explanatory. However, in order to assist users the following text sets out guidance as to the sense in which selected terms are used throughout the document.

Carrier: For the purposes of the INCOTERMS 2010 rules, the carrier is the party with whom carriage is contracted.

Customs Formalities: These are requirements to be met in order to comply with any applicable customs regulations and may include documentary, security, information or physical inspection obligations.

Delivery: This concept has multiple meanings in trade law and practice, but in the INCOTERMS 2010 rules, it is used to indicate where the risk of loss of or damage to the goods passes from the seller to the buyer.

Delivery document: This phrase is now used as the heading to article A8. It means a document used to prove that delivery has occurred. For many of the INCOTERMS 2010 rules, the delivery document is a transport document or corresponding electronic record. However, with EXW, FCA, FAS and FOB, the delivery document may simply be a receipt. A delivery document may also have other functions, for example as part of the mechanism for payment.

Electronic record or procedure: A set of information constituted of one or more electronic messages and, where applicable, being functionally equivalent with the corresponding paper document.

Packaging: this word is used for different purposes:

(1) The packaging of the goods to comply with any requirements under the contract of sale.

(2) The packaging of the goods so that they are fit for transportation.

(3) The stowage of the packaged goods within a container or other means of transport.

In the INCOTERMS 2010 rules, packaging means both the first and second of the above. The INCOTERMS 2010 rules do not deal with the parties' obligations for stowage within a container and therefore, where relevant, the parties should deal with this in the sale contract.

Chapter 2 Name and Quality of Commodity

2.1 Name of Commodity

Usually, the parties to a contract specify the name of the product under the subject "Name of Commodity". This clause is a main component of the Description of Goods. As the basis of a transaction, it concerns the rights and obligations of the buyer and the seller. If the goods delivered by the seller are not in accordance with the agreed name of commodity, the buyer reserves the right to lodge a claim, reject the goods or even cancel the contract. Therefore, as a main clause of a sales contract, the name of commodity should be clearly stipulated. When giving the name, try to be specific and adopt the widely accepted name agreed by both parties. To some products, we should be cautious in selecting suitable names, either reducing customs duties, or saving freight.

2.2 Quality of Commodity

2.2.1 Ways of Describing the Quality of Goods

Quality is the most important factor in the sale of goods, the seller must deliver the goods as required by the contract. Otherwise, the buyer may claim for damages, require delivery of substitute goods, or require the seller to remedy, or even reject the goods and cancel the contract. The quality agreed upon in the contract is the basis of the seller's delivery. In international transactions, there are different ways of describing the quality of goods in a contract:

1. Sale by Actual Quality

Products are showed to buyers in factory, then business will be done after buyer's inspection on spot. Through this method, the quality of the product must be based on the inspection result. If the seller delivers the inspected products to buyer, he has no right to refuse them. In general, such practice is suitable to the situation, which the quantity of these products is not so large that buyer can inspect them on spot. Therefore, expensive goods such as arts and crafts can adopt this kind of way.

2. Sale by Sample

Samples are either offered by the seller or the buyer. They are described as "sale by seller's sample", and the "sale by buyer's sample" respectively.

(1) Counter sample: When sale is made by buyer's the goods delivered by the seller, may

sometimes not be in conformity with the buyer's sample and thus the buyer may refuse to accept the goods. In order to avoid disputes over the quality of goods in the days to come, a wise seller should first send a copied piece of product for confirmation before putting into production. This copied product is called "counter sample" or "confirming sample", on which the seller's delivery will be based.

(2) Sealed sample: Before sending samples or delivering the goods to the buyer, the seller may select some samples and seal them in the presence of the buyer on notary. This sealed sample is for checking the quality of the shipments in the future.

(3) Safeguard clauses: When sale by buyer's sample, to prevent disputes upon the third party's intellectual properties, safeguard clauses are usually stipulated in the contract. The following is an example:

"It is the buyer rather from the infringement of the third party's intellectual properties."

(4) Reference sample: When sale is made by description, either the seller or the buyer may send a physical sample to the other party to let him know more clearly about the products. This sample is often marked "for reference only". It is not the basis of delivery.

3. Sale by Description

(1) Sale by specification, grade or standard: some indices such as chemical composition, contents, length, sizes, etc. can reflect the quality of the goods sufficiently. Describing quality by specification is simple as well as accurate. That's why it is most widely used. Some products can be divided into different grades based on different specifications.

e. g fresh hen eggs, shell light brown and clean.

Grade AA	60-65 gm per egg
Grade A	55-60 gm per egg
Grade B	50-55gm per egg
Grade C	45-50 gm per egg

Standards are formulated either by government or commercial organizations. Some of them are national, others are international. Many countries have their own standards, for example, BS in Britain, ANSI in the USA and Japan. The typical international standard is ISO standard. When sale is made by standard, it is important to mark the publication year of the standard.

(2) Sale by trademark or brand: some products may have been sold in the market for many years and enjoy high popularity. Their quality can be represented by their trademarks and brands, such as Coca Cola, White rabbit Creamy Candy.

However, some well-known brand products cannot be traded only by their marks and brands owing to their varieties and complexities. Take SONY as an example, there are Sony television,

Sony walkman, Sony DVD, and so on. In this case, detailed quality indices or technical descriptions must be clearly stated.

(3) Sale by descriptions and illustrations: Some products like machinery, instruments, equipments, and transportation tools are complicated in structure. It is difficult to describe the full aspects of their quality, thus sale by descriptions and illustrations is applicable. In the contract, the clause of quality contains not only the name of commodity, the brand but also the instructions to illustrate the structure and functions of the product. Clauses like "quality and technical data to be strictly in conformity with the description submitted by the seller" are to be stipulated.

(4) Sale by name of origin: this method is limited only for native products with traditional arts or special local flavor. It is usually used together with brands or specifications. e. g. Shichuan Preserved.

2.2.2 Quality Clause in Contract

In quality clause, the name and specification, grade, or the serial number and data of the sample, etc, should be clearly stated. We may use description or sample separately or together to describe quality, depending on the product features.

(1) When sale is made by sample, sometimes it is not easy for the goods shipped to be in complete conformity with the sample, or we are not quite sure of the quality. In this case, clauses like "the quality of the shipped to be about equal to the sample" may be stipulated.

(2) Flexible quality range for some primary products including range and allowing more or less.

(3) Quality Tolerance

It is very unavoidable for some industrial products such as instruments, mechanical products to have some tolerance. e. g. Soybean, if the oil content of the goods shipped is 1% higher, the price will be accordingly increased by 2%.

Chapter 3 Quantity of Commodity

3.1 Counting Method of Commodity

3.1.1 Metrical Units

In international trade, as different products have different characteristics and different countries may adopt different systems of weights and measures, units and ways of quantity calculation are varied. There are International System of Units, Metric System, British System and U. S. System. While the British system's long ton, L/T equals to 2200 pounds, the U. S. system's short ton, S/T equals to 2000 pounds. Besides, some capacity units like gallon and bushel are of the same names under the Britain system and the U. S. system, but the actual capacities are different. There are two categories of metric units which are used to show the quantity of commodity in international trade. One is metrical units, including weight, length, area, volume and capacity. The other is numbers, including some customary units such as dozen, ream, and some packing units like barrel (petroleum, oil), bale (cotton), etc.

3.1.2 Methods for Calculating Weight

In international trade, a lot of products are measured by weight according to general commercial practices and rules, the following are the methods of calculating weight:

1. Gross Weight

Gross weight refers to the weight of the product itself plus the package of this product, such method is suitable for calculating low value goods.

2. Net weight

Net weight means the weight of the product itself. According to international rules and practices, weight is calculated by net weight unless otherwise stated in the contract. Some products can be weighted only when they are packed, and this weight including package is called gross weight. For some less valued products, we may stipulate in called gross for net. If net weight has to be used, we must deduct the weight of package, i. e. the weight of tare. The following are some methods of calculating tare:

(1) Real tare. The package is actually weighted.

(2) Average tare. When the package is in the same sizes, we may select some of them to weight in the balance, and calculate the average weight.

(3) Customary tare. This is suitable for standardized package is known to everyone and it is unnecessary to weight.

(4) Computed tare. The weight of the package is agreed upon by both sides.

3. Conditioned weight

Some products like wool, cotton, raw silk have unstable moisture contents. In order to determine the moisture contents accurately, the universal conditioned weight is used. Conditioned weight equals to dry weight plus standard moisture content.

4. Theoretical weight

Some products are of uniform sizes and/or specifications, so the weight of each unit is almost the same. We can get the total weight by multiplying the total number and the weight of each unit.

3.2 Quantity Clause in Contract

3.2.1 The Importance of Quantity Clause

The quantity of commodity is a major indispensable clause in a contract. The CISG states that the seller must deliver goods which are of the quantity required by the contract. If the seller delivers a quantity of goods greater than that provided for in the contract, the buyer may take delivery or refuse to take delivery of the excess quantity. If the buyer takes delivery of all or part of the excess quantity, he must pay for it at the contract rate.

3.2.2 More or Less Clause

In practice, it is sometimes hard to control strictly the quantity of some bulk cargoes like farm products, mineral products. Besides, owing to change to supplies and limitation to processing conditions, the actual quantity may be somewhat more or less than the contracted quantity. Under such circumstances, more or less clause is usually stipulated in the contract so that the seller can fulfill the contract more smoothly. The more or less clause is a clause which stipulates the quantity delivered can be more or less within certain extent. The most commonly used way is allowing some percentage more or less. For example, 2000 M/T, 5% more or less at seller's option. However, if the quantity is related with transportation, we may stipulate as "at carrier's option", or "at buyer's option" when the ship is arranged by the buyer.

Settlement for the more or less part is usually based on the contract price. If the parties are concerned about the great changes in price at the time when delivery is made, they may stipulate that settlement or this part is based on the market price at the time when the goods are shipped on board the vessel.

Chapter 4 Packing of Commodity

4.1 Types of Commodity Packing

Commodity is usually connected with certain kinds of packing. Some packing is a constitutional part of a product. In international trade, packing is especially significant. Packing clause is often one of the major trade clauses in a contract. Packing can be divided in to selling packing and transport packing according to their different functions in commodity circulation. Selling packing is also called small or inner or immediate packing. It is mainly used to protect products, make the products convenient to use, and to promote sales. Inner packing should be in conformity with the laws and regulations of the purchase countries. Transport packing is also called big or outer packing. Its main functions are to protect goods, and make the goods easy to store and ship. In this section, we shall mainly discuss transport packing.

In transit, not all goods are necessarily packed. With the development of transportation, more and more small and roundish cargoes like grain, cement and liquid cargoes like petroleum are in bulk, i. e. they can be loaded directly into the transportation vehicles with mechanical operation. In this way, the costs of carriage are saved, and the carriage is speeded up. Some cargoes like steel, timber, etc. need only to be bundled up. Which are described as goods in naked packing. But for most cargoes, packing is essential in transportation. There are two kinds of transportation packing:

4.1.1 Unit packing

(1) Bale: Bale is a heap of material pressed together and tied with rope or metal wire, suitable for paper, wool, cotton, and carpets, etc; Bag: Bag is made of cotton, plastic, paper or jute, ideal for cement, fertilizer, flour, chemicals, etc; Barrel/drum: Barrel/drum is made of wood, plastic or metal used for liquid or greasy cargoes; Box/case: Box/case is wooden in structure and of various sizes, and some airtight, providing strong protection for cargoes as equipment and car accessories;

(2) Glass container: Glass container is used for dangerous liquid cargoes such as acid which needs careful handling; Carton: Carton is a very common form of packing particularly for consumer-type of products. It can promote sales to some extent as words can be printed on them; Crate/skeleton case: Wooden structure between a bale and a case used for light weight goods of large cubic capacity as machinery.

4.1.2 Unionization (or combined) packing

When we put the individual packing together and place them into a lager container, it is called unionization packing. Pallet, flexible container and container all are combined packing. The combined packing has such advantages as to protect goods effectively, improve efficiency, and to save packing costs as well as freight.

4.2 Marks of Commodity Packing

Marks on transport packing help to identify goods, and facilitate correct operation. According to their functions, marks on transport packing can be divided into shipping mark, indicative mark, warning mark, weight/volume mark, and origin mark.

4.2.1 Shipping Mark

Shipping mark facilitates the identification and count of the goods in the process of loading and unloading, shipping and storing. Shipping marks can also prevent the goods from being wrongly delivered or shipped. Shipping marks are usually composed of numbers, alphabets, and simple words. The UN has recommended a type of standard shipping mark to all countries, which cover four parts: the English abbreviation of the receiver; reference number, such as order number, invoice number; destination; serial number.

e. g. ABCCO
SC9750
LONDON
NO. 4-20

Shipping mark is usually indicated in export documents like invoice, bill of landing. and insurance policy.

4.2.2 Indicative Mark

It is a caution mark, which reminds people of carefulness in handling or carrying goods. It is composed of graphs and words, such as HANDLE WITH CARE, THIS WAY UP, KEEP DRY, USE NO HOOK.

4.2.3 Warning Mark

It is also called dangerous mark and is used to indicate explosive, poisonous, inflammable goods. It is also composed of graphs or pictures and words.

4.3 Packing Clause in Contract

4.3.1 Neutral Packing

Neutral packing is a special type of packing, which means the origin of the product is not shown on the inner and outer packages. Chinese export product are usually marked with words like "Made in the People's Republic of China", "Made in China". But sometimes, at the request of the buyer, the seller would accept neutral packing. Neutral packing is divided into neutral packing with designated brand and neutral packing without designated brand. Neutral packing with designated brand means the brand and/or trade mark designed by the buyer are marked out on the product and/or package, but with no indication of the country of origin. Neutral packing without designated brand means neither brand and/or trademark nor country of the origin are marked out on the product and/or package. Neutral packing is a usual practice in international trade, but in recent years it has been restricted by some countries. Exporters should be cautions in adopting it.

4.3.2 Packing Clause in Contract

In contract, we usually stipulate the packing material and the way of packing.

e. g. Packing: in cartons containing 30 doz. each

Packing: in wooden cases of 50 kilos net each

Ambiguous terms like "seaworthy packing" or "customary packing" are not applicable, since disputes may arise. Usually, there is no need to stipulate packing marks in the contract, as they are usually decided by the seller. But on condition that the buyer nominates it, it is necessary to stipulate the details of the shipping mark. Packing charges are usually included in price. But if the buyer asks for special packing, we should make it clear as to who shall bear the additional charges. The time and methods of payment should also be stated.

Chapter 5 Price of Commodity

5.1 Principle of Pricing

5.1.1 Choice of Currency for Payment

Pricing is one of the most important and complex tasks in business, and even more of a problem when linked with exporting. An exporter should sell his products at a price acceptable to the customers and, at the same time, generate enough revenue to cover all its costs. Appropriate pricing is not easy, which requires much skill and must be treated seriously and carefully.

Currency for account is the currency used for price calculation. Currency for payment is the currency for settlement. Normally, the currency for account is the currency for payment if no otherwise is stipulate in contract. Currency for account and payment can be the home currency of the exporter the importer's currency or a third currency if only these currencies are convertible. When choosing the currency, the exporter and importer should take foreign exchanges rates into consideration, and the fluctuations of exchange rates may influence their interests.

Theoretically, use of hard currency (currency that is reliable and stable and more in demand) as payment currency is more favorable to the exporter, while the importer prefers to pay in soft currency (currency that is not readily convertible to gold, or into other currencies which are less in demand and that is unstable in value).

Which currency is to be used depends on the consultation between the buyer and the seller. If one seller has to adopt an unfavorable currency as payment currency, he should take some measures to offset the foreign exchange exposures.

1. Try to reduce the import price and raise the export price

When sign the contract, take the trend of currency into consideration. If you are an importer, while the currency used is likely to float upward (Note: this is your forecast), you should try to press the seller to reduce the price. If you are an exporter, while the currency is likely to float downward, you should try to raise the price. Usually such measure is used within a short period, because it is rather difficult to forecast the tendency of foreign exchange for a long period.

2. Stipulate exchange proviso clause

In the case that the currency for account and payment are the same soft currency, i. e. the change of the exchange rate between the present date and the settlement date might be for the seller. To product its firm from suffering loss, the seller should define in the contract its firm from suffering loss, the seller should define in the contract the equivalent contractual amount in another strong currency according to the rate between this soft currency and another strong currency on the day of concluding the contract. On the date of payment, the amount in hard currency shall be converted into soft currency at the rate of that date accordingly. This converted amount of soft currency is what the buyer should pay to the seller.

5.1.2 Clause of Price in Contract

Price clause includes unit price and total amount. A unit price is composed of four parts; currency unit, unit price figure, measurement unit and delivery term. For example, USD 500 per barrel FOB Dalian.

1. Fixed price

The common way of price stipulation is to define a fixed price mutually agreed. The fixed price is so clear a definite as to facilitate accounting.

2. Flexible price

Because of the uncertainty of the market situation, price may be flexibly stipulated as "price to be agreed on the date of XXX" or only part of the price is fixed.

3. Price adjustment (revision) clause

For contracts of machinery and equipment which require long production time, a "Price Adjustment Revision Clause" is added to a fixed price and normally only an "Initial Price" is decided upon at the time of contract stipulation. Under this clause, the price can be added according to the changes of salaries, and prices of raw materials, etc.

5.2 Commission and Discount

5.2.1 Commission

Commission will be specifically stipulated when an intermediary is involved in the deal. It refers to the money received by an agent for his intermediary service. Commission may or may not be include in the price, which may be expressed in different ways, such as USD 1000 per M/T CFR Seattle, including 2% commission, or USD 1000 per M/T CFRC 2% Seattle, or USD 1000 per M/T CFRC 2% Seattle, or USD 1000 per M/T CFRC2 Seattle. The commission included in a price is called plain commission, otherwise it's called secret commission. Chinese foreign trade enter prices usually make quotations with commissioners, while collecting secret commission when they act as agents of domestic enterprises in import and export, that is, the amount of commission is not shown in the quotation. Contract price with commission is called commission-included price. We get commission by multiplying this price with commission rate.

5.2.2 Discount

Discount is a certain percentage of price reduction, a special favor given by the exporter to the importer. There are different types of discount such as "quantity discount", "cash discount", and "special discount" for some special purposes. Discount is also specified in the price clause, such as "USD2000per metric ton CIF London less 3% discount". Discount is usually used as a means of promoting and expanding sales.

Chapter 6 Transport of Commodity

6.1 Type of Transport

International cargo transport is an important link in international trade. Shipping documents are one of the essential documents in international settlement. Clause of shipment is one of the major clauses of the contract. Transport allows goods to be conveyed from one place to another. Without transport, international trade would not be possible. Carriage of goods can take place by sea, rail, air, road, inland waterway, parcel post, container and multimodal transportation.

6.1.1 Sea Transportation (Ocean Transportation)

Ocean transport is the most widely used mode of transport in international trade. It accounts for 90% of international transport, In China, ocean transport is in the overwhelmingly majority. The advantages of ocean transport are easy passage, large capacity and low cost. However, ocean transport is slow, vulnerable to bad weather and less punctual if compared with road or air transport. According to ways of operation, ocean transport can be divided into liner transport and charter transport.

1. Liner Transport

(1) Characteristics of liner transport

①Fixed sailing date, fixed route, making calls at scheduled ports and relatively fixed freight rate.

②Liner freight covers loading and unloading charges, so the carrier is responsible for the loading and unloading.

(2) Freight rate

Freight rate is stipulated in the tariff. It contains basic freight rate and various kinds of surcharges.

①Standards of collecting freight:

a. Weight: For items marked with "W" in the tariff, the freight thereon is to be calculated per metric ton on weight (weight ton).

b. Measurement: For items marked with "M", the freight is to be calculated per cubic meter on measurement of the cargo (measurement ton).

c. Weight or measurement: For items marked with "W/M", the freight is to be calculated on basis of either weight or measurement ton, subject to the higher one.

d. "Ad Val.": For items marked with "Ad Val.", the freight is to be calculated on the basis of the price or value of the cargo concerned. For some valuable goods like gold, platinum, silver, precision instrument, expensive fur, usually 1%~5% of the price.

e. "W/M or Ad val.": For items marked "W/, or Ad val." The highest rate is adopted.

②Various kinds of surcharges

In addition to be the basic freight rates, there are many kinds of surcharges that can not be ignored:

a. bunker adjustment factor

b. port surcharges

c. transshipment surcharges

d. heavy lift and long length additional

2. Charter Transport

Charter here refers to the practice of paying money to a shipping company to use their boats. Charter rate is much cheaper than that of the liner. Shippers may choose direct route. Therefore it is widely used in transport of bulk cargo. There are two types of charter transport, i. e. voyage charter transport and time charter transport.

(1) Voyage charter transport

A voyage charter is the hire of a ship for a particular voyage. It can be further divided into single voyage charter, consecutive voyage charter and so on. The ship owner is responsible for fulfilling transportation according to the stipulated voyage, and for the operation and management of the ship, and should bear all costs in transit. The freight rate is usually charged by quantities of the goods carried, or a fixed rate, no matter how much is the quantity.

A charter party is a contract for the hire of an entire ship for a particular voyage or a set period of time. It provides the rights and obligations of the two sides. It should be made clear as to who will bear the loading and unloading charges. If the ship owner is not prepared to bear these charges, the deadline or rate of loading and unloading should be set down. Stipulation of loading and unloading charges is as follows:

①Liner terms: The freight includes loading and unloading charges. The ship owner shall be responsible for loading and unloading.

②Free out: The freight includes loading charges.

③Free in: The freight includes unloading charges.

④Free in and out: If the ship owner is neither responsible for loading and unloading nor for stowed and trimmed charges, "F. I. O. S. T." is applicable.

(2) Time charter transport

A time charter is the charter of a ship for a definite period of time. The ship owner is responsible for providing seaworthy ship and the related charges. The renter has the right to dispatch the ship, but should bear all expenditures in transit, such as charges for fuels, port and loading and unloading.

6.1.2 Rail transport

Rail transport is a major mode of transport in terms of capacity, only second to ocean transport. It is capable of achieving relatively high speed and is very economical especially if it provides the complete trainload for a shipper on a regular basis. Besides, it is less prone to interruption by poor weather. But it is confined to railroads and therefore less flexible. Rail transport can be divided into international combined rail transport and domestic rail transport.

6.1.3 Air transport

1. The Features of Air Transport

Air transport is one of the youngest forms of distribution. The most obvious advantage of air freight is quick transit. The following are its pros and cons:

(1) Quick, reliable transits: This eliminates the need of extensive warehouse accommodation and reduces the risk of stockpiling, obsolescence, deterioration and capital tied up in warehouse and stock provision.

(2) Low risk of damage and pilferage, competitive insurance premium.

(3) Ideal mode for consumer-type cargoes such as fresh flowers and fruits which deteriorate easily, fashionable articles that have a short selling lie, seasonal goods or merchandise of high value to low weight ratio.

(4) High operating cost and initial cost of air when compared to overall capacity. Average aircraft capacity is only 2,000 ~ 25,000kg.

2. Types of Air Transport

Air transport services are divided into three categories: scheduled airlines, chartered carriers, and consolidated consignments by freight forwarders

(1) Scheduled airlines: scheduled airlines operate on a scheduled service, over a fixed airline and between fixed airports. They are suit able for conveying fresh, emergent and seasonal goods.

(2) Chartered carriers: Chartered carriers are the hire of an air craft by a shipper or several shippers to deliver cargoes. They are ideal for carrying cargoes of large quantities or carrying

cargoes of different shippers to the same destination.

(3) Consolidate consignments: Consolidated consignments mean that the air freight forwarder usually assembles a number of individual shipments into one consignment and dispatches them on one air way bill. A consolidated shipment made up by several shipments can be dispatched to one common destination, Many shippers prefer this kind of shipment as the freight rate is 7%~10% lower than that of a scheduled airline published by IATA.

6.1.4 Container Transport

Container transport is a method of distributing merchandise in a unitized form, suitable for ocean, rail and multi-modal transport. It is the most modern form of physical international distribution and overall is highly efficient in terms of reliability, cost, quality of service and so on.

The advantages of container transport are as follows.

(1) It can be handled quickly and easily by standardized equipment and can thus save labors and loading and unloading charges.

(2) The low risk of cargo damage and pilferage enables more favorable cargo premium to be obtained, compared with break-bulk cargo shipments.

(3) Less packing is required for containerized consignments, no packing is required. This produces substantial cost savings in the international transit and raises service quality.

(4) Faster transit, coupled with more reliable maritime schedules, and ultimately increased service frequency, produces savings in warehouse accommodation needs, lessens risks of obsolescent stock and speeds up capital turnover.

6.1.5 International Multi-modal Transport

Following the containerization of international transport, a brand new mode of transport "international multi-modal transport" has been introduced in the transport industry. International multi-modal transport means the carriage of cargo by at least two modes of transport on the basis of a multi-modal transport contract from a place at which the cargoes are collected in one country to a place designed for delivery in another country. Although different models of transport (sea, air, rail, etc.) are combined, only one multi-modal transport operator is responsible for taking the cargo from the consignor and delivering them to the consignee.

The use of containers in multi-modal transport means high efficiency. Better quality of transport, lower cost and less time required for cargo movement between the point of origin and place of delivery. Multi-model transport document is the only document to use, which also adds to the economy and simplicity of the documentation process.

6.2 Transport Document

6.2.1 Bill of lading (B/L)

A bill of lading is a transportation document which is issued by an ocean carries to a shipper with whom the carrier has entered into a contract for the carriage of goods.

1. Purposes Served by Bill of Lading

A bill of lading serves there purpose: First, it is a carrier's receipt for goods. Second, it's evidence of a contract of carriage. Finally it's a document of title, that is, the person rightfully in possession of the bill is entitled to possess, use, and dispose of the goods the bill represents. The B/L is a receipt for goods shipped on board a vessel, signed by the person (or his agent) who contract to carry them, and stating the conditions in which the goods were delivered to the ship.

(1) Receipt for the goods

A bill of lading describes the goods put on board a carrier, states the quality, and their condition . The form itself is normally filled out in advance by the shipper; then, as the goods loaded comply with the goods listed. The carrier, however, is responsible only to check for out ward compliance that is, that the labels comply and that the packages are not damaged. If all appears proper, the appropriate agent of the carrier will sign the bill and return it to the shipper.

(2) Evidence of the contract of carriage

Between the shipper and the carrier the bill of lading is evidence of their contract of carriage.

(3) Document of title to the goods

T he named consignee of the holder of a bill of lading, provided he has received it in good faith through due negotiation, has a claim to title and, by surrendering the bill, to delivery of the goods.

2. Types of bill lading

There are a number of different types of bill of lading. The following lists those encountered the most often.

(1) Shipped (on board) bill of lading and received for shipment bill of lading.

Shipped B/L is issued by the shipping company after the goods are actually shipped on board the designed vessel and the date of issue of the B/L are indicated on the shipped B/L. And the date of issue is the date of shipment. Since shipped bill of lading provides better guarantee for the consignee to receive the cargo at the destination, the importer will normally required exporter to produce shipped B/L and most bill of lading forms are preprinted as "Shipped Bill".

Receive for Shipment B/L arises where the word "shipped" does not appear on bill of lading. It merely confirms that the goods have been over to and are in the custody of the ship owner.

(2) Clean bill of lading and unclean bill of lading

A clean bill of lading is the one issued by a carrier for goods which were received in good condition. A clean bill of lading provides proof that up until the time goods were transferred to the carrier, no damage has occurred. This assists in placing responsibility if in fact goods are eventually in other than undamaged condition.

When goods are received in damaged condition for shipment on a vessel, the master of the ship will note the damage on the bill of lading. A bill of lading with such a notation is referred to as an unclean bill of lading. Unclean B/L is usually not acceptable to the buyer and bank.

(3) Straight B/L, Blank B/L and order B/L

Straight bill of lading has designed consignee. Under this bill, only the consignee at the destination is entitled to take delivery of the cargo. As it is not transferable, it is not commonly used in international trade and normally applies to high-value shipments or goods for special purposes.

Blank B/L also called Open B/L or bear B/L, means that there is no definite consignee of the goods. There usually appear in the box of consignee word like "to bear". Anyone who holds the bill is entitled to the goods the bill represents. NO endorsement is needed for the transfer of the blank bill. Due to the exceedingly high risk involved, this bill is rarely used.

Order B/L: is widely used in international trade. It means that the goods are consigned or destined to the order of a named person. In the box of consignee, "to order", "to order the shipper", or "To order of the consignee" is marked . this type of bill of lading is a negotiable instrument. That is it may be used to transfer title to goods being shipped to another party. The transfer may occur at any time during the transit process simply by conveying the order bill to another party. Order B/ L can be transferred only after endorsement is made. If it is made out to order of the consignee, the consignee will endorse the bill to transfer it.

(4) Direct transshipment and through bill of lading

Direct B/L means the goods are shipped from the port of lading direct to the port of destination.

Through bill of lading is something necessary to employ two or more carriers to get the goods to their final destination. In this case, usually the fast carrier will sign and issued a through bill of lading the on-carriage may be either by a second vessel or by a different form of transport.

(5) Long form bill of lading and short form bill of lading

Long form bill of lading is more detailed with shipping contract clauses printed on the back of the page.

Short form B/L, as the name implied, is an abbreviated type of document, not containing the long list of detailed clauses that generally appear on bills of lading.

6.3 Transport Clause in Contract

6.3.1 Time of Shipment and Delivery

Shipment clause includes time of delivery, port (place) of shipment and destination, etc.

The seller fulfills his obligation of delivery when the goods are shipped on board the vessel or delivered to the carrier. All these contracts are shipment contracts. The time of delivery in the contract is the time of shipment is a very important clause in a contract. Any delay or advance of delivery constitutes violation of contract. There are several ways of stipulating time of delivery in contract:

(1) time of shipment definitely stated

for example: shipment during December 2011

shipment not later than 31st december, 2011

(2) shipment within xx days after receipt of L/C

For a contract in which payment is made by L/C, in order to avoid the risks of losses resulted from the buyer's failure in opening L/C, or for taking use of L/C as a means of delivery this way. Under this circumstance, the seller would wait for the arrival of the L/C before getting the goods ready. Therefore the time of delivery is related with the time of receipt of L/C.

6.3.2 Partial Shipment and Transshipment

1. Partial shipment

Partial shipment, also described as shipment by installments, means the goods in one contract are to be shipped in lots. In international trade, sometimes partial shipment has to be made because of large quantity of the transaction, or the limitation of supplies and transportation. If no such clause is stated in the contract, it is regarded as "partial shipment is not allowed". But some international rules stipulate oppositely, for example, UCP 500 stipulates that partial drawings and/or shipments are allowed unless the credit stipulates otherwise. In view of the above differences, we should make it clear in the contract as to whether partial shipment is allowed to avoid misunderstandings. Stipulate allowing partial shipment only. The exact time of delivery and the quantities of each lot and the total lots are not stipulated in the contract. This way of stipulating is favorable to the seller since he can decide how much and when the goods are to be shipped based on the supplies of goods an the transportation conditions. State in detail the time of delivery and quantity of each lot. This way is usually adopted when the buyer need to resell the goods or has some special requirements in use. This way strictly limits the seller. If he fails to carry out any one lot, he shall be responsible for breaking the contract. According to UCP 500, transportation documents which appear on their face to indicate that shipment has been made on the same means of conveyance and for the same journey, provided they indicate the same destination, will not be regarded as covering partial shipments, even the transport documents indicate different dates of shipment and/or different ports of loading.

2. Transshipment

According to UCP 500, transshipment means a transfer and reloading during the course of carriage from one conveyance or vessel to another conveyance or vessel, within the same mode of transport or from one mode of transport to another mode of transportation. Unless transshipment is prohibited by the terms of the credit, it is allowed. However, in the absence of terms as to whether transshipment is allowed or not in the contract, transshipment is to be construed as not allowed.

Chapter 7 Insurance of Commodity

7.1 Perils of the Sea

Perils of the sea are some of the causes of losses which may affect property on an ocean voyage. Generally speaking, perils of the sea are those causes over which the captain of a vessel has no control. Thus if a peril of the sea causes damage to cargo, whether the carrier may be responsible depends upon the nature of the loss. If there was no negligence on the part of the captain of the ship, the carrier could probably not be held responsible for compensating cargo owners for loss or damage. Cargo insurance coverage is available to cover for such losses for the benefit of the cargo owner. Perils of the sea include:

(1) Natural calamities: Natural calamities cover bad weather, thunder and lightening, flood, floating, drift ice, earthquake, tsunami and other irresistible disasters.

(2) Fortuitous accident: Fortuitous accidents mainly include stranded (get aground), striking a rock, sunk, collide, fire, exploding and missing and other accidents with sea characteristics.

(3) Extraneous risks: Extraneous risks refer to risks outside perils of the sea. General extraneous risks include theft, breakage, leakage, contamination, sweat and heating, taint of odor, hook damage, shortage, and rust. Special extraneous risks refer to risks resulting from military affairs, political and administrative rules such as war, strike, failure to deliver, rejection, etc.

7.2 Ocean Average

7.2.1 Total Loss

Average means loss sustained in sea transportation. According to the extent of the loss, it is divided into total loss and partial loss.

1. Actual total loss

Where the subject matter insured is destroyed, or so damaged as to cease to be a thing of the kind insured, or where the assured is irretrievably deprived thereof, there is an actual total loss. Furthermore, actual total loss, within the meaning of the definition, may be construed in three distinct ways, namely:

(1) When the subject matter is totally destroyed.

(2) When the subject matter is so damaged as to cease to be a thing of the kind insured, and

(3) When the assured is irretrievably deprived thereof.

2. Constructive total loss

There is a constructive total loss where the subject matter insured is reasonably abandoned on account of its actual total loss appearing to be unavoidable, or because it could not be preserved from actual loss without an expenditure which would exceed its value when the expenditure had been incurred.

7.2.2 Partial Loss

A partial loss is any loss other than a total loss. A partial loss may include a particular average loss, a general average loss and particular charges.

1. A particular average loss

If the average (damage) is accidently occasioned by some perils insured against, and not by the deliberate act of a person for the common benefit, that loss must be sustained exclusively by the person upon whom the damage falls and is termed a particular average. Or we may say it is the accidental damage to part of the cargo. For instance, ten per cent of the cotton yarn cargo was burned when the ship caught fire.

2. General average loss

Where parts of a ship or cargo are sacrificed, or expenses are incurred by a ship in order to preserve the property of others who are parties to the common adventure, then the act is said to be a general average act, and the loss incurred is then spread "generally" amongst the beneficiaries. Thus, for there to be a general average act, certain criteria must be met.

(1) The peril must be real and actually exist.

(2) "Reasonably made" infers that the master of a vessel must act reasonably when making a sacrifice for which others will eventually be partly liable.

(3) There is a general average act where any extraordinary sacrifice or expenditure is voluntarily and reasonably made or incurred in time of peril for the purpose of preserving the property imperiled in the common adventure.

(4) For there to be a general average loss, there must be an "extraordinary" sacrifice or expenditure which is made for the benefit of all the parties to the common adventure.

(5) The sacrifice may take the fore of cargo or ship's apparel being deliberately case away for the benefit of the whole venture.

(6) The actions of the ship's master should be successful in saving the voyage

7.3 Insurance Clause in Contract

Ocean Marine Cargo Clause of the People's Insurance Company of China was constituted in 1972 and revised in 1976 and 1981. There are mainly two types of insurance coverage: basic coverage and additional coverage, the additional coverage includes general additional coverage and special additional coverage.

7.3.1 Basic Coverage

1. FPA (free from particular average)

FPA is a limited form of cargo insurance cover under which partial loss or damage resulted from natural calamities is not recoverable, unless these natural calamities occur before or after fortuitous accidents. It provides coverage for total losses and general average.

2. WPA or WA (with particular average, with average)

WPA is a wider cover than FPA. It provides cover against all loss or damage due to marine perils throughout the duration if the policy, including partial loss or damage which may be attributed to natural calamities like heavy weather.

3. All Risks

All Risks is the most comprehensive of the three basic coverage under which the insurer is responsible for all total or partial loss of, or damage to the goods insured either arising from sea perils or general external causes, However, it does not cover loss, damage or expense caused by delay, inherent or nature of the goods, or special external risks of war, strike, etc.

7.3.2 Additional Risks

1. General additional risks

The following general extraneous risks are to be covered subject to additional premium.

(1) Risk of theft, pilferage and non-delivery (TPND), Risk of theft and pilferage refers to the risk against the cargo's being stolen in transit of voyage. Risk of non-delivery refers to the risk against loss of complete packages (including box, case, drum etc.) due to improper unloading or for some unknown reason.

(2) Risk of fresh water and / or rain damages (FWRD). The risk of damage to the goods by fresh water and /or rain is covered by this coverage.

(3) Risk of clean and breakage. Under this coverage is the risk of breakage of the fragile goods by vibration, clash or pressing.

(4) Risk of leakage. It covers the risk of seepage and leakage of the liquid goods caused by

the damaged container.

(5) Risk of shortage. This risk covers the shortage of weight for the goods due to the external packing broken. However, normal short age of weight in transit is not covered.

(6) Risk of intermixture and contamination. Damage to the goods caused by its being intermixed or contaminated with each other is covered by this risk.

(7) Risk of taint of odor. Edibles, herbal medicine, cosmetics or raw materials may sometimes be tainted by odor of their own. Such a risk is under this coverage.

(8) Risk of sweating and heating. Under this coverage is the risk of damage of the goods by sweat and heating as a result of the sudden change of temperature or the ventilation on the vessel being out of order, etc.

(9) Risk of rust. It covers the risk of damage to the goods by rust caused by contamination with sea water. But goods getting rusty by itself or due to its own flaw is exclude.

(10) Risk of breakage of packing. Damage to the goods caused by rough handling is covered by this risk.

(11) Hook damage. It covers damage to the goods caused by hooks in the process of loading and unloading, such as the losses of cereals due to the damage of packing bags by hooks.

General additional risks cannot be covered independently and should go with FPA or WPA. They are included in All Risks coverage.

2. Special addition risks

Special additional risks cover the damage or losses arising from special additional reason such as political event, military affairs, national policies and acts, and administrative measures. The special additional risks include (1) war risk; (2) strike risk; (3) failure to delivery risk; (4) import duty risk; (5) on deck risk (6) rejections risk.

These additional coverage are usually taken out together with FPA, WPA and All Risks.

Chapter 8 International Trade Payment

8.1 Instruments of Payment

In international trade, it is hardly possible for the seller to deliver the goods and the buyer to make the payment face to face. Usually, the seller delivers the goods and hands over the documents. Banks are intermediaries. Bills are instruments of payment. These are the features of modern international trade payment. Nowadays non-cash payment is universally adopted all over the world. Under non-cash payment, negotiable instruments to be commonly used as payment instruments are bills of exchange, promissory notes and checks, among which bills of exchange are the most widely used ones. No export transaction can be said to be successful until payment has been received for the goods delivered overseas, and the proceeds have been safely credited to the exporter's account. Compared with payment arrangements for domestic transactions, international payment arrangements are much more complicated and difficult. This chapter will focus on instruments of payment, methods and terms of payment in international trade of goods.

8.1.1 Bills of exchange (draft)

1. Definition of bills of exchange (Chart 8 -1)

A bill of exchange is a written, dated and signed instrument that contains an unconditional order from the drawer that directs the payer to pay a definite sun of money to a payee on demand or at a specified future date. It is a useful instrument because it allows one party to direct another to pay money either to himself, to his agent, or to a third party. Of course, the order is valid only if the payer has an underlying obligation to pay money to the drawer. This can arise in situations where the drawer is holding money on account of the drawer, where the drawer lent money to a drawee, or where the drawer has sold goods to the drawee and the drawee owes the sale price to the drawer.

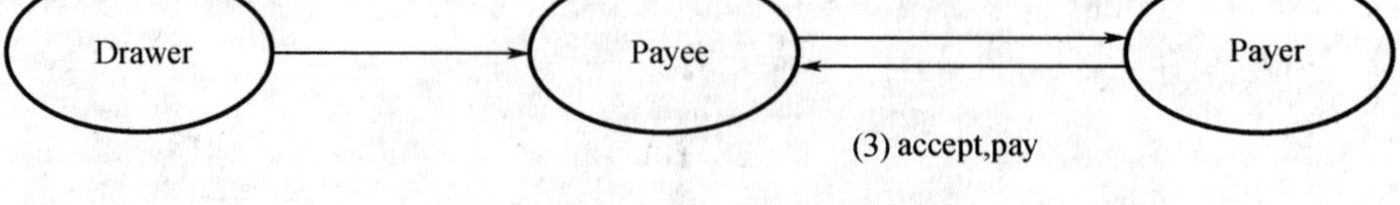

Chart 8 -1 Procedure of Draft

2. Contents of bills of exchange

(1) Parties related to Draft

①Drawer—person who issues the draft, in international trade, the person is usually the exporter.

②Drawee—the payer of the draft, in international trade, the person is usually the importer.

③Payee—person who accepts the draft, in international trade, the person is usually the exporter or his or her nominated person.

(2) Amount and Monetary

It specifies definitely the amount drawee should pay, and the monetary be used. In international trade, the amount of draft should be within the range that of contract or L/C, if there is no special condition, the amount and monetary should be as same as that of invoice, otherwise, the drawee have right to refuse it.

(3) Payment Time

It specifies definitely the payment time, such as "payment at sight", "payment in 30 days", etc.

(4) Place of Issue and Payment

It specifies the place of issue and payment. Usually it marks by the place in which drawer and drawee living.

(5) Signature of drawer

3. Types of bills of exchange

Draft can be classified as the follows according to different views:

(1) Commercial draft: It is a bill issued by a trader on another trader or on a bank.

Banker's draft: It is a draft drawn by a bank on another bank. Both the payer and payee are banks.

(2) Clean draft: It is a bill without shipping documents attached thereto.

Documentary draft: It is a bill with shipping documents attached thereto.

(3) Sight draft or demand draft: It is a bill payable on demand or at sight or on presentation.

Time draft or usance draft: It is a bill payable at a fixed or determinable future time. The time may be expressed in the following three ways:

①at... days after sight.

②at... days after date.

③at a fixed date.

4. Application of bills of exchange

In international trade, the drawer draws and signs and delivers it to the payee. Upon issuance, the drawer has the responsibility to ensure the draft be accepted and paid. If the draft is dishonored, the drawer shall be recourse by the bearer and reimburse the amount, interest and the relevant charges. Acceptance means the drawee of the bill writes down the word "accept", marks the date and signs his name across the face of the bill. This action means the payer promise to pay at the date of payment. In doing so, the drawee (acceptor) commits himself to pay the bill upon presentation at maturity. After accepting the bill, the drawee should return it to the holder who will present it for payment at maturity. On the expiry date of draft, the payer makes sufficient payment to the legal bearer, the latter then writes off the draft and return it to the payer as a receipt. The act of a payee, drawee, or holder of a draft in signing the back of the draft to transfer rights in the draft to another. In financial market, the typical endorsement is discount of draft, i. e. , the bearer transfers a time and accepted draft to a bank or a discounting company, who, as transferee, will deduct the interest as discount rate and pay the remaining sum to the bearer. Dishonor means the payer refuses or fails to pay or accept the bill when the holder makes presentment to him. When dishonored, the holder shall pursue the right of recourse by giving notice of dishonor to the drawer and each endorser. Protest is a written statement under seal drawn up and signed by a Notary Public or other authorized person for the purpose of giving evidence that a bill of exchange has been presented by him for payment but dishonored. After a bill is dishonored by non-acceptance or by non-payment, and a notice of dishonor is sent, the holder may hand the bill to a Notary Public who will present it again for acceptance or for payment as the case may be, so as to obtain a legal proof of the act of dishonor. As it is dishonored again, the Notary Public then draws up a protest, i. e. , an official certificate evidencing the act of dishonor and stating the reason for the protest, demands made on the drawee (or the acceptor) and the response received.

8.1.2 Promissory note (Chart 8 -2)

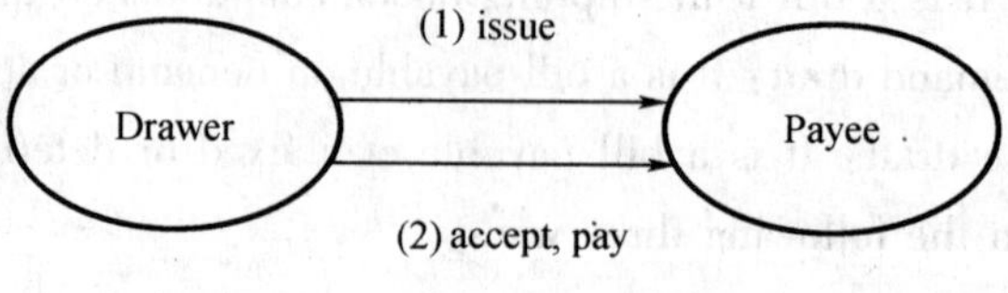

Chart 8 -2 Procedure of Promissory Vote

A written promise to pay a determinate sum of money made between two parties is a promissory note, or simply a note. The party who promises to pay is called the maker; the party who is to be paid is the payee.

8.1.3 Check(Chart 8 -3)

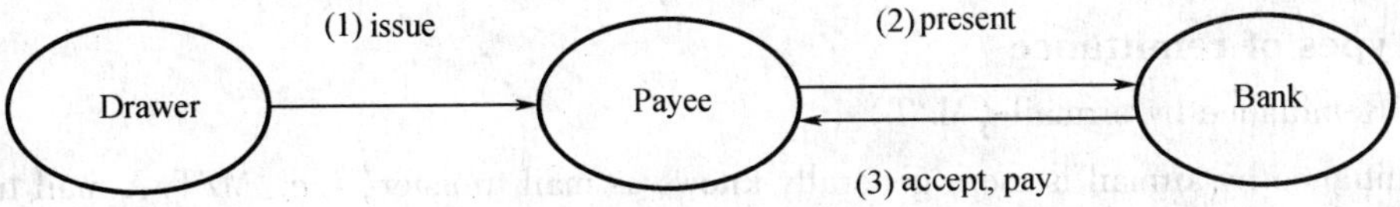

Chart 8 -3 Procedure of Check

A check is a special type of draft, the drawer is the person signing the check, the drawee is the bank where the drawer has an account, and the payee is the beneficiary, that is, the person in whose favor the check is made out. Thus, a check is an unconditional order by the drawer or maker asking his bank to pay a certain amount of money to a third party on demand. In simple terms, a check is a demand draft drawn in a bank. When the drawer signs a check, he should see to it that his deposit in the bank is not lower than the amount of the check. If the drawer has not enough deposit in the bank for the check amount, the check will be dishonored, and this kind as check is called "bounced check", which in not allowed.

8.2 Methods of Payment

8.2.1 Remittance

1. Definition of remittance(Chart 8 -4)

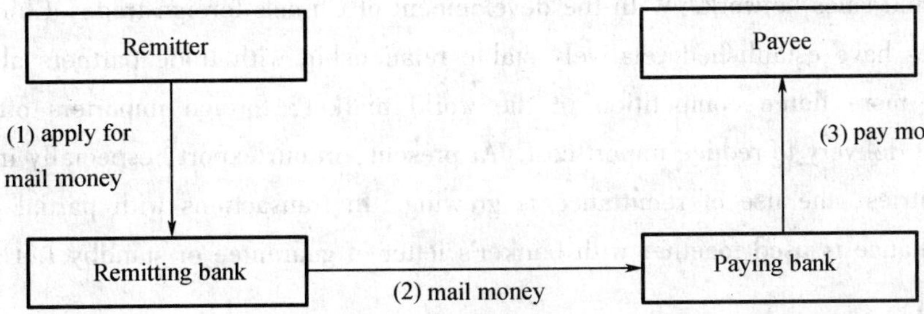

Chart 8 -4 Procedure of Remittance

Remittance refers to the transfer of funds from one party to another between different countries, that is, a bank (the remitting bank), at the request of its customer, transfers a certain sum of money to its overseas branch to correspondent bank (the paying bank) instructing them to pay to a named person or corporation (the payee as beneficiary) domiciled in that country. There are three basic ways for a bank to transfer founds for its client from home country to abroad. They are remittance by airmail, remittance by cable and remittance by demand draft.

2. Types of remittance

(1) Remittance by airmail (M/T)

Remittance by airmail is more generally knows as mail transfer, i. e. M/T. A mail transfer is to transfer funds by means of a payment order or a mail advice to sometimes a debit advice issued by a remitting bank, at the request of the remitter. A payment order, mail advice or debit advice is an authenticated order in writing addressed by one bank to another instructing the latter to pay a sum certain in money to a specified person or a beneficiary named thereon.

(2) Remittance by cable/telex/SWIFT (T/T)

Remittance by cable/telex/SWIFT is often referred to as cable transfer or telegraphic transfer, namely T/T. It is exactly the same as a mail transfer, except that instructions from the remitting bank to the paying bank are transmitted by cable instead of by air mail. It is therefore faster, but more expensive than the mail transfer. It is often used when the remittance amount is large and the transfer of founds is subject to a time limit.

(3) Remittance by banker's demand draft (D/D)

Remittance by banker's demand draft is often referred to as D/D. A banker's draft is a negotiable instrument drawn by a bank on its overseas bank.

In our foreign trade practice, remittance is only adopted in making down payments, commissions, etc. It is not the major method of payment. But it is a major method in developed countries, because of the substantial internal transactions of transnational companies and reliable trade partners and sales network. With the development of China's foreign trade, Chinese foreign trade enterprises have established relatively stable relationship with trade partners abroad. And with more and more fierce competition in the world market, foreign importers often ask for payment against delivery to reduce import cost. At present, in our export, especially in trade with developed countries, the use of remittance is growing. In transactions with partial or deferred payment, remittance is used together with banker's letter of guarantee or standby L/C.

8.2.2 Collection

1. Definition of collection

After he has shipped the goods to his customers abroad, the exporter draws a bill of exchange on the latter with or without shipping documents attached thereto and then gives the draft to his bank together with his appropriate collection instructions. In simple terms, a collection means that the creditor entrusts the bank to collect payment from the debtor. The bank acts as the intermediary.

2. Parties related to collection (Chart 8 -5)

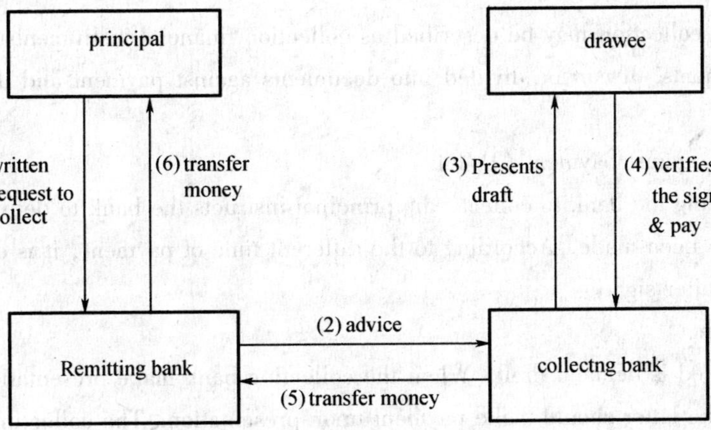

Chart 8 -5 Procedure of Collection

Usually there are four parties related to collection, that is principal (exporter), remitting bank, collecting bank and drawee.

(1) principal

It is the exporter or the seller who entrusts the collection items to his bank.

(2) drawee

It is the buyer or the importer to whom the collection items are to be presented for acceptance or payment.

(3) remitting bank

It is the bank to which the drawer entrusts the collection items. Upon receipt of the collection items from the exporter, the bank for wards them to the collection bank, in accordance with the collection instruction given by the principal.

(4) collecting bank

It is the bank entrusted by the remitting bank to present the collection items to the drawer. The collecting items of drawer, the collection bank is generally a branch of a correspondent or an agent of the remitting bank.

3. Types of collection

(1) clean collections

Clean collections are collections on financial instruments without being accompanied by commercial documents. Such as invoice, bill of lading, insurance policy etc.

(2) documentary collections

Documentary collection may be described as collection financial instruments accompanied by commercial documents. It can be divided into documents against payment and document against acceptance.

①documents against payment (D/P)

When entrusting the bank to collect, the principal instructs the bank to deliver the document when payment has been made. According to the different time of payment, it is divided into D/P at sight and D/P after sight

a. D/P at sight

The draft issued is demand draft. When the collecting bank make presentation to the drawer (the importer), the latter should make payment upon presentation. The collecting bank will then deliver the documents to him.

b. D/P after sight

Time draft is used in D/P after sight. When the collecting bank makes presentation, the buyer shall first make acceptance after checking the documents and will make payment in the date of expiry of payment

②document against acceptance (D/A)

But there are some differences between D/A and cash on delivery: In cash on delivery, the seller can only sue the buyer on basis contract but also on draft accepted by the buyer. The relationship between the creditor and the debtor defined by the draft is simple and stable, and the seller is relatively in favorable position.

8.2.3 Letter of Credit

1. Definition of letter of credit (Chart 8 -6)

In international sales transaction, the seller, undoubtedly, would prefer to be paid in advance. The buyer, on the other hand, would like to make sure, before paying, that

(1) The goods are actually shipped and that;

(2) The goods shipped meet his contractual specifications;

(3) To take delivery before paying. Depending on the relative bargaining power of the buyer and seller, any of these possible arrangements can be included as a term in the sales contract, If

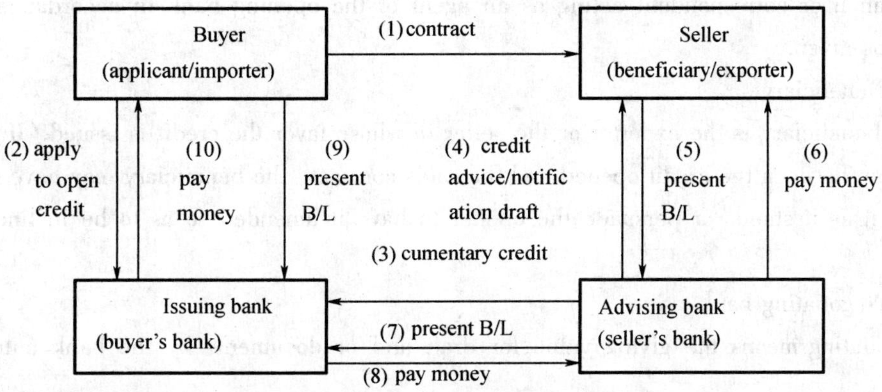

Chart 8－6　Procedure of L/C

the seller is unable to determine the buyer's creditworthiness, he may insist upon " cash in advance". If the buyer wants to confirm that the goods have been shipped, the term documents against payment can be used. If the buyer insists upon taking delivery before making payment, a document against acceptance term can be used. None of these terms are used very often. In part, this is because they imply that both sides distrust each other, To avoid this, contracting parties use a "letter of credit" A letter of credit or L/C is a conditional undertaking of payments by a bank.

2. Parties to letter of credit

Probably the parties related to L/C include opening bank, applicant, advising bank, beneficiary, negotiating bank and paying bank.

(1) Applicant or opener

The applicant or the opener is always an importer or a buyer, who fills out and signs an application form, requesting the bank to issue a letter of credit in favor of an exporter or a seller abroad.

(2) Issuing bank or opening bank

The issuing bank is one which issues a letter of credit at the request of an applicant. It is located in the same place with the applicant. It undertakes to pay to the beneficiary. If the applicant fails to pay after the issuing bank makes payment, the latter has the right to sell the goods and claim from the applicant if the proceeds are not sufficient.

(3) Advising bank

The advising bank is one which advises the credit to the beneficiary in accordance with stipulations on the credit. It is located in the place of the beneficiary, which is usually the issuing bank's branch or correspondent acting as an agent of the opening bank in accordance with the instructions given.

(4) Beneficiary

The beneficiary is the exporter or the seller in whose favor the credit is issued. If there is a discrepancy between the credit opened and the sales contract, the beneficiary may have the option to accept it as it stands or persuade the opener to have it amended so as to be in line with the contract.

(5) Negotiating bank

Negotiating means the giving value for draft and/or documents by the bank authorized to negotiate.

(6) Paying bank

The paying bank is always the drawee of a draft stipulated in the credit. Or we may say it is a bank nominated by the issuing bank to make payment under the credit. Sometimes the paying bank is the issuing bank itself.

3. Procedures of letter of credit operations

The documentary credit procedure involves the following steps:

(1) The buyer and seller agree on the terms of sale: ①specifying a documentary credit as the means of payment, ②naming an advising bank (usually the seller's bank), ③ listing required documents.

(2) The buyer applies to his bank (issuing bank) to open a documentary credit naming the seller as the beneficiary based on specific terms and conditions that are listed in the credit.

(3) After accepting the application, the opening bank shall stipulate L/C clauses strictly conforming to the instructions of application form and mail or send by SWIFT to the advising bank named in the credit.

(4) After verifying the authenticity of the credit, the advising bank shall advise the beneficiary of L/C or just transferring the L/C to him. And a copy is usually kept for file. There are two ways of advising: one is to deliver the L/C directly to the beneficiary, attached with a signed advice note. Another one is when the addressee of the L/C is the advising bank, the advising bank shall copy word by word in its own advice note, sign, and deliver it to the beneficiary.

(5) The seller (beneficiary) ships the goods to the buyer and obtains a negotiable transport document (negotiable bill of lading) from the shipping firm/agent.

(6) The seller prepares and presents a document package to the advising bank consisting of documents such as negotiable transport document, commercial invoice, insurance policy,

inspection certificate, etc.

(7) The advising bank reviews the document package making certain the document are in conformity with the terms of the credit and pays the seller. In the case of a credit available by negotiation, the negotiating bank (usually be the advising bank) negotiates the documents with recourse to the beneficiary. After negotiation, the negotiating bank will claim reimbursement from the issuing bank or the reimbursing bank in accordance with the reimbursement terms indicated in the credit and documents will be sent to the issuing bank. The advising bank sends the document package by mail or by courier to the issuing bank. The issuing bank reviews the document package making certain the documents are in conformity with the terms of the credit, pays the advising bank and advising the buyer that the documents have arrived. The buyer reviews the document package making certain the documents are in conformity with the terms of credit, and makes a cash payment (with a sight draft) to the issuing bank, or signs an acceptance (promising to pay at a future date). The issuing bank sends the document package by mail or courier to the buyer who then takes possession of the shipment. At present, most L/Cs are opened by telecommunication. Although the forms are different their contents are, in the main, the same.

4. Characteristics of letter of credit business

(1) A banker's credit

The issuing bank undertakes to effect payment, provided the documents presented are in compliance with the terms and conditions of the letter of credit. Thus the bank assumes a primary liability rather than a secondary liability for payment.

(2) Banks deal with documents

In letter of credit business, banks deal with documents and not with goods, services and/or other performances to which the documents may relate. They examine exclusively on the basis of the credit are fulfilled. They are not in a position to verify whether the goods supplied actually conform with those specified in the credit. They are not to be held liable for a discrepancy between the goods invoiced and those actually delivered. If the documents presented are not in compliance with the terms and conditions of the credit, the bank will refuse to pay no matter whether the goods shipped are agreed with those mentioned in the contract.

(3) A letter of credit is a self-sufficient instrument

Although the credit is issued on the basis of the sales contract, banks are in no way concerned with or bound by such contract, even if any reference whatsoever to such contract is included in the credits. The bank, when issuing the credit has no regard for the sales contract but follows an application handed in by the buyer.

5. Classification of letters of credit

(1) According to the revocability of credit

A credit may be either revocable or irrevocable. Every credit should clearly indicate whether it is revocable or irrevocable. In the absence of such indication the credit shall be deemed to be irrevocable.

①Irrevocable credit

An irrevocable credit is a credit which constitutes a definite undertaking of the issuing bank and can be amended or cancelled by the issuing bank only on condition that all parties concerned, that is, the issuing bank, the beneficiary and the confirming bank, if any, do agree. This credit gives the beneficiary greater assurance of payment.

②A revocable credit

A revocable credit is a credit which can be amended or cancelled at any moment by the issuing bank without prior notice to the beneficiary. However, under such a credit, if the payment, acceptance, or negotiation has been effected by the banks concerned prior to their receipt of notice of amendment or cancellation, the issuing bank will still have to reimburse them.

(2) According to the method of payment

All credits must clearly indicate whether they are available by payment, by acceptance or by negotiation.

①payment L/C

A payment credit is a credit available by payment, under which a bank specifically nominated there in is authorized to pay against the shipping documents with or without a draft presented in conformity with the terms of the credit.

②Acceptance credit

An acceptance credit is a credit available by acceptance, under which a bank specifically nominated therein is authorized to accept.

③Negotiation credit

A negotiation credit is a credit under which a bank specifically nominated there in is authorized to negotiate or a credit which is freely negotiable by any bank.

(3) Special credits

①Revolving credit

This is a type of credit that renews itself after amount is drawn. To define it more clearly, it is a credit where, under the terms and conditions thereof, its amount is renewed or reinstated without any specific amendment made thereto.

②Back-to-back credit

This is a new credit opened on the basis of an already existing nontransferable credit. It is used by traders to make payment to the ultimate supplier. A trader receives a little of credit from the buyer and then opens another letter of credit in favor of the supplier .

6. Letter of Credit Clause in contract

(1)Sight L/C

The buyers shall arrange with × × bank for opening an irrevocable(transferable divisible) letter of credit (confirmed by × × Bank) in favor of the Sellers before-(or within—days after receipt of the Sellers' advice or within—days after signing of this contract). The said letter of credit shall be available by sight draft for full invoice value and remain valid for negotiation in China until the 15th day after date of shipment.

(2)Draft L/C

The letter of credit must stipulate that reimbursement is to be made telegraphically upon receipt of the cable advice of negotiation. The buyers shall arrange with × × bank for opening an irrevocable(transferable) banker's acceptance letter of credit in favor of the sellers before-(or within—days after receipt of Sellers advice, or within—days after signing of this Contract). The said letter of credit shall be available by draft at—sight(or after shipment) and remain valid for negotiation in China until the 15th day after the aforesaid time of shipment.

8.2.4 Banker's Letter of guarantee

In international trade, each party of the contract wants to be ensured that the other party is in a position to honor its commitment as contracted. Such security may be obtained through banks in the form of letter of guarantee. A Banker's Letter of guarantee (L/G) or bond is a contract by which a bank (the guarantor) agrees to pay another's debt or to perform another's obligation only if that other individual or legal entity fails to pay or perform. A banker's letter of guarantee is usually a separate contract from the principal agreement, and therefore the letter of guarantee is secondarily liable to the third person.

Chapter 9 Inspection, Claim, Force Majeure and Arbitration

9.1 Commodity Inspection

9.1.1 Purpose of commodity inspection

In international trade, inspection is an absolutely necessary step in the transfer of the goods form the seller to the buyer. United Nations Convention on Contracts for the International Sale of Goods (hereinafter called CISG) and the laws of various countries have made similar stipulations on the buyer right of inspection. In actuality, in order to clarify the responsibilities, clauses regarding inspection are ally stipulated in the contract, which cover the place and time of inspection, basis for inspection, inspection organization, and so on. In order to solve disputes arising from breach of contract by any party, claim clauses regarding validity of claim , basis for claim, and even the amount for claim are included in the contract. If, however, the, breach of contract by any party is due to force majeure, the party concerned shall hold no liability. In order to ascertain whether an event is force majeure, we may stipulate the scope of majeure in the advance. In the event that both parties have different interpretation on some facts or clauses or any party shirks liabilities intentionally, mediation and arbitration are usually required. Sometimes a law suit may be taken. Among the ways of settling international trade disputes, arbitration is favored by most businessmen.

In international trade, the quality and quantity of the goods delivered by the seller should be in the manner requires by the contract. In this sense, inspection of commodity and the issuance of certificate of inspection are necessary steps in the transfer of goods. Inspection may be made by the seller and the buyer themselves. But on most occasions, the seller does not transfer the goods to the buyer face to face. In addition, during the long distance transit, loading and unloading operation, losses of or damage to the goods may occur owing to the various kinds of risks or the carriers' fault. For the purpose of identifying liabilities and ascertaining facts, inspection by authoritative, impartial inspection bodies is required, by whom the certificates of inspection are issued. There certificates have been the major basis for transferring the goods, making payments, lodging and settling claims in international trade.

9.1.2 Time and places of inspection

There are three ways of stipulating the and time of inspection in the contract

(1) Shipping quality and weight

This means that inspection at the seller's factory or the port of shipping is final. Buyers can re-inspect the goods at the port destination, but normally he cannot claim for compensation. Thus it is favorable to the seller.

(2) Landed quality and weight

This means inspection carried out at the port of destination is final . This arrangement is favorable to the buyer.

(3) Inspection at the port of shipment and re-inspection at the port of destination

It means after inspection at port of shipment, the buyer retains the right to re-inspect and claim for compensation if the merchandise doesn't comply with the contract. This method is favorable to both sides and therefore is widely used in international trade.

9.1.3 Inspection body

There are mainly two types of inspection body: government and non-governmental. The governmental inspection bodies such as the Food and Drugs Administration (FDA) in the USA specialize in inspection of particular merchandise (grain, drug, etc.) The international inspection of commodity is mainly undertaken by nongovernmental bodies which have the same legal status as notary organizations.

According to the Law of the of People's Republic of China on Import (hereinafter referred to as This law) and Export Commodity Inspection and the Regulations for the Implementation of the law of the people's Republic of China on Import and Export Inspection (hereinafter referred to as the Regulations), the State Commodity Inspection Authorities are in charge of the inspection of import and export commodities throughout the country. Their basic tasks are as follows:

(1) Statutory inspection on import and export

Import and export commodity inspection can be divided into two types: statutory inspection and non-statutory inspection. In the light the need in the development of foreign trade, the state inspection agency formulates, adjust and publishes a List of Import and Export Commodities Subject to Inspection Enforced by the Commodities Inspection Authorities (hereinafter referred to as the List of Commodities) for those commodities which involve social and public interests. The list of Commodities varies with the development of foreign trade. For example, the list adopted on July 1,1995, involves 18 categories, covering 2012 commodity codes widely used in Harmonized

Description and Coding System. The statutory inspection on imports and exports includes the following items:

①inspection of import and export commodities included in the List of Commodities

②hygiene inspection on the foods for export

③testing and inspection on the performance and employment of the packages and containers for dangerous export goods

④ cargo worthiness inspection on such means of transportation as vessels' holds and containers for carrying perishable foods and frozen goods for export

⑤inspection of imports and exports to be conducted by the commodity inspection authorities according to relevant international treaties

⑥inspection of import and exports to be carried out by the commodity inspection regulations.

(2) Survey of import and export commodities

The State Inspection Authorities and their designated or the international trade interested parties, relevant units in china, and export commodities within the specified scope may issue certificates of survey. The commonly issued inspection certificates are Inspection Certificate of Quality, Weight, Health, Inspection Certificate Damaged Cargo, and Disinfection Inspection Certificate.

(3) Supervision and control

This Law and the Regulations hold that the State commodity Inspection Authorities exercise supervision and control over the inspection conducted by the inspection agencies and personnel designated or accredited by the consignees, consignors, manufacturers, trading units, storage and transport units of import and export commodities. The principal measures of supervision and control include:

①System of import safety license and export quality license. No import commodities subject to the import safety license system shall be allowed for import unless they have been granted an import safety license by the State Commodity Inspection Authorities. No export commodities subject to the export quality license system shall be allowed for export unless they have been granted an export license.

②Hygiene registration system. Manufacturers of foods for export which are subject to a hygiene registration system shall apply to the commodity inspection authorities for hygiene registration; they shall not be allowed to produce, process or store foods for export unless they have obtained the approval from the State Commodity Inspection Authorities .

③Quality certification marks. The State Commodity Inspection Authorities shall conclude quality certification agreement on import and export commodities with relevant foreign bodies and shall conduct quality certification for import and export commodities according to the relevant agreements or upon entrustment by relevant foreign bodies.

④Commodity inspection marks. The commodity inspection authorities may affix commodity inspection marks on the import and export commodities found up to standard through inspection.

9.1.4 Inspection standards

Inspection on import and export commodities performed by the commodity inspection authorities shall cover quality, specifications, quantity, weight, packing and the requirements for safety and hygiene. The commodity inspection authorities shall conduct inspection according to the following standards:

(1)The inspection shall be performed according to the standards of seller's country.

(2)The inspection shall be performed according to the standards and methods agreed upon both by the seller and the buyer.

(3)The inspection shall be performed according to the international standards of international conventions.

9.2 Commodity Claim

There are generally three types of claim: claim regarding selling and buying, claim regarding transportation, claim regarding insurance. In the section, only the claim regarding selling and buying is discussed.

9.2.1 Definition of Claim

(1)Breach of contract committed by the seller

Breach of contract committed by the seller mainly covers: ①The seller fails to deliver the goods; ②The documents relating to goods are incomplete; ③The goods do not conform with the contract, etc.

(2)Breach of contract committed by the buyer

Breach of contract committed by the buyer mainly covers: ①The buyer fails to pay the price; ②The buyer fails to take delivery of the goods, etc.

9.2.2 Claim clause in contract

(1)claim clause

This is the commonly adopted claim clause in a sales contract.

①Basis for claim; evidences to be provided.

②Term of validity of claim.

(2) Penalty clause

Sometimes a penalty clause should be included in the contract in case the buyer fails to delay in opening of L/C, or the seller fails to deliver the goods on time. Under this clause, the party who fails to fulfill the contract must pay a fine, a certain percentage of total contractual value.

The following are two example of penalty clause:

①Penalty clause regarding the seller's delay in delivery

should the sellers fail to make delivery on time as stipulated in the contract, the Buyers shall agree to postpone the delivery on condition that the Sellers agree to pay a penalty which shall be deducted by the paying bank from the payment under negotiation, or by the Buyers direct at the time of payment. The rate of penalty is charged at 0.5% of the total value of the goods whose delivery has been delayed for every seven days, less than seven days should be counted as seven days. But the total amount of penalty, however, shall not exceed 5% of the total value of the goods involved in the late delivery. In case the sellers fail to make delivery ten weeks later than the time of shipment stipulated in the contract, the buyers shall have the right to cancel the contract and the sellers, in spite of the cancellation, shall still pay the aforesaid penalty to the buyers without delay.

②Penalty clause regarding the buyer's delay in opening of L/C

should the buyers for its own sake fail to open the letter of credit on time stipulated in the contract, the buyers shall pay a penalty to the sellers. The penalty shall be charged at the rate of 0.5% of the amount of the letter of credit for every ten days of delay in opening the letter of credit. Any fractional days less than ten days for the calculation of penalty. However, the penalty shall not exceed 5% of the total value of the credit which the buyers should have opened. The penalty shall be the sole compensation for the damage caused by such delay.

9.3 Force Majeure of Commodity

9.3.1 Definition of force majeure

Force majeure (french: "superior force") is an event or effect that cannot be reasonably anticipated nor controlled. A party is not liable for any damage resulting from his failure to perform the contract if he can show that his failure was "due to an impediment beyond his control, that the impediment was not something he could have reasonably taken into account at the time of contracting, and that he remains unable to overcome the impediment or its consequences. Force majeure is not only narrowly defined, but also limited in its application. It applies to situations-such as natural disasters, war, embargoes, strikes, break downs, and the bankruptcy of a supplier—that frustrate both the party attempting to perform and the party expecting performance because neither party is really at fault, the breaching party is excused from paying damages. He is not, however, exempted from the application of any other appropriate remedy such as suspension of performance of avoidance.

There are usually two consequences of force majeure: termination of the contract and postponement of the contract. Whether terminating the contract or postponing the performance of the contract depends on what degree the force majeure event has affected the performance of the contract, or on the detailed stipulations in the contract. Generally speaking, the contract can be avoided only if the occurrence of the force majeure event makes it impossible to perform the contract such as the loss of or damage to specifically designated goods, or the event is so serious that it is impossible to recover within a short period of time. Otherwise, the suffering party can only make amendments to the contract to reduce the possible losses to the other party.

9.3.2 Force majeure clause in contract

The force majeure clause usually contains:

(1) the scope of force majeure events: since there is still no definite explanation as to which events should be regarded as force majeure, the seller and the buyer usually stipulate in their contract the scope of force majeure events. Force majeure events include certain natural disasters such as fire, flood, storm, heavy snow, earthquake, etc. and social disturbances like war, strikes, sanction, etc.

(2) time limit of notifying the other party: in case of a force majeure event, the party seeking to use the clause of farce majeure has a duty to promptly notify the other party of the impediment and its effect on his ability of perform.

(3) the issuer of the certificate: a force majeure event should be verified by a certificate that attests such an event. The issuer of the certificate should be mentioned in the clause.

9.4 Arbitration of Commodity

9.4.1 The ways of settlement of disputes

When disputes arise between exporter and importer, they can be settled though friendly consultation, arbitration, or litigation. Friendly negotiation is an important tool in the process of dispute settlement, and undoubtedly the one most commonly relied on. The majority of the disputes are settled this way and friendly business relations are thus maintained between exporters. Arbitration is the next best alternative. It is a means of settled between two parties though the medium of a third party to compel anther to do him justice. It is usually costly and time-consuming. This section will focus on arbitration. Arbitration means a method of resolving disputes arising from the two-side of parties who voluntarily render their disputes to a third party agreed by themselves to deal with in accordance with certain arbitration rules and make a final decision binding each of the parties based on the arbitration clause concluded previously by them or based on the arbitration agreement the parties have reached after the disputes arose.

(1) Voluntarily: the litigants submit themselves voluntarily to an arbitrator. The arbitrator is a private, disinterested person, or nonofficial government organization chosen by the parties to a disputed question.

(2) An arbitration agreement in written form between the parties concerned is prerequisite for arbitration. An arbitration agreement is a contract between two or more parties whereby they agree to refer the subject in dispute to others and to be bound by their award.

(3) More simple in procedures, less costly and time-consuming than litigation

(4) The award is final and binding on both parties .

9.4.2 Arbitration procedures

Arbitration mainly refers to the procedures and methods of arbitration, which includes the application of arbitration, nomination of arbitrators, arbitration tribunal, arbitration award and the payment of arbitration fees. There are arbitration procedures in the arbitration organizations of countries in the world. In order to promote arbitration smoothly, it should be made clear which kind of arbitration procedure should be adopted in the contract.

The parties must automatically execute the arbitral award within the time limit specified in the arbitral award. In case one party fails to execute the arbitral award, the other party may apply to the competent court for enforcement. If the residence or the properties of the losing party is located within the territory of china, the other party may apply to the Intermediate People's Court in the place where the residence of the losing party or the property of the losing party is located for enforcement of the award; if the residence of the losing party or the property of the losing party is located outside China, the other party may apply to the competent court in that country for enforcement in accordance with the Convention.

9.4.3 Arbitration place

The arbitration place can be anywhere in the seller's country, the buyer's country or a third country. The status of arbitration place is as important as that of arbitration body in an arbitration agreement. The country where an arbitration place is or an arbitral award is made is the country of the nationality of a foreign arbitral awards, therefore, it is the arbitration place that is in the first important place in recognition and enforcement of an arbitral award.

9.4.4 Arbitration bodies

There are two forms of arbitration: institutional arbitration and ad hoc arbitration. What the major difference between an ad hoc arbitration and an institutional arbitration falls on the fact that it is unnecessary for an ad hoc arbitration to have an institutional arbitration body to administrate a case. Generally it is not essential to stipulate an arbitration body in an arbitration clause for an ad hoc arbitration. But things are different in China, there is no ad hoc arbitration in China at present. So in China, it is necessary to indicate an arbitration body (an arbitration commission), otherwise the arbitration clause may be considered as an invalid clause. The China International Economic and Trade Arbitration Commission (CIETAC) in Beijing, and its chapters in Shenzhen and Shanghai, and liaison offices in Dalian, Fuzhou, Changsha, Chengdu and Chongqing accept arbitration cases according to arbitration rules and regulations, and use the unified Arbitration Rules and Panel of Arbitrators. The name of the arbitration body should be written correctly otherwise it will have a bad result. For example, when an arbitration clause provides an arbitration body never existed, the desire for arbitration will be frustrated.

9.4.5 Arbitration Clause in contract

In international arbitration contract, there are arbitration place, arbitration body, arbitration procedure, arbitration effect and arbitration fees, etc. The foreign trade contract of our country includes the following three arbitration clauses:

(1) Arbitration clause in our country

All disputes arising from the execution of, or in connection with this contract, shall then be settled amicably through negotiation. In case no settlement can breached through negotiation, the case shall then be submitted to the Foreign Economic and Trade Arbitration commission of the China Council for the Promotion of International Trade, Beijing for arbitration in accordance with its Provisional Rules of Procedure. The arbitral award is final and binding upon both parties.

(2) Arbitration clause in counterparty's country

All disputes arising from the execution of , or in connection with this contract, shall be settled amicably through negotiation. In case no settlement can be reached through negotiation, the case shall then be submitted for arbitration. The location of arbitration shall be in the country of the domicile of the sued party. If in China, the arbitration shall be conducted by the Foreign

Economic and Trade Arbitration Commission of the China Council for the Promotion of international Trade, Beijing in accordance with its Provisional Rules of Procedure. If in the arbitration shall be conducted by in accordance with its arbitral rules of procedure, the arbitral award is final binding upon both parties.

(3) Arbitration clause in the third country

All disputes arising from the execution of, or in connection with this contract, shall be settled amicably through negotiation, incase no settlement can be reached through negotiation, the case shall then be submitted to in accordance with its arbitral rules of procedure, The arbitral award is final and binding upon both parties.

Chapter 10 Negotiation on Contracts for International Sales of Goods

10.1 Negotiation Procedure

Contracts are formed through negotiations between the buyer and the seller. The process of negotiation usually includes enquiry, offer, counter-offer and acceptance, among which offer and acceptance are the two integral steps in forming a contract. International trade negotiations may be conducted through letters, faxes, e-mails, etc. Negotiations may also be carried out face-to-face. Whatever is chosen for the negotiation, four procedures are generally involved.

10.1.1 Enquiry

Enquiry is also known as invitation to offer. Both importers and exporters can make use of this step to initiate a potential transaction. By making an enquiry, the exporter may aim find out certain terms for a desired transaction.

The seller should attach much importance to the enquiries sent by the buyer, who might by a potential customer of the seller. Each enquiry stands for a sales opportunity, an opportunity to foster a potential long-term relationship. An enquiry may be made in a way like:

e. g. By cable: INTERESTED IN BUTTERFLY BRAND SEWING MACHINE PLEASE QUOTE.

10.1.2 Offer

An offer is a proposal that is made to a certain individual or legal entity to enter into a contract, which is definite in its terms, and which indicates the offer's intent to be bound.

An offer may be made by the seller or the buyer. The former is called "selling offer"; whereas the latter is called "buying offer" which usually described as a "bid". The following is an example of an offer by cable: OFFER 2000DOZEN SPORT SHIRTS SAMPLED MARCH 15TH USD90 PER DOZEN CIF NEW YORK EXPORT STANDARD PACKING MAY/JUNE SHIPMENT IRREVOCABLE SIGHT L/C SUBJECT REPLY HERE 20 TH

10.1.3 Counter-offer

A counter-offer is a reply to an offer that adds to, limits, or modifies materially the terms of the offer. A seller, for example, who accepts a buyer' offer but informs the buyer that goods will be a different color, has made a counter-offer.

Virtually, a counter-offer is a new offer made by the offer. The original offer becomes null and void and its original offer or is not bound any more. Counter-offers may be made repeatedly between the buyer and the seller. The following are two examples of counter-offers made by telegram.

Outgoing telegram: YOURTLX THIRD REGRET UNABLE ACCERT COMPETITORS QUOTING SIMILAR QUALITY USD55 PLEASE REPLY IMMEDIATELY.

Incoming telegram: OURS THIRD RENEW OFFER SUBJECT REPLY TENTH OUR TIME.

10.1.4 Acceptance

AN acceptance is an unconditional assent to an offer or an assent to an offer conditioned on only minor changes that do not affect any material terms of offer. For example, a cable reading "YOURS FOURTEENTH WE ACCEPT" is a typical acceptance.

10.2 Formation of the Contract

10.2.1 Offer

AN offer is a proposal addressed to specific persons indicating an intention by the offeror to be bound to the sale or purchase of particular goods for a price, a proposal for concluding a contract addressed to one or more specific persons constitutes an offer if it is sufficiently definite and indicates the intention of the offeror to be bound in case of acceptance.

1. The constitution of an offer

(1) To one or more specific persons

For a proposal to be an offer, it must be addressed to "one or more specific persons." Proposals made to the public are ordinarily intended to be nothing more than invitations to negotiate. For example, an advertisement in a newspaper for the sale of goods at a particular price might put the advertiser in the awkward position of having to deliver more goods than he has on hand because of heavier than expected demand, or of absorbing a substantial loss because of an increase in the cost of the goods between the advertisement was placed and the time it appeared.

(2) Sufficiently definite

A proposal is sufficiently definite if it indicates the goods and expressly or implicitly fixes or makes provision for determining the quantity and the price. Other terms and conditions, if not definitely stipulated in the contract, should be added

2. Term of validity

There is a term of validity for each offer, a period within which the offeree can make acceptance, and the offeror is only bound. The offeror may clearly define it in the offer, otherwise a reasonable time should be regarded as the term of validity. But it is hard to tell what a reasonable time is. So we'd better state it clearly in the offer. The ways of stipulating term of validity are:

(1) The latest time: e. g. REPLY REACHING HERE BEFORE 15th.

(2) A period of time: e. g. This offer is valid for 3 days.

3. Withdrawal and revocation of an offer

(1) Withdrawal

An offer becomes effective only after it reaches the offeree. Thus, offersincluding offers that promise they are irrevocable can be withdrawn prior to their reaching the offeree.

(2) Revocation

Until a contract is concluded an offer may be revoked if the revocation reaches the offeree before he has dispatched an acceptance.

10.2.2 Acceptance

A contract comes into existence at the point in time an offer is accepted. Acceptance is a statement or conduct by the offeree indicating assent that is communicated to the offeror.

1. The constitution of an acceptance

(1) The acceptance must be made by the offeree.

Any acceptance made by others is not effective.

(2) The contents of an acceptance must conform to that of an offer.

As a rule, only the complete conformity indicates that the two parties of a transaction reached an agreement, i. e. the meeting of minds.

Article 19 of CISG states that

"①A reply to an offer which purports to be an acceptance but contains additions, limitations or other modifications is a rejection of the offer and constitutes a counter-offer." This provision, however, does not mean that the offeree is not allowed to make any additions, limitations or other modifications when making an acceptance. The question is whether the alteration is fundamental or not.

"②However, a reply to an offer which purports to be an acceptance but contains additional or different term which do not materially alter the terms of the offer constitutes an acceptance, unless the offeror, without undue delay, object orally to the discrepancy or dispatches a notice to effect, If he does not so object, the terms of the contract are the terms of the offer with the modifications contained in the acceptance."

"③Additional or different terms relating, among other things, to the price, payment, quality and quantity of the goods, place and time of delivery, extent of one party's liability to the other materially."

(3) The acceptance must be made within the period of time for acceptance. An offer usually contains the term of validity, implying the offer or is bound within this term.

(4) An acceptance must be indicated. Silence or inactivity does not, in and of itself constitute acceptance.

2. The withdrawal of acceptance

Article 22 of CISG state that "An acceptance may be withdrawn if the withdrawal reaches the offeror before or at the same as the acceptance would have become effective." A contract comes into effect at the moment when an acceptance of an offer becomes effective.

中文部分

第一章 国际贸易术语

第一节 国际贸易术语概述

一、贸易术语的作用

贸易术语也被称为价格术语或交货术语,是指在销售合同中用一个标准的术语来说明商品从卖方手中转移到买方的地点和方式。例如:船上交货(FOB)以及成本、保险、加运费(CIF),就可以表示商品的价格构成,风险从卖方转移到买方的时间,以及运费和保险费。因此贸易术语大大简化了洽谈业务的过程,节省了时间和费用。

二、有关贸易术语的国际惯例

贸易术语虽然已经在实践中应用很多年,但由于各国对贸易术语的理解互有差异,因而容易误解。为了避免争议,有些商业团体便制定了一些统一解释贸易术语的规则或标准。

1.《1932 年华沙 - 牛津规则》

这一规则由国际法协会在 1932 年起草。它包含 21 个条款,规定了 CIF 贸易术语的本质,以及买卖双方应该承担的费用、风险和责任。

2.《1941 年美国对外贸易定义修订本》

1941 年由 9 家美国商会共同起草了该规则。尽管这一套对外贸易术语已经过时,但有时仍在美国国内使用。它包括 6 个贸易术语。

3.《2000 年国际贸易术语解释通则》

早在 1936 年,国际商会(ICC)即制定了《国际贸易术语解释通则》(International Commercial TERMS,简称 INCOTERMS)。此后该通则几经修订,于 2000 年 1 月 1 日生效。该通则共解释了 13 种贸易术语,并将其分成以下 4 种不同的基本类型。

(1)E 组(EXW),卖方/出口商在其自己的所在地把货物交给买方。

(2)F 组(FCA,FAS 和 FOB),卖方/出口商须将货物交至买方指定的承运人。

(3)C 组(CFR,CIF,CPT 和 CIP),卖方/出口商必须签订运输合同并支付运费,但装船和起运后货物灭失或损坏的风险或其他费用,卖方不承担责任。C 组术语证明是装运合同(与“到达”相反)。

(4)D 组(DAF,DES,DEQ,DDU 和 DDP),卖方/出口商必须承担把货物运至目的地国家所需的全部费用和风险。D 组术语证明是到达合同。

4.《国际贸易术语解释通则 2010》

全球经济一体化使得商业通向世界各地市场的途径空前宽广,各种各样的货物被销售到世界各地。然而,随着全球贸易数额的增加和贸易复杂性的加强,因贸易合同起草不当而带来的误解和高代价争端也可能随之增加。

《国际贸易术语解释通则》在国内和国际贸易用语的使用促进了全球贸易的进行。在贸易合同中引用《国际贸易术语解释通则 2010》可明确界定各方义务并降低法律纠纷产生的风险。

自从 1936 年国际商会制定出《国际贸易术语解释通则》之后,此项在全球范围内被采用的合同标准就经常性地更新换代,与国际贸易的发展步调一致。《国际贸易术语解释通则 2010》考虑了免税贸易区的不断增加,电子沟通在商务中的不断增多,以及被更加重视的货物运输中的安全和变化等问题。《国际贸易术语解释通则 2010》更新并加强了交货规则,将规则总量从 13 条减少到了 11 条,并使所有规则的表述更加简洁明确。《国际贸易术语解释通则 2010》同时也是第一个使得所有在买卖双方中的适用保持中立的第一个国际贸易术语解释版本。

国际商会的商法和实践委员会成员来自世界各地和多个贸易部门,该委员会广泛的专业技能确保了《国际贸易术语解释通则 2010》与各地的商贸需求相适应。

国际商会向 Fabio Bortolotti(意大利)的商法和实践委员会的成员表示谢意,向由 Charles Debattista(副组长,英国)、Christoph Martin Radtke(副组长,法国)、Jens Bredow(德国)、Johnny Herre(瑞典)、David Lwee(英国)、Lauri Railas(芬兰)、Frank Reynold(美国)、Miroslav Subert(捷克)组成的起草小组致谢,并且向对 11 条规则的表述给予帮助的 Asko Raty(芬兰)致谢。

第二节 国际惯例

一、《国际贸易术语解释通则》的宗旨和范围

《国际贸易术语解释通则》的宗旨是为国际贸易中最普遍使用的贸易术语提供一套解释的国际规则,以避免因各国不同解释而出现的不确定性,或至少在相当程度上减少这种不确定性。

合同双方当事人之间互不了解对方国家的贸易习惯的情况时常出现,这就会引起误解、争议和诉讼,从而浪费时间和费用。为了解决这些问题,国际商会(ICC)于 1936 年,以后又于 1953 年、1967 年、1976 年、1980 年、1990 年和 2000 年对通则进行了修订,现在通用的是在 2000 年版本基础上作出补充和修订的版本,以便使这些规则适应当前国际贸易实践的发展。需要强调的是,INCOTERMS 涵盖的范围只限于销售合同当事人的权利义务中已

售货物(指“有形的”货物,不包括“无形的”货物,如电脑软件)交货有关的事项。

关于 INCOTERMS,有两个非常普遍的误解。一个是常常认为 INCOTERMS 适用于运输合同而不适用销售合同;第二个是人们有时错误地认为它规定了当事人可能希望包含在销售合同中的所有责任。

首先,正如 ICC 一贯强调的那样,INCOTERMS 只涉及销售合同中买卖双方的关系,并且只限于一些非常明确的方面。对于进口商和出口商来讲,考虑那些为完成国际销售所需要的各种合同之间的实际关系当然是非常必要的。完成一笔国际贸易不仅需要销售合同,而且需要运输合同、保险合同和融资合同,而 INCOTERMS 只涉及其中的一项合同,即销售合同。虽然如此,当合同双方当事人统一使用某一具体的贸易术语时,将不可避免地对其他合同产生影响。举例说明,卖方同意在合同中使用 CFR 和 CIF 术语时,他就只能以海运方式履行合同,因为在这两个术语下他必须向买方提供提单或其他海运单据,而如果使用其他运输方式,这些要求是无法满足的。而且,跟单信用证要求的单据也必然将取决于准备使用的运输方式。

其次,INCOTERMS 涉及货物进口和出口清关、货物包装的义务,买方受领货物的义务,以及提供证明各项义务得到完整履行的义务。尽管 INCOTERMS 对于销售合同的执行有着极为重要的意义,但销售合同中可能引起的许多问题却并未涉及以及某些情况下的免责等。需要强调的事,INCOTERMS 无法取代那些完整的销售合同所需要订入的标准条款或商定条款。通常,INCOTERMS 不涉及违约的后果或由于各种法律阻碍导致的免责事项,这些问题必须通过销售合同中的其他条款和适用的法律来解决。INCOTERMS 一直主要用于跨国境的货物销售交付,因此它是一套国际商业术语。然而,有时 INCOTERMS 也被用于纯粹国内市场的货物销售合同中,在此情况下,INCOTERMS 中的 A2、B2 以及任何与进口有关的条款当然就变成多余了。

二、《国际贸易术语解释通则》修订的原因

连续修订 INCOTERMS 的主要原因是使其适应当代商业的实践。1980 年修订本引入了货交承运人(现在为 FCA)术语,其目的是为了适应在海上运输中经常出现的情况,即交货点不再是传统的 FOB 点(货物越过船舷),而是在将货物装船之前运到陆地上的某一点,在那里将货物装入集装箱,以便经由海运或其他运输方式(即所谓的联合或多式运输)继续运输。

在 1990 年的修订本中,涉及卖方提供交货凭证义务的条款在当事方同意使用电子方式通信时,允许用电子数据交换(EDI)信息替代纸面单据。毫无疑问,为了使 INCOTERMS 更利于实务操作,其草拟和表述一直都在改进。

三、INCOTERMS 2000

在为期两年的修订过程中,ICC 尽其最大努力通过 ICC 各国家委员会吸取了各行业国

际贸易从业者的意见和建议,完成了修订稿的多次修改。令人高兴的是,INCOTERMS 2000 这个版本与 INCOTERMS 1990 相比看上去变化很小。原因很明显,即 INCOTERMS 当前已得到世界承认,所以 ICC 决定巩固 INCOTERMS 在世界范围内得到的承认,并避免为了变化而变化。另一方面,在修订过程中,ICC 尽量保证 INCOTERMS 2000 中的语言清楚准确地反映出国际贸易实务。新的版本在下面两个方面作出了实质性改变:

(1)在 FAS 和 DEQ 术语下,办理清关手续和缴纳关税的义务;

(2)在 FCA 术语下装货和卸货的义务。

无论是内容变化还是形式变化都是在对 INCOTERMS 的使用者广泛调查的基础上作出的,而且对 1990 年以来 INCOTERMS 专家小组(专门为 INCOTERMS 使用者提供额外服务的机构)收到的咨询意见给予了充分考虑。

四、在销售合同中订入 INCOTERMS

鉴于 INCOTERMS 不断修订,所以如果合同当事方意图在销售合同中订入 INCOTERMS 时,清楚地指明所引用的 INCOTERMS 版本是很重要的,人们很容易忽略这一点。例如当在标准合同或订货单中引用了早期版本时,未能引用最新版本,可能会对当事方的意图是在合同中引用新版本还是早期版本引起纠纷。希望使用 INCOTERMS 2000 时,应在合同中明确规定该合同受 INCOTERMS 2000 的约束。

五、INCOTERMS 的结构

1990 年,为了便于理解,将所有的术语分为 4 个基本不同的类型。第一组为"E 组"(EX WORKS),指卖方仅在自己的地点为买方备妥货物;第二组为"F 组"(FCA,FAS 和 FOB),指卖方须将货物交至买方指定的承运人;第三组为"C 组"(CFR,CIF,CPT 和 CIP),指卖方须订立运输合同,但对货物灭失或损坏的风险以及装船和起运后发生意外所发生的额外费用,卖方不承担责任;第四组为"D 组"(DAF,DES,DEQ,DDU 和 DDP),指卖方须承担把货物交至目的地国所需的全部费用和风险。表 1-1 反映了这种分类方法。

表 1-1　2000 年国际贸易术语解释通则

E 组(发货)	
EXW	工厂交货(……指定地点)
F 组(主要运费未付)	
FCA	货交承运人(……指定地点)
FAS	装运港船边交货(……指定装运港)
FOB	装运港船上交货(……指定装运港)
C 组(主要运费已付)	
CFR	成本加运费(……指定目的港)

CIF	成本、保险费加运费(……指定目的港)
CPT	运费付至(……指定目的地)
CIP	运费、保险费付至(……指定目的地)
D组(到达)	
DAF	边境交货(……指定地点)
DES	目的港船上交货(……指定目的港)
DEQ	目的港码头交货(……指定目的港)
DDU	未完税交货(……指定目的地)
DDP	完税后交货(……指定目的地)

在 INCOTERMS 2000 中,所有术语下当事人各自的义务均用 13 个项目列出,卖方在每一项目中的地位对应了买方在同一项目中相应的地位。

六、用于说明

在起草 INCOTERMS 2000 过程中,力求使这 13 个术语的不同表达尽可能地做到连贯一致,这样就避免了用不同表述表达相同的意思。而且,只要可能,应尽量使用 1980 年《联合国国际货物销售合同公约》中的表述。

1. 托运人(shipper)

在一些情况下,需要用同一个词表示两个不同的意思,这只是由于无法找到合适的代替词的缘故。商人们在销售合同和运输合同中经常遇到这种困难。例如,"托运人"一词既可以表示将货物交付运输的人,又可表示与承运人订立合同的人,而这两个"托运人"可能是不同的人。如在 FBO 合同中,卖方将货物交付运输,而买方则与承运人订立运输合同。

2. 交货(delivery)

需要特别注意的是,"交货"这个词在 INCOTERMS 中有两种不同含义。首先,"交货"一词被用来判断卖方何时完成了其交货义务,这一规定在所有 INCOTERMS 的 A4 条款中。其次,"交货"也被用于买方受领或接受货物的义务,这一规定在所有 INCOTERMS 的 B4 条款中。用于第二种含义时,"交货"首先意味着买方"接受"C 组术语的基本宗旨,即卖方在将货物交运时即完成其义务;其次,"交货"一词还意味着买方有受领货物的义务。为避免因买方提取货物前支付不必要的储藏费,后一种义务是很重要的。例如,在 CFR 和 CIF 术语的合同中,买方有义务接受货物并从承运人处领取货物,若买方未履行该义务,就可能对于承运人订立运输合同的卖方损失承担赔偿责任,或者向承运人支付货物滞期费以使承运人放货。在这方面,说买方必须"受领货物"并不表示买方将其作为符合销售合同而接受货物,而只是指买方接受这一事实,即卖方按 C 组术语 A3 1)款订立运输合同,完成了将货物交付运输的义务。如果买方在目的地收到货物后,发现货物与销售合同规定不符,买方可使用销售合同和适用的法律给予的任何一种补救办法向卖方寻求补偿。如前所述,此项事宜已完全超出 INCOTERMS 的使用范围。

当货物在某一特定地点可以交给买方时,INCOTERMS 2000 在适当之处使用了"将货物交给买方处置"的表达。这种表达与《联合国国际货物销售合同公约》中"将货物交与"的表述含义相同。

3. 通常(usual)

"通常"一词在很多术语中出现,如在 EXW 术语中表示交货时间的条款(A4)中,在 C 组术语下关于卖方必须提供的单据和必须订立的运输合同的条款(A8,A3)。当然,说清楚"通常"的含义并非易事,然而在很多情况下,是有可能认定该行业内人士通常是如何行事的,这种行事惯例即可作为参照。在此意义上,"通常"这个词比"合理的"一词更有帮助。"合理的"要求的不是根据日常实践的评估,而是根据更难界定的善意和公平交易原则的评估。在一些情况下,可能还是需要判断什么是"合理的",尽管如此,由于上述原因,在 INCOTERMS 中,一般使用"通常"一词而不是用"合理的"一词。

4. 费用(charges)

在涉及到办理货物进口手续的义务时,判断货物进口时要支付的"费用"包括哪些内容是很重要的。在 INCOTERMS 1990 中,DDP 术语 A6 使用的是"出口和进口中所需缴纳的官方费用"。而在 INCOTERMS 2000 中,删去了"官方"一词,其原因是在决定某项收费是否是"官方"收费时,"官方"一词会造成某种不确定性,虽然删去了"官方"一词,但本意并非改变这一条款的实质意义。必须支付的"费用"仅涉及进口必然发生并按适用的进口管理规定必须支付的费用,其他任何由私人机构在货物进口时收取的费用不应包括在"费用"中,如与清关义务无关的储存费,然而,若承诺义务的一方非亲自履行该义务时,则履行此义务可能发生付给海关经纪人或运输行(freight forwarders)的一些费用。

5. 港口(port)、地点(place)、点(point)和所在地(premise)

在交货地点的问题上,INCOTERMS 中使用了不同的表达方法。只适用于海运的术语,如 FAS,FOB,CFR,CIF,DES 和 DEQ,使用了"装运港"和"目的港"两种表达。在所有其他的术语中使用的是"地点"(place)一词。在某种场合,有必要指明在"港口"和"地点"(place)内的某"点"(point),因为卖方不仅需要知道他要把货物交至一个特定地区,例如某个城市,而且也要知道在该地区的什么地点将货物交给买方处置。销售合同经常缺少这一方面的信息,于是 INCOTERMS 规定如果在指定地点没有约定交货点,并且有几个点可以选择,卖方可选择对其最有利的点交货(见 FCA 术语中的 A4 条款)。当交货点是卖方"地点"时,则使用了"卖方所在地"(见 FCA 术语中的 A4 条款)。

6. 船只(ship 和 vessel)

在使用海上运输货物的术语中,"ship"和"vessel"被当作同义词使用。无须说明,当"ship"作为贸易术语的组成部分时,如"船边交货"(FAS)和"目的港船上交货"(DES),必然要使用"ship"一词。同样,由于 FOB 术语中传统上使用"越过船舷"的表达,因而必然会将"ship"一词用于相关内容。

7. 查对(checking)和检验(inspection)

在 INCOTERMS 中,A9 和 B9 条款分别使用"查对、包装和标记"和"货物检验"作为条款标题。尽管"checking"和"inspection"是同义词,但是人们普遍认为运用下述方法来区别使用比较合理:在涉及卖方按 A4 交货的义务时使用查对(checking),而后者则用于一些特殊情况,即进行"装运前检验",因为在通常情况下只有当买方或货物出口(或进口)国当局希望货物装运前保证货物符合合同或官方规定时才要求进行"检验"。

七、卖方的交货义务

INCOTERMS 将重点放在卖方的交货义务上,对与卖方交货有关联的责任和费用的准确分配在各当事方有持续商业关系的情况下一般不会有什么问题。他们会在相互之间确立一种习惯做法,而且他们会按这种方式处理以后的交易。然而,当建立一种新的商业关系或通过经纪人的中介订立合同时,当事人一定要按合同规定办事,在将 INCOTERMS 2000 订入合同时,按照 INCOTERMS 2000 的规定划分责任、费用和风险。

当然,人们希望 INCOTERMS 能够尽可能细致地划分与交货有关的各当事方的义务。与 INCOTERMS 1990 相比,INCOTERMS 2000 在某些具体情况下在这方面作了进一步努力(见 FCA 术语中 A4 条款)。但在 FAS 和 FOB A4 中,不可避免地要援用行业惯例("按港口的习惯方式"),其原因是,在 FAS 或 FOB 合同下将货物尤其是农矿产品交运的具体做法在不同的海港是不一样的。

八、与货物有关的风险和费用的转移

当卖方交货后,货物灭失或损失的风险,以及负担与货物有关的费用的义务便从卖方转移到买方。由于不应给予买方任何拖延风险和费用转移的机会,因此,所有术语都应作出规定,当买方没有按约定受领货物或没有给予卖方完成交货义务的必要指示(有关装船时间和或交货地点)时,风险和费用甚至在交货之前就可转移。这种提前转移风险和费用的条件就是货物一直为买方准备的,或如术语所规定,已为买方划出。

在 EXW 术语下,这一点尤为重要,因为在所有其他术语下,当采取措施为交运、发送货物(F 组和 C 组)或在目的地作交货准备时(D 组),但在一些例外场合,如当卖方散装发运货物且未确定每一个买方的数量时,则在货物按前述规定特定化前,风险和费用不发生转移(参见《1980 年联合国国际货物销售合同公约》第 69.3 条)。

九、术语

1. E 组术语

E 组术语下卖方的义务最小:卖方只要将货物在约定地点,通常是在卖方所在地,交给

买方处置即可。但是,另一方面,在实务中,卖方经常在帮助买方将货物装至买方的运输工具上。如果将卖方的义务扩大到包括装货,那么 EXW 术语将更好地反应这一实务。但是,人们认为理想的是仍然保留 EXW 下卖方义务的传统原则,其目的是使其适用于那些卖方不愿意承担任何装货义务的情况。若买方希望卖方负担更多的义务,应在销售合同中写明。

2. F 组术语

F 组术语是与要求卖方的指示将货物交运。在 FCA 术语下,当事各方所希望的交货点造成了困难,其原因是此术语所涉及的合同可能会遇到各种各样的情况。货物可能装上买方派往卖方所在地提取货物的车辆;或者货物也许需要从卖方派往买方指定交货地点的车辆上卸下。INCOTERMS 2000 考虑到了上述可能,规定若合同中指定交货地点是卖方所在地,当货物装上买方的装货车辆时即完成交货,在其他情况下,当货物在卖方的车辆上尚未卸货而交给买方处置时,即完成交货。在 INCOTERMS 1990 中,FCA 术语 A4 条款中提到的各种不同运输方式在 INCOTERMS 2000 中未再重复。

FOB 术语中的交货点与 CFR 和 CIF 术语中的相同,尽管对此有很多争议,但在 INCOTERMS 2000 中仍未作改动。虽然 FOB 术语中的"越过船舷"交货的原则在当前许多情况下已不再适合,但是既然已为商人们所深知,并根据货物的特点和可用的装卸设备的具体情况加以运用,更改 FOB 的交货点可能会造成不必要的混乱,尤其对于租船合同进行产品运输来说,更是如此。

可惜的是,FOB 术语被一些商人用来表示"任何"交货点,如"FOB 工厂""FOB 工场""FOB 卖方工厂"或其他内陆地点,这样做就失去了 FOB 术语是"Free on Board"的缩写的意义了。这样使用 FOB 术语会造成混乱,应该避免。

FAS 术语办理货物出口手续的义务出现了重要的变化,因为最普通的做法是由卖方而不是由买方承担这项义务。为了保证这一变化得到足够的重视,在 FAS 序言中已使用了黑体字标出。

3. C 组术语

C 组术语要求卖方按照通常条件自付费用订立运输合同。因此,卖方支付运费运到的地点,必须在 C 组每一项术语后指明。按照 CIF 和 CIP 术语,卖方还要负责办理保险和负担保险费用,由于费用划分地点确定为目的地国家的某个点,因此 C 组术语往往被误认为是到货合同,在到货合同中,卖方要承担货物实际被运到约定地点之前的全部风险和费用。在此必须强调,C 组术语与 F 组术语具有相同性质,就在于卖方是在装运国或发货国进行合同履行。因此,C 组术语的销售合同和 F 组术语的销售合同一样,属于装运合同。

装运合同的特点是,卖方要支付将货物按照惯例航线和习惯方式运至约定地点所需的通常运输费用,而货物灭失或损坏的风险以及在货物以适当方式交付运输之后发生意外而发生的额外费用则由买方承担。因此,C 组术语包含两个区别于其他所有术语的"分界点”:一是指明卖方必须安排运输,并承担其费用;二是风险的划分点。为此,凡增加卖方在C组术语下的义务而扩大卖方的责任超出上述风险划分的“分界点”时,应特别注意。按照CIF和CIP术语,卖方在履行其合同义务、订立运输合同,将货物交付承运人并办理保险后,应免除卖方任何进一步的风险和费用,这正是C组术语的实质所在。

C组术语作为装运合同的本质也通过在此组术语下广泛使用跟单信用证作为人们喜爱的付款方式显现出来。若销售合同的当事方同意,卖方凭跟单信用证向银行提交约定的运输单据后收取货款,则如果卖方在按照跟单信用证得到货款或在货物起运或发货后以其他方式得到货款之后,仍承担进一步的风险和费用,就与跟单信用证的中心目的地支付(运费到付),卖方必须支付运输合同的费用;然而,在货物装船或发货后的事件所发生的额外费用必须由买方承担。

如果卖方需要提供包括缴纳关税、税款和其他费用在内的运输合同,那么,在合同约定这些费用由卖方支付时,这一点在所有C组术语的A6条款中已作出明确规定。

若按习惯要订立几份运输合同,以便货物中途转运以抵达约定的目的地,则卖方必须支付所有的费用,包括货物从一种运输工具转到另一种运输工具而发生的费用。但是,若承担人依据转运合同或类似条款的规定形式及权利以避免意外的阻碍(例如冰块、堵塞、劳工动乱、政府禁令、战争或类似战争行为),则由此发生的所有额外费用应由买方承担,因为卖方的义务只限于订立通常的运输合同。

销售合同的当事人往往希望明确卖方应在什么程度内订立运输合同,包括卸货费用由谁负担。由于当货物由通常的班轮运输时,这些费用一般包括在运费之内,因此,销售合同经常规定,货物必须由班轮运输或至少按“班轮条件”运输。有时在CFR和CIF术语后加上“到岸上(landed)”。然而,最好不要在C组术语中使用缩用语,除非在有关行业中,该缩写语为合同当事人或适用的法律或行业惯例所明确理解和接受的。

具体而言,卖方不应当(在不改变C组术语本质的情况下,实际上也不能够)承担任何保证货物抵达目的地的义务,因为在运输途中任何迟延的风险应由买方承担。因此,涉及时间的任何义务必须表明装船地或发货地,例如“装运(发货)不迟于……”。像“CFR汉堡不迟于……”这样的一份协议术语用法不当,并会引起不同的解释:当事人的意思可能被认为是货物必须在规定的日期抵达汉堡,在这种情况下该合同不是装运合同而是到货合同;另一种可能理解是,卖方发运货物的时间必须使其在通常情况下能在规定的时间前抵达汉堡,除非发生意外事件耽误运输。

在产品贸易中,若是购买的货物正在海上运输途中,在这种情况下,贸易术语后应加上“在途(afloat)”一词。根据CFR和CIF术语,货物的灭失或损坏的风险这时已从卖方转移到买方,这就可能引起解释上的困难。一种可能是,维持CFR和CIF术语有关买卖双方风险划分的通常含义,即风险在装运时转移。这意味着买方也许不得不承担销售合同生效时已发生的事件的后果;另一种可能性是让风险的转移和合同订立的时间相一致。前一种可能性也许更切合实际,因为确定正在运输途中货物的状况往往是不可能的。鉴于这个原因,《1980 年联合国国际货物销售合同公约》第 68 条规定"如果情况表明由此需要,从货物交付给签发体现运输合同的单据的承运人时起,风险就由买方承担",但是有一例外,即当"卖方知道或理应知道货物已经灭失或损坏,而不将这一事实告知买方"时。因此,CFR 或 CIF 术语后加上"在途"一词的解释应取决于销售合同适用的法律。建议当事人弄清适用的法律及其可能导致的解决方法。如有疑问,当事人应在合同中加以明确规定。

在实务中,甲、乙方继续频繁使用 C&F(或 C and F,C + F)这样传统的术语。然而,在绝大多数情况下,交易方视这些传统术语等同于 CFR。为了避免解释和同时的困难,交易方应使用 CFR 术语,因为 CFR 术语是全球广泛接受的"成本加运费(……指定目的港)"的唯一的缩写。

在 INCOTERMS 1990 中,CRF 和 CIF 的 A8 条款要求:只要卖方提供的运输单据(通常是提单)中援引了租船合同,例如,通常用的表达方式"所有其他条款和条件均按租船合同",这时卖方就有义务提供租船合同的副本。尽管签约人最好是在定立合同时能够确知合同中所有条款的内容,但是这种提供租船合同的做法带来了一些问题,尤其是在跟单信用证业中。所以,在 INCOTERMS 2000 中,删去了 CRF 和 CIF 术语下卖方要随运输单据提供租船合同副本的义务。

虽然 INCOTERMS 中 A8 条款目的在于保证卖方向买方提供"交货凭证",但应该指出,这里强调的只是卖方提供了"通常"的凭证,卖方就完成了这项义务。在 CRF 和 CIF 术语下,卖方要提供"通常的运输单据",即在 CRF 和 CIF 术语下,卖方要提供提单和海运单,运输单据必须是"清洁的",即运输单据上不能出现声明货物和(或)其包装有与合同不符的条款或批注。若单据中出现这样的条款或批注,那么这个单据就被认为是"不清洁的",而在跟单信用证交易中则会被银行拒收。但是,一份运输单据,即使上面没有这样的条款或批注,对买方来说通常也不能成为对抗承运人的无可置疑的证据,证明货物在装运时是符合销售合同内容的。一般情况下,承运人会在运输单据的正面以标准文句指明,在运输单据中加入的细节是托运人的声明,因此货物情况只是"据称"如其添加的细节所述。承运人以此拒绝承担有关货物状况的责任。根据大多数援助的法律或原则,承运人必须使用合理的方法检验货物是否正确,否则对收货人负有责任。然而,在集装箱中承运人无法检查集装箱内货物,除非承运人负责将货物装入集装箱。

涉及保险的术语只有两个,即 CIF 和 CIP。在这两个术语下,卖方有义务为买方的利益办理保险。在其他情况下,则是由当事方自己决定是否要办理保险以及投保到什么程度。由于卖方要为买方的利益办理保险,卖方不一定知道买方的详细需求。根据由伦敦保险人协会(Institute of London Underwriters)拟订的《协会货物保险条款》(Institute Cargo Clauses)规定办理"最低程度"的保险,规定办理中等程度保险,规定办理最高险别。在 CIF 术语下的产品销售中,买方或许希望将在途货物卖给新的买方,而这个新的买方也许希望再将货物售出,所以,买方不可能了解这些后继买方的保险需求。因此,在 CIF 术语下,传统上选择最低保险的程度,买方可以要求卖方办理附加保险。但最低保险对制成品货物的销售可能不太适宜,因为对制成品而言存在偷盗、不可搬运或保管的风险。由于 CIP 不同于 CIF,所以采用 CIP 下的最高险别而不是 CIF 下的最低险别,将会是可行的。但若在 CIF 和 CIP 术语下对卖方办理货物保险义务的要求不同,则容易导致混乱。所以,这两个术语要求卖方只限于办理"最低程度"的货物保险。对于 CIP 术语下的买方来说,注意到这一点是非常重要的。如果买方要求附加险别,它可以与卖方协议由卖方办理或自行安排办理个别高的保险。在某些情况下,买方也许会要求获得比《协会货物保险条款》(A)更高的保险,比如战争险、动乱险、民变险、罢工或其他劳工动乱险。若买方希望卖方安排这样的保险,买方必须明示卖方,而卖方必须在可能情况下负责安排这些保险。

4. D 组术语

D 组术语与 C 组术语有着本质区别。根据 D 组术语,卖方负责将货物运至边境或进口国内的约定目的地或点。卖方必须承担货物运至该地前的全部风险和费用,因此,D 组术语属于到货合同,而 C 组术语则属于离港(装运)合同。

在 D 组术语下,除了 DDP,卖方在目的地国交货时无须办理进口手续。传统的做法是,在 DEQ 术语下,卖方有义务办理货物的进口清关手续,因为货物需要搬运到码头,这样就进入了进口国。但是,由于大多数国家的清关手续发生了变化,因此在有居住地的一方办理进口清关手续并缴纳关税和其他费用更为合适。所以,DEQ 术语有了一些改变,与前面提到的 FAS 术语的变化一样,DEQ 术语中的变化在序言中以黑体字标出。

看来,很多国家使用一些没有收进 INCOTERMS 中的贸易术语,尤其是在铁路运输中。然而,在这些术语下,通常并不想让卖方承担将货物运至边境前的货物灭失或损坏的风险。在这些情况下,最好使用 CPT 指明边境。另一方面,如果他们希望让卖方负担运输中的风险,使用指明边境的 DAF 术语将更合适。

DDU 术语是在 INCOTERMS 1990 中新加入的。当卖方准备在目的国交货但不办理进口手续、不缴纳关税时,该术语就发挥了重要作用。在那些办理海关手续很困难而且耗时很久的国家里,卖方承担在完成海关清关手续后交货的义务将是有风险的。尽管按照 DDU 术语的 B5 和 B6 条款,买方要承担其为完成货物进口手续情况时可能发生的额外风险和费用,但我们仍然建议在办理货物进口手续可能会有困难的国家的交易中,卖方不使用 DDU 术语。

十、"无义务"的表示

"卖方须知"和"买方须知"这样的表达方法体现出 INCOTERMS 只涉及当时双方对对方承担的义务。这样,"无义务"则被用于一方对另一方不承担义务的情况。如果按该术语中 A3 条款卖方须安排并支付运输费用,则在 B3 的"运输合同"项目下"无义务"的字样即规定了买方的地位。同样，当任何一方对对方都不承担义务时，在双方名下都会出现“无义务”一词，例如有关“保险”的情况。

在上述任何一种情况下，重要的是要指出，即使一方“无义务”为另一方履行某项任务，这并不意味着履行该任务不符合它的利益。例如，CFR 的买方按照 B4 对卖方并无投保的责任，但很明显买方投保符合其利益，因为在该术语下按照 A4 卖方也没有义务获取保险。

十一、INCOTERMS 的变体

在实务中，当事双方经常在 INCOTERMS 术语基础上添加词句以求得比术语更精确的约定。需要强调的事，INCOTERMS 对任何这种添加的内容不提供任何规定。这样，如果当事双方无法依赖一个公认的行业惯例来揭示其新增内容时，他们可能会由于无法就新增内容证明有一贯的理解而面临严重的问题。

以常用的“FOB 理舱”和“EXW 装车”为例，卖方的义务不仅被扩大至包括负担将货物分别装到船上或装上车辆的费用，而且也包括在装舱和装货期间货物意外的灭失或损坏的风险，这就无法在全世界达成一致的理解。由于上述原因，强烈建议当事双方明确表示他们是否只打算由卖方承担装舱和装车的任务及费用，还是卖方也需要承担装舱和装车全部结束之前的风险。对此 INCOTERMS 并无答案。假如合同也未对双方意图加以明确的话，双方就将面临不必要的麻烦和费用。

尽管 INCOTERMS 2000 未对许多这样的普遍使用的变体作出规定，某些术语的序言确实在提醒双方，如希望超出 INCOTERMS 的规定来分配双方义务，则需要使用特殊的合同条款。例如：

EXW	关于卖方将货物装上买方的运输工具的额外义务
CIF/CIP	关于买方安排货物额外保险的需要
DEQ	关于卖方支付卸货之后的费用的额外义务

在一些情况下，卖方和买方援引班轮和租船合同中的商业惯例，这样就需要明确区分当事双方在运输合同中的义务和彼此在销售合同中的义务。但是，对于“班轮条件”和“终点站搬运费”等表达法尚无权威解释。在这些条款下，费用的划分因地点的不同而不同，而且经常变化。建议当事方在销售合同中明确规定如何划分双方应承担的费用。

在租船合同中经常使用的表达法如“FOB 理舱”“FOB 理舱和平舱”等，有时被用在销售合同中以明确在 FOB 术语下卖方要在何种程度内负担理舱和平舱的义务。当时用此类附加语时，有必要在销售合同中明确额外的义务只限于费用还是包括费用和风险。

如上所述，我们尽量使 INCOTERMS 反映出最通行的国际商业做法。然而，在某些情况下，尤其是 INCOTERMS 2000 与 INCOTERMS 1990 有不同之处时，当事方也许会希望以不同方式使用贸易术语。在贸易术语的序言中，以“但是”作句子的开头专门提醒注意这些可能性。

十二、港口或特定行业的习惯做法

因为贸易术语要在不同行业和不同地区使用,对双方的义务不能总是规定得很精确。因此,在某种程度上,有必要参考港口的或特定行业的习惯做法,或当事方在先前的交易中已经建立的习惯做法(参见《1980 年联合国国际货物销售合同公约》第 9 条)。对于卖方和买方而言,当协商销售合同时,使自己及时了解这些习惯做法,并在不能确定时,通过在销售合同中适当的条款澄清当事方的法律地位是值得推荐的做法。在具体合同中这些特别条款将取代或改变 INCOTERMS 规定的任何解释规则。

十三、买方关于装运地的选择

在一些情况下,在订立销售合同时可能无法准确地确定卖方将货物交运的点甚至地点。比如,在这一阶段,可能只约定在“某一范围”或一个较大的地点,如海港。在这种情况下,通常规定买方随后有权或有义务在这一范围内或地点内指定更精确的地点。若如上文所述买方有义务提供精确点而没做到,则买方就要承担由这种未尽义务而造成的任何额外的风险和费用(如所有术语中 B5 和 B7 条款规定)。除此之外,若买方没能使用自己的权力指示交货点,则卖方可以选择在对卖方最合适的点交货(FCA 中的 A4 条款)。

十四、清关

不少人对“清关”这个词有一些误解,本书明确指出,“清关”是指无论何时当卖方或买方承担将货物运过出口国或进口国的海关的义务时,这项义务不仅包括缴纳关税和其他费用,而且包括履行一切与货物通过海关有关的行政事务以及向当局提供必要信息并缴纳相关费用。在某些地区,如欧盟内部或其他自由贸易区,当不再有缴纳关税的义务和对进出口的限制时,有人认为使用规定办理货物清关手续义务的术语时不恰当的,尽管这是错误的认识。为此,“在需要办理海关手续时”的用语被加入了相关术语的 A2 和 B2、A6 和 B6 条款,这样,在无须办理海关手续的情况下,使用该用语就可以避免模棱两可的情况。

清关手续由住所在该国的一方或其代表办理通常是可取的。因此,出口商通常应办理出口清关手续,进口商应办理进口清关手续。

INCOTERMS 1990 中的 EXW、FAS(要求买方办理货物出口清关手续)和 DEQ(要求卖方办理进口清关手续)与上述原则不一致。INCOTERMS 2000 给卖方和买方,但表示卖方最小义务的术语 EXW 却未被改动(买方仍承担办理出口清关的义务)。DDP 术语的字面含义即完税后交货,采用该术语表示卖方明确同意完成该术语的义务,即办理进口清关手续并缴纳全部相关费用。

十五、包装

大多数情况下,当事人事先知道货物安全运至目的地需要何种包装。但是,由于卖方包装货物的义务可能因具体的运输方式和期限而大相径庭，因而有必要规定卖方有义务使货物的包装适合运输方式的要求，但只限于在订立销售合同前已经知道有关运输的情况（参阅《1980 年联合国国际货物销售合同公约》第 35 条 1 款和第 35 条 2 款 b 项规定，即货物包装必须"适用于订立合同时曾明示或默示地同意卖方的任何特定目的，除非情况表明买方并不依赖卖方的技能和判断力，或者这种依赖是不合理的"）。

十六、货物检验

在许多情况下，人们会建议买方在卖方把货物交付运输前或交付运输是安排货物检验（称为"装运前检验"）。除非合同另有规定，买方应承担检验费用，且这种检验是为了他自身利益安排的。但是，若进行的检验是为了使卖方履行在其本国时用于出口货物的任何强制性规定，则卖方应支付检验费用，除非使用的是 EXW 术语，这使买方应负担检验费用。

十七、运输方式和相应的 INCOTERMS 2000 术语（见表 1－2）

表 1－2　运输方式和相应的 INCOTERMS 2000 术语

（1）适用于任何运输方式

E 组	
EXW	工厂交货（……指定地点）
F 组	
FCA	货交承运人（……指定地点）
C 组	
CPT	运费付至（……指定目的地）
CIP	运费、保险费付至（……指定目的地）
D 组	
DAF	边境交货（……指定地点）
DDU	未完税交货（……指定目的地）
DDP	完税后交货（……指定目的地）

（2）只适用于海运及内河运输

F 组	
FAS	装运港船边交货（……指定装运港）
FOB	装运港船上交货（……指定装运港）
C 组	

CFR	成本加运费(……指定目的港)
CIF	成本、保险费加运费(……指定目的港)
D组	
DES	目的港船上交货(……指定目的港)
DEQ	目的港码头交货(……指定目的港)

十八、推荐使用

在某些情况下,在选择FCA和FOB时,应注意条款的序言推荐使用或者推荐不使用某个术语,遗憾的是,商人们依然不适当地使用FOB,使得卖方在将货物交给买方指定的承运人之后依然会遇到风险。FOB仅在下列情况下适用,即当卖方只打算越过船舷交货,无论怎样都要交到船上,而不是将货物交给承运人以使货物能被继续运输和装载到船上,例如装到集装箱内或装到卡车等所谓集装运输工具上。所以,前言中有强烈的警告,若当事方无意超过船舷交货则不应使用该术语。

有时也会出现这样的情况,即当买卖双方考虑使用其他运输方式时却错误地使用了适合于海运的术语。这将会使卖方处于不利的处境,即无法完成向买方提交适合单据的义务(如提单、海运单或有同等作用的电子信息)。上述图表显示了不同运输方式适用的INCOTERMS 2000的术语,而且各个术语的序言也提示该术语是适用于所有运输方式或仅适用于海运。

十九、提单和电子商务

在CFR和CIF术语下,传统做法是装船提单是卖方应提供的唯一可接受的单据,提单起到了以下三个重要的作用:

(1)将货物交付至船上的证明;

(2)运输合同的证明;

(3)一种通过将纸面单据交给另一方,将在途货物的权利转移给另一方的方式。

除提单外的其他运输单据可以完成上述三项作用的前两项,但却无法控制货物在目的地交货或使买方能够通过将纸面单据交付给买方。而其他运输则将指明在目的地有权接受货物的当事方的名字。为保证在目的地能够向承运人提取货物,拥有提单是必要的,这使得用电子通信方式取代提单变得尤其困难。

另外,习惯上签发数份正本提单,这时,买方或按其指示向卖方付款的银行,确信所有正本都已由卖方提交(所谓"全套")至关重要。这也是ICC有关跟单信用证的规则(即《跟单信用证统一规则》,在INCOTERMS 2000出版时其版本为UCP 500)的要求。

运输单据不仅必须证明货物已经交付承运人,而且要证明在承运人能够确定的范围内货物被收到时状况良好。在运输单据中任何表示货物并非呈良好状态的批注将会使该单据成为“不清洁”单据，这样的单据根据 UCP 将无法接受。

尽管提单具有特定的法律性质，但预计在不远的将来其会被电子方式替代。INCOTERMS 1990 充分估计了这种可以预期的发展。根据 A8 条款，若当事方同意以电子方式通信，则可以用具有同等作用的电子信息取代纸面运输单据。这些电子信息可以被直接或经由提供增值服务的第三方传送至有关当事人。一种第三方可以提供的有用的服务时登记单的一系列持有人。提供这种服务的系统，如图 BOLERO 的服务，或许需要得到像《国际海运委员会电子提单 1990 年规则》第 16 条、17 条和 1996 年 UNCITRAL《电子商务示范法》那样的法律规范和原则的进一步支持。

二十、不可转让的运输单据替代提单

近几年，简化单据的做法取得了很大的进展。提单经常被不可转让的运输单据所代替，其类似于海运以外的其他运输方式所使用的运输单据。这些单据被称为“海运单”“班轮运单”“货运收据”或其他名称。使用这些不可转让单据也是可以的，但当买方希望通过提交单据给新的买方来出售在途货物时就不行了。为了使出售在途货物成为可能，有必要在 CFR 和 CIF 术语下保留卖方提供提单的义务。然而，如果合同当事人知道买方不打算销售在途货物，他们可以达成明确协议来免除卖方提供提单的义务，或者在不需要提供提单时采用 CPT 和 CIP 这两种术语。

二十一、对承运人给予指示的权利

在 C 组术语中 ，买方支付货款时应确信卖方收款后无权就货物的处置对承运人作出新的指示。有些用于特殊运输方式（空运、公路或铁路）的运输单据通过向买方交付特定的运单正本或两联中的一联，使买方有排除卖方对承运人作出新指示的可能性。但在海运中用以替代提单的运输单据通常并不包含这种“阻止”功能。国际海事委员会为弥补这一缺陷，引入《1990 海运单统一规则》，使当事方可以加入一“无处置权”条款，卖方据此放弃指示承运人向其他人或在运单中指定地点之外的地点交货的权利。

二十二、ICC 仲裁

若合同当事人愿意在相互间发生争议时提交 ICC 仲裁，则应在合同或当没有单独的合同文本时，在达成协议的相互往来函电中明确清楚地约定采用 ICC 仲裁。合同中或与之有关的来往函电中订入一种或几种 INCOTERMS 术语本身并不构成采用 ICC 仲裁条款。

以下是 ICC 推荐使用的标准仲裁条款：

“与本合同有关的一切正义应根据 ICC 仲裁规则，由根据该规则指定的一名或几名仲裁员最终裁决。”

第三节 2010 通 则

本术语适合于任何运输方式。

一、EXW(工厂交货(……指定地点))

该术语可用于各种运输方式,包括多式联运。该术语适合国内贸易,FCA 通常更适合国际贸易。

"工厂交货(……指定地点)"是指当卖方在其所在地或其他商定的地点(如工场、工厂或仓库等)将货物交给买方处置时,即完成交货,卖方不负责将货物装上任何运输工具,也不负责出口清关手续。

建议双方清楚地界定交货地点,因为涉及到卖方所承担的费用和风险。买方在指定的地点接货后,便承担所有的费用和风险。

该术语是卖方承担责任最小的术语。使用该术语时应该注意以下几点:

(1)卖方不负责为买方将货物装上任何运输工具,即使在实践中卖方装载货物会更为有利。但是,若卖方负责装载货物,买方应承担装载货物的全部费用和风险。如果卖方装载货物更为有利,则应使用 FCA,该术语下卖方同意装载货物并承担费用和风险。

(2)使用 EXW 术语时,买方应该注意,如果买方要求卖方办理出口报关手续,卖方可提供协助,但卖方没有义务进行出口报关。在买方不能直接或间接地办理出口手续时,不应使用该术语。

A　卖方义务

A1　卖方的一般义务

卖方必须提供符合销售合同规定的货物和商业发票,以及合同可能要求的证明货物符合合同规定的其他任何凭证。

A2　许可证和其他手续

在需要办理出口手续时,应买方要求并由其承担风险和费用,卖方必须给予买方一切协助,以帮助买方取得为货物出口所需的出口许可证或其他官方许可。

A3　运输合同与保险合同

(1)运输合同

卖方无义务订立运输合同。

(2)保险合同

卖方无义务订立保险合同。然而,应买方的要求,卖方必须提供有关取得保险相关风险和费用的信息。

A4　交货

卖方必须按照合同约定的点，或如果未约定，按照交付此类货物的惯常时间，在指定的地点将未置于任何运输车辆上的货物交给买方处置。若在指定的地点内未约定具体交货点，或有若干个交货点可使用，则卖方可在交货地点中选择最适合其目的的交货点。

A5　风险转移

除 B5 规定者外，卖方必须承担货物灭失或损坏的一切风险，直至已经按照 A4 规定交货为止。

A6　费用划分

除 B6 规定者外，卖方必须支付与货物有关的一切费用，直至已按照 A4 规定交货为止。

A7　通知买方

卖方必须给予买方有关货物将于何时何地交给买方处置的充分通知。

A8　交货凭证

卖方无此义务。

A9　查对、包装、标记

卖方必须支付为了货物交给买方处置所需进行的查对费用（如查对货物品质、丈量、过磅、点数的费用）。卖方必须自付费用提供按照卖方在订立合同前已知的有关该货物运输所要求的包装，除非按照相关行业惯例，合同所指货物通常无需包装。包装应作适当标记。

A10　其他义务

应买方要求并由其承担风险和费用，卖方必须给予买方一切协助，以帮助其取得由交货国和（或）原产地国所签发或传送的为买方出口和（或）进口货物可能的要求的和必须要从他国过境所需要的任何单据。

B　买方义务

B1　买方的一般义务

买方必须按照销售合同规定支付价款。

B2　许可证和其他手续

买方必须自担风险和费用，取得任何出口和进口许可证或其他官方许可，并在需要办理海关手续时，办理货物出口的一切海关手续。

B3　运输合同与保险合同

（1）运输合同

买方有义务订立运输合同。

（2）保险合同

买方有义务订立保险合同。

B4　受领货物

买方必须在卖方按照 A4 和 A7 规定交货时受领货物。

B5　风险转移

买方必须按照下述规定承担货物毁灭或损坏的一切风险：自按照 A4 条款规定交货之时起，及由于买方未按照 B7 条款规定通知卖方，则自约定的交货日期或交货期限届满之日起，但以该项货物已正式划归合同项下，即清楚地划出或以其他方式确定为合同项下的货物为限。

B6　费用划分

买方必须支付：

(1)自按照 A4 规定交货之时起与货物有关的一切费用；

(2)在货物交给买方处置而买方未受领货物或未按照 B7 规定给予卖方相应的通知而发生的任何额外费用，但以该项货物已正式划归合同项下，即清楚地划出或以其他方式确定为合同项下的货物为限；

(3)在需要办理海关手续时，货物进口应缴纳的一切关税、税款和其他费用以及办理海关手续的费用；

(4)买方必须偿付卖方按照 A2 规定给予协助时所发生的一切费用。

B7　通知卖方

一旦买方有权确定在约定的期限内受领货物的具体时间(或)地点时，买方必须就此给予卖方充分的通知。

B8　交货凭证

买方必须向卖方提供已受领货物的适当凭证。

B9　货物检验

买方必须支付任何装运前的检验费用，包括出口国有关当局强制进行的检验。

B10　其他义务

买方必须支付因取得 A10 所述单据而发生的一切费用，并偿付卖方给予协助时所发生的费用。

二、FCA(货交承运人(……指定地点))

该术语可用于各种运输方式，包括多式联运。

"货物承运人"是指卖方只要将货物在指定的地点交给由买方指定的承运人、另外一个人或另一个指定地点。双方应清楚已界定的交货地点，因为从那一点起，风险已转移到买方。FCA 术语要求卖方负责并办理出口清关手续。然而，卖方无义务进口报关，缴纳进口关税或执行其他进口报关手续。

A　卖方义务

A1　卖方的一般义务

卖方必须提供符合销售合同规定的货物、商业发票，以及合同可能要求的、证明货物符合合同规定的其他任何凭证。

A2 许可证和其他手续

卖方必须自担风险和费用，取得任何出口许可证或其他官方许可，并在需要办理海关手续时办理货物出口所需要的一切海关手续。

A3 运输合同与保险合同

(1)运输合同

卖方无义务订立运输合同。但若买方要求，或者如果是商业惯例而买方未适时给予卖方相反指示，则卖方可按照通常条件订立运输合同，费用和风险由买方承担。在任何一种情况下，卖方都可以拒绝订立此合同，如果拒绝，则应立即通知买方。

(2)保险合同

卖方无义务订立保险合同。然而，应买方的要求，卖方必须提供有关取得保险相关风险和费用的信息。

A4 交货

卖方必须在指定的交货地点，在约定的交货日期或期限内，将货物交付给买方指定的承运人或其他人。

交货在以下时候完成：

(1)若指定的地点是卖方所在地，则当货物被装上买方指定的承运人或代表买方的其他提供的运输工具时；

(2)若指定的地点是买方指定的承运人或其他人，则当货物在卖方的运输工具上，尚未卸货的承运人或其他人的处置时。

若在指定的地点没有约定具体交货点，且有几个具体交货点可供选择时，卖方可以在指定的地点选择最适合其目的的交货点。

A5 风险转移

除 B5 规定者外，卖方必须按照下述规定承担货物毁灭或损坏的一切风险，直至已经按照 A4 规定交货为止。

A6 费用划分

除 B6 规定外，卖方必须支付以下费用：

(1)与货物有关的一切费用，直至已按照 A4 规定交货为止；

(2)在需要办理海关手续时，货物出口应办理的海关手续费用及出口应缴纳的一切关税、税款和其他费用。

A7 通知买方

卖方必须给予买方说明货物已按照 A4 规定交付给承运人的充分通知。若在约定时间内承运人未按照 A4 规定接受货物，则卖方必须相应地通知买方。

A8 交货凭证

卖方必须自担费用向买方提供证明按照 A4 规定交货的通常单据。

应买方要求并由其承担风险和费用,卖方必须给予买方一切协助,以取得有关运输合同的运输单据。

A9 查对、包装、标记

卖方必须支付为按照 A4 交货所需进行的查对费用(如核对货物的品质、丈量、过磅、点数的费用)。

卖方必须自付费用提供按照卖方在订立销售合同前已知的有关该货物运输所要求的包装,除非按照相关行业惯例,合同所述货物无需包装发运。包装应作适当标记。

A10 其他义务

应买方要求并由其承担风险和费用,卖方必须给予买方一切协助,以帮助买方取得装运地或原产地国所签发或传送的,为买方进口货物可能要求的或必要时从他国过境所需的任何单据。

B 买方义务

B1 买方的一般义务

买方必须按照销售合同规定支付价款。

B2 许可证和其他手续

买方必须自担风险和费用,取得任何进口许可证或其他官方许可,并在需要办理海关手续时办理货物进口和从他国过境的一切海关手续。

B3 运输合同与保险合同

(1)运输合同

买方必须自付费用订立自指定的地点运输货物的合同,卖方按照 A3(1)订立了运输合同时除外。

(2)保险合同

买方有义务订立保险合同。

B4 受领货物

买方必须在卖方按照 A4 规定交货为止。

B5 风险转移

买方必须按照自按照 A4 规定交货之时起规定承担货物毁灭或损坏的一切风险。由于买方未按照 A4 规定指定承运人或其他人,或其指定的承运人或其他人未在约定的时间接管货物,或买方未按照 B7 规定给予卖方相应的通知,则自约定的交货日期或交货期限届满之日起,但以该项货物已正式划归合同项下,即清楚地划出或以其他方式确定为合同项下的货物为限。

B6　费用划分

买方必须支付:

(1)自按照 A4 规定交货之时起与货物有关的一切费用;

(2)由于买方未能按照规定指定承运人或其他人,或由于买方指定的人未在约定的时间内接管货物,或由于买方未按照 B7 规定给予卖方相应的通知而发生的任何额外费用,但以该项货物已正式划归合同项下,即清楚地划出或以其他方式确定为合同项下的货物为限;

(3)在需要办理海关手续时,货物进口应缴纳的一切关税、税款和其他费用以及办理海关手续的费用及从他国过境的费用。

B7　通知卖方

买方必须就按照规定指定的人的名称给予卖方充分通知,并根据需要指明运输方式和向该项指定的人交货的日期或期限,以及依情况在指定的地点内具体交货。

B8　交货凭证

买方必须接受按照 A8 规定提供的交货凭证。

B9　货物检验

买方必须支付任何装运前检验的费用,但出口国有关当局强制进行的检验除外。

B10　其他义务

买方必须支付因取得 A10 所述所发生的一切费用,并偿付卖方按照该款给予协助以及按照订立运输合同所发生的费用。

三、CPT(运费付至(……指定目的地))

该术语可用于各种运输方式,包括多式联运。

“运费付至”是指卖方向其指定的承运人交货,但卖方还必须支付将货物运至目的地的运费,亦即买方承担交货之后一切风险和其他费用。

这一规则有两个关键点,因为风险和费用在不同的地点转移,建议双方在合同中精确地规定交货地点,风险在哪里转移到买方,卖方订立运输合同的指定目的地。如果需要许多承运人负责将货物运抵到目的地,双方又没有指定具体的交货点,卖方可以把货物交到第一承运人手中。如果双方希望在以后的阶段转移风险(例如港口或机场),他们需要在销售合同中指定。同时建议双方尽可能指定交货地点,以及到达那一点位置时卖方应该承担的费用。卖方应该准确地订立运输合同。如果运输合同中规定卖方在指定目的地卸货,卖方应该按照合同规定承担此项费用,除非双方另有规定。

CPT 术语要求卖方办理出口清关手续。然而,卖方不需要进行进口报关,缴纳进口关税和履行任何进口报关手续。

A　卖方义务

A1　卖方的一般义务

卖方必须提供符合销售合同规定的货物、商业发票,以及合同可能要求的用于证明货物符合合同规定的其他任何凭证。

A2　许可证和其他手续

卖方必须自担风险和费用,取得任何出口许可证或其他官方许可,并在需要办理海关手续时办理货物出口所需的一切海关手续。

A3　运输合同与保险合同

(1)运输合同

卖方必须自付费用,按照通常条件订立合同,依照常规路线及习惯方式,将货物运至指定的目的地或约定点。如未约定或按照惯例也无法确定具体交货点,则卖方可在指定的目的地选择最适合其目的的交货点。

(2)保险合同

卖方无义务订立保险合同。然而,应买方的要求,卖方必须提供有关取得保险相关风险和费用的信息。

A4　交货

卖方必须向按照 A3 规定订立合同的承运人交货,以使货物在约定的日期或期限内运至指定的目的地约定点。

A5　风险转移

除 B5 规定者外,卖方必须承担货物灭失或损坏的一切风险,直至已经按照 A4 规定交货为止。

A6　费用划分

除 B6 规定外,卖方必须支付以下费用:

(1)直到按照 A4 规定交货之时与货物有关的一切费用;

(2)按照 A3(1)规定所发生运费和其他一切费用,包括根据运输合同规定由卖方支付的装货费和在目的地的卸货费;

(3)在需要办理海关手续时,货物出口需要办理的海关手续费用,及出口应缴纳的一切关税、税款和其他费用,以及根据运输合同规定,由卖方支付的货物从他国过境的费用。

A7　通知买方

卖方必须给予买方说明货物已按照 A4 规定交货的充分通知,以及要求的任何其他通知,以便买方能够为受领货物而采取通常必要的措施。

A8　交货凭证

卖方必须自担费用向买方提供证明按照 A4 规定交货的通常单据。

应买方要求并由其承担风险和费用,卖方必须给予买方一切协助,以取得有关运输合同的运输单据。

A9 查对、包装、标记

卖方必须支付为按照 A4 交货所需进行的查对费用(如核对货物品质、丈量、过磅、点数的费用)。卖方必须自付费用,提供符合其安排的运输所要求的包装,除非按照相关行业惯例合同所述货物无需包装发运。包装应作适当标记。

A10 其他义务

应买方要求,卖方必须给予买方一切协助,以帮助买方取得由装运地国和(或)原产地国所签发或传送的,为买方进口货物可能要求和必要时从他国过境所需的任何单据。

B 买方义务

B1 买方的一般义务

买方必须按照销售合同规定支付价款。

B2 许可证和其他手续

买方必须自担风险和费用,取得任何进口许可证或其他官方许可,并在需要办理海关手续时办理货物进口和从他国过境所需的一切海关手续。

B3 运输合同和保险合同

(1)运输合同

买方无义务订立运输合同。

(2)保险合同

买方有义务订立保险合同。

B4 受领货物

买方必须在卖方按照 A4 规定受领货物,并在指定的目的地从承运人处收受货物。

B5 风险转移

买方必须承担按照 A4 规定交货时起货物灭失或损坏的一切风险。如买方未按照 B7 规定给予卖方通知,则买方必须从约定的交货日期或交货期限届满之日起,承担货物灭失或损坏的一切风险,但以该项货物已正式划归合同项下,即清楚地划出或以其他方式确定为合同项下的货物为限。

B6 费用划分

买方必须支付:

(1)自按照 A4 规定交货之时起与货物有关的一切费用;

(2)货物在运输途中直至到达约定目的地为止的一切费用,除非这些费用根据运输合同应由卖方支付;

(3)卸货费,除非这些费用根据运输合同应由买方支付;

(4)如买方未按照 B7 规定给予卖方通知,则自约定的装运日期或装运期限届满之日起,货物所发生的一切额外费用,但以该项货物已正式划归合同项下,即清楚地划出或以其

他方式确定为合同项下货物为限;

(5)在需要办理海关手续时,货物进口应缴纳的一切关税、税款和其他费用,及办理海关手续的费用,以及从他国过境的费用,除非这些费用已包括在运输合同中。

B7 通知卖方

一旦买方有权决定发送货物的时间和(或)目的地,买方必须就此给予卖方充分通知。

B8 交货凭证

买方必须接受按照 A8 规定提供的运输单据。

B9 货物检验

买方必须支付任何装运前检验的费用,但出口国有关当局强制进行的检验除外。

B10 其他义务

买方必须支付因获取 A10 所述单据所发生的一切费用,并偿付卖方因给予协助而发生的费用。

四、CIP(运费和保险费付至(……指定目的地))

该术语可适用于各种运输方式,包括多式联运。

"运费和保险费付至(……指定目的地)"是指卖方向其指定的承运人交货,但卖方还必须支付将货物运至目的地的运费,亦即买方承担卖方交货之后的一切风险和额外费用。

但是,按照 CIP 术语,卖方还必须办理买方货物在运输途中灭失或损坏风险的保险。因此,由卖方订立保险合同并支付保险费。买方应注意到,CIP 术语只要求卖方投保最低限度的保险险别。如买方需要更高的保险险别,则需要与卖方明确地达成协议,或者自行作出额外的保险安排。

这一规则有两个关键点,因为风险和费用在不同的地点转移。建议双方在合同中精确地规定交货地点,风险在哪里转移到买方,卖方订立运输合同的指定目的地。如果需要许多承运人负责将货物运抵到目的地,双方又没有指定具体的交货点,卖方可以把货物交到第一承运人手中。如果双方希望在以后的阶段转移风险(例如港口或机场),他们需要在销售合同中指定。同时建议双方尽可能的在交货地点指定点,以及到那一点位置卖方应该承担的费用。卖方应该准确的订立运输合同。如果运输合同中规定卖方在指定目的地卸货,卖方应该按照合同规定承担此项费用,除非双方另有规定。

CIP 术语要求卖方办理出口清关手续。然而,卖方不需要进行进口报关,缴纳进口关税和履行任何进口报关手续。

A 卖方义务

A1 卖方的一般义务

卖方必须提供符合销售合同规定的货物和商业发票,以及合同可能要求的用于证明货物符合规定的其他任何凭证。

A2　许可证、其他手续

卖方必须自担风险和费用,取得任何出口许可证或其他官方许可,并在需要办理海关手续时办理货物出口所需的一切海关手续。

A3　运输合同和保险合同

(1)运输合同

卖方必须自负费用,按照通常条件订立运输合同,依照常规路线及习惯方式,将货物运至指定的目的地的约定点。若未约定或按照惯例也不能确定具体交货点,则卖方可在指定的目的地选择最适合其目的的交货点。

(2)保险合同

卖方必须按照合同规定,自付费用取得货物保险,并向买方提供保险单或其他保险证据,以使买方或其他对货物具有保险利益的人有权直接向保险人索赔。卖方应按照最低限度保险险别投保。最低保险金额应包括合同规定价款另加 10%(即 110%),并应采取合同货币。

A4　交货

卖方必须在约定日期或期限内向按照 A3 规定订立合同的承运人交货,或如有接运的承运人时,向第一承运人交货,以使货物运至指定的目的地的约定点。

A5　风险转移

除 B5 规定外,卖方必须承担货物灭失或损坏的一切风险,直至已经按照 A4 规定交货为止。

A6　费用划分

卖方必须支付以下费用:

(1)与货物有关的一切费用,直至已经按照 A4 规定交货为止;

(2)按照 A3(1)规定所发生的运费和其他一切费用,包括装船费和根据运输合同应由卖方支付的目的地的卸货费;

(3)按照 A3(2)发生的保险费用及在需要办理海关手续时,货物出口需要办理的海关手续费用,以及根据运输合同由卖方支付的货物从他国过境的费用。

A7　通知买方

卖方必须给予买方说明货物以按照 A4 规定交货的充分通知,以及要求的任何其他通知,以便买方能够为受领货物而采取通常必要的措施。

A8　交货凭证

卖方必须自付费用向买方提供按照 A3 订立的运输合同所涉及的通常运输单据。

A9　查对、包装、标记

卖方必须支付为按照 A4 规定交货所需进行的查对费用(如核对货物品质、丈量、过磅、点数的费用)。

卖方必须自付费用,提供符合其安排的运输所要求的包装,除非按照相关行业惯例该合同所描述的货物无需包装发运。包装应作适当标记。

A10 其他业务

应买方要求并由其承担风险和费用,卖方必须给予买方一切协议,以帮助买方取得由装运地国和(或)原产地国所签发或传送的,为买方进口货物可能要求的和从他国过境所需的任何单据。

B 买方义务

B1 买方的一般义务

买方必须按照销售合同规定支付价款。

B2 许可证和其他手续

买方必须自担风险和费用,取得任何进口许可证或其他官方许可,并在需要办理海关手续时办理货物进口和从他国过境所需的一切海关手续。

B3 运输合同和保险合同

(1)运输合同

买方无义务订立运输合同。

(2)保险合同

买方无义务订立保险合同。

B4 受领货物

买方必须在卖方按照 A4 规定交货时受领货物,并在指定的目的地从承运人处受领货物。

B5 风险转移

买方必须按照 A4 规定交货后货物灭失或损坏的一切风险。买方如未按照 B7 规定通知卖方,则必须从约定的交货日期或交货期限届满之日起,承担货物灭失或损坏的一切风险,但以该项货物已正式划归合同项下,即清楚地划出或以其他方式确定为合同项下之货物为限。

B6 费用划分

除 A3 规定外,买方必须支付以下费用:

(1)自按照 A4 规定交货之时起与货物有关的一切费用;

(2)货物在运输途中直至到达约定目的地为止的一切费用,除非这些费用根据运输合同应由卖方支付;

(3)卸货费,除非这些费用根据运输合同应由买方支付;

(4)如买方未按照 B7 规定给予卖方通知,则自约定的装运日期或装运期限届满之日起,货物所发生的一切额外费用,但以该项货物已正式划归合同项下,即清楚地划出或以其他方式确定为合同项下货物为限;

(5)在需要办理海关手续时,货物进口应交纳的一切关税、税款和其他费用和办理海关手续的费用,以及从他国过境的费用,除非这些费用已包括在运输合同中。

B7　通知卖方

一旦买方有权决定发运货物的时间和(或)目的地,买方必须就此给予卖方充分通知。

B8　交货凭证

买方必须接受 A8 规定提供的运输单据,但要在该单据符合合同规定的情况下。

B9　货物检验

买方必须支付任何装运前检验的费用,但出口国有关当局强制进行的检验除外。

B10　其他业务

买方必须支付因获取 A10 所述单据所发生的一切费用,并偿付卖方因给予协助而发生的费用。

五、DAT(目的地交货(……指定目的港或目的地))

该术语可适用于各种运输方式,包括多式联运。

“目的地交货”是指当卖方在指定的目的港或目的地将货物从运输工具上卸下交给买方处置。目的地包括任何地点,如码头、仓库、集装箱集散地、铁路或空运货物终点站。

卖方应承担在指定的目的港或目的地将货物从运输工具上卸下交给买方为止的所有风险。建议双方在合同中精确地规定目的地,如果可能,指定目的地的港口或地点,以及到那一点位置卖方应该承担的风险。卖方应该准确地订立运输合同。而且,如果双方希望卖方承担把货物从目的地继续运往另一个地点,应该使用 DAP 或 DDP。

DAT 术语要求卖方办理出口清关手续。然而,卖方不需要进行进口报关,缴纳进口关税和履行任何进口报关手续。

A　卖方义务

A1　卖方的一般义务

卖方必须提供符合销售合同规定的货物和商业发票,以及合同可能要求的、证明货物符合合同规定的其他任何凭证。

A2　许可证和其他手续

卖方必须自担风险和费用,取得任何出口许可证或其他官方许可或其他必要文件,以便交给卖方处置,并在需要办理海关手续时办理货物出口并运至指定的边境交货地点以及从他国过境所需的一切海关手续。

A3　运输合同与保险合同

(1)运输合同

卖方必须自付费用订立运输合同,将货物运至边境指定的目的港或目的地。如未约定或按照惯例也无法确定边境指定的交货地点的具体交货点,则卖方可在指定的交货地点选择最适合其目的的交货地点。

(2)保险合同

卖方无义务订立保险合同。然而,应买方的要求,卖方必须提供有关取得保险相关风险和费用的信息。

A4 交货

卖方必须在约定日期或期限内,在指定的目的港或目的地,将货物从交货工具上未卸下交给买方处置。

A5 风险转移

除 B5 规定外,卖方必须承担货物灭失或损毁的一切风险,直至已经按照 A4 规定交货位止。

A6 费用划分

除 B6 规定外,卖方必须支付以下费用:

(1)按照 A3(1)规定发生的费用,及初次之外与货物有关的一切费用,直至已经按照 A4 规定交货为止。

(2)在需要办理海关手续时,货物出口需要办理的海关手续费用,及货物出口时应缴纳的一切关税、税款和其他费用,以及按照 A4 规定交货之前从他国过境的费用。

A7 通知买方

卖方必须给予买方有关预期到达时间的充分通知,以及要求的任何其他通知,以便买方能够为受领货物而采取通常必要的措施。

A8 交货凭证

卖方必须自付费用向买方提供说明货物已按照规定交付至指定的地点的通常单据或其他凭证。

A9 查对、包装、标记

卖方必须支付为按照 A4 规定交货所需进行的查对费用(如核对货物品质、丈量、过磅、点数的费用)。卖方必须自付费用提供包装,除非约定或按照相关行业惯例,合同所指货物通常无须包装即可交货),此项包装应按照卖方订立销售合同前一直的有关运输的要求,适合在边境交货及接运运输。包装应作适当标记。

A10 其他义务

应买方要求尤其承担风险和费用,卖方必须给予买方一定协助,以帮助买方取得由装运地国和(或)原产国所签发或传送的,为买方进出口货物可能要求的和必要时从他国过境所需的任何单据。

B 买方义务

B1 买方的一般义务

买方必须按照销售合同规定支付价款。

B2 许可证和其他手续

买方必须自担风险和费用,取得任何进口许可证或其他官方许可或其他文件,并在需要办理海关手续时办理货物进口所需的一切海关手续,及后继运输所需的一切海关手续。

B3 运输合同和保险合同

(1)运输合同

买方无义务订立运输合同。

(2)保险合同

买方有义务订立保险合同。

B4 受领货物

买方必须在卖方按照 A4 规定交货时受领货物。

B5 风险转移

买方必须承担按照 A4 规定交货之时起货物灭失或损坏的一切风险。

如买方未按照 B7 规定通知卖方,则必须从约定的交货日期或交货期限届满之日起,承担货物灭失或损坏的一切风险,但以该项货物已正式划归合同项下,即清楚地划出或以其他方式确定为合同项下的货物为限。

B6 费用划分

买方必须支付以下费用:

(1)自按照 A4 规定交货时起与货物有关的一切费用;

(2)如按照 A4 规定交货而买方未受领货物或未按照 B2 规定给予卖方通知,因此发生的一切而外费用,但以该项货物已正式划分归合同项下,即清楚地划出或以其他方式确定为合同项下的货物为限;

(3)在需要办理海关手续时,办理海关手续的费用及货物进口时应缴纳的一切关税、税款和其他费用,以及办理后继续运输的费用。

B7 通知卖方

一旦买方有权决定在约定期限内的时间和(或)在指定的目的地受领货物的点,买方就必须就此给予卖方充分通知。

B8 交货凭证

买方必须接受按照 A8 规定提供的运输单据和(或)其他交货凭证。

B9 货物检验

买方必须支付任何装运前检验的费用,但出口国有关当局强制进行的检验除外。

B10 其他义务

买方必须支付因获取 A10 所述单据或有同等作用的电子信息所发生的一切费用,并偿付卖方因此给予协助而发生的费用。必要时,应卖方要求,买方必须负担风险和费用,向卖方提供外汇管制许可、许可证件、其他单据或经认证的副本,或提供取得联运单据所需的进口国最终目的地地址中所指的任何其他单据。

六、DAP(所在地交货(……指定目的地))

该术语可适用于各种运输方式,包括多式联运。

“所在地交货”是指当卖方在指定的目的港或目的地将货物未从运输工具上卸下交给买方处置。卖方承担货物到达指定地点的一切风险。

建议双方在合同中精确地规定指定地点的点,以及到那一点位置卖方应该承担的风险。如果卖方要承担在指定目的地将货物从运输工具上卸下的费用,应该在运输合同中确定,否则卖方无义务承担卸货费。

DAP 术语要求卖方办理出口清关手续。然而,卖方不需要进行进口报关,缴纳进口关税和履行任何进口报关手续。如果双方希望卖方负责进口报关,缴纳进口关税和进口手续,应使用 DDP 术语。

A　卖方义务

A1　卖方的一般义务

卖方必须提供符合销售合同规定的货物和商业发票,以及合同可能要求的、证明货物符合合同规定的其他任何凭证。

A2　许可证和其他手续

卖方必须自担风险和费用,取得任何出口许可证或其他官方许可或其他必要文件,以便交给卖方处置,并在需要办理海关手续时办理货物出口并运至指定的边境交货地点以及从他国过境所需的一切海关手续。

A3　运输合同与保险合同

(1)运输合同

卖方必须自付费用订立运输合同,将货物运至边境指定的目的港或目的地。如未约定或按照惯例也无法确定边境指定的交货地点的具体交货点,则卖方可在指定的交货地点选择最适合其目的的交货地点。

(2)保险合同

卖方无义务订立保险合同。然而,应买方的要求,卖方必须提供有关取得保险相关风险和费用的信息。

A4　交货

卖方必须在约定日期或期限内,在指定的目的港或目的地,将货物从交货工具上未卸下交给买方处置。

A5　风险转移

除 B5 规定者外,卖方必须承担货物灭失或损毁的一切风险,直至已经按照 A4 规定交货位止。

A6 费用划分

除 B6 规定者外，卖方必须支付以下费用：

(1)按照 A3(1)规定发生的费用，及初次之外与货物有关的一切费用，直至已经按照 A4 规定交货为止；

(2)在需要办理海关手续时，货物出口需要办理的海关手续费用，及货物出口时应缴纳的一切关税、税款和其他费用，以及按照 A4 规定交货之前从他国过境的费用。

A7 通知买方

卖方必须给予买方有关预期到达时间的充分通知，以及要求的任何其他通知，以便买方能够为受领货物而采取通常必要的措施。

A8 交货凭证

卖方必须自付费用向买方提供说明货物已按照规定交付至指定的地点的通常单据或其他凭证。

A9 查对、包装、标记

卖方必须支付为按照 A4 规定交货所需进行的查对费用(如核对货物品质、丈量、过磅、点数的费用)。卖方必须自付费用提供包装(除非约定或按照相关行业惯例，合同所指货物通常无需包装即可交货)，此项包装应按照卖方订立销售合同前一直的有关运输(如运输方式、目的地)的要求，适合在边境交货及接运运输。包装应作适当标记。

A10 其他义务

应买方要求尤其承担风险和费用，卖方必须给予买方一切协助，以帮助买方取得由装运地国和(或)原产国所签发或传送的、为买方进出口货物可能要求的和必要时从他国过境所需的任何单据。

B 买方义务

B1 买方的一般义务

买方必须按照销售合同规定支付价款。

B2 许可证和其他手续

买方必须自担风险和费用，取得任何进口许可证或其他官方许可或其他文件并在需要办理海关手续时办理货物进口所需的一切海关手续，及后继运输所需的一切海关手续。

B3 运输合同和保险合同

(1)运输合同

买方无义务订立运输合同。

(2)保险合同

买方有义务订立保险合同。

B4 受领货物

买方必须在卖方按照 A4 规定交货时受领货物。

B5　风险转移

买方必须承担按照 A4 规定交货之时起货物灭失或损坏的一切风险。如买方未按照 B7 规定通知卖方,则必须从约定的交货日期或交货期限届满之日起,承担货物灭失或损坏的一切风险,但以该项货物已正式划归合同项下,即清楚地划出或以其他方式确定为合同项下的货物为限。

B6　费用划分

买方必须支付以下费用:

(1)自按照 A4 规定交货时起与货物有关的一切费用;

(2)如按照 A4 规定交货而买方未受领货物或未按照 B2 规定给予卖方通知,因此发生的一切额外费用,但以该项货物已正式划归合同项下,即清楚地划出或以其他方式确定为合同项下的货物为限;

(3)在需要办理海关手续时,办理海关手续的费用及货物进口时应缴纳的一切关税、税款和其他费用,以及办理后继续运输的费用。

B7　通知卖方

一旦买方有权决定在约定期限内的时间和(或)在指定的目的地受领货物的点,买方就必须就此给予卖方充分通知。

B8　交货凭证

买方必须接受按照 A8 规定提供的运输单据和(或)其他交货凭证。

B9　货物检验

买方必须支付任何装运前检验的费用,但出口国有关当局强制进行的检验除外。

B10　其他义务

买方必须支付因获取 A10 所述单据所发生的一切用,并偿付卖方因此给予协助而发生的费用。必要时,应卖方要求,买方必须负担风险和费用,向卖方提供外汇管制许可、许可证件、其他单据或经认证的副本,或提供取得联运单据所需的进口国最终目的地地址中所指的任何其他单据。

七、DDP(完税后交货(……指定目的地))

该术语可适用于各种运输方式,包括多式联运。

"完税后交货(……指定目的地)"是指卖方在指定的目的地,办理完进口清关手续,将在交货运输工具上尚未卸下的货物交与买方,即完成交货。卖方必须承担将货物运至目的地的一切风险和费用,包括在需要办理海关手续时在目的地应交纳的任何进口"税费",包括办理一切海关手续、交纳海关手续费、关税、税款和其他费用的责任和风险。

DDP 术语下卖方承担最大责任。建议双方在合同中精确地规定指定地点,以及到那一点位置卖方应该承担的风险。如果卖方要承担在指定目的地将货物从运输工具上卸下的费用，应该在运输合同中确定，否则卖方无义务承担卸货费。

若卖方不能直接或间接地取得进口许可证，则不应使用DDP术语。

如果双方希望买方承担进口报关所有的风险和费用，应该使用DAP术语。

如果当事方希望将任何进口时所要支付的一些费用（如增值税）从卖方的义务中排除，则应在销售合同中明确写明。

A 卖方义务

A1 卖方的一般义务

卖方必须提供符合销售合同规定的货物和商业发票，以及合同可能要求的用于证明货物符合合同规定的其他凭证。

A2 许可证和其他手续

卖方必须自担风险和费用，取得任何出口和进口许可证或其他官方许可或其他文件，并在需要办理海关手续时办理货物出口和进口以及从他国过境所需的一切海关手续。

A3 运输合同与保险合同

(1)运输合同

卖方必须自付费用订立运输合同，将货物运至指定的目的地。如未约定或按照惯例也无法确定具体交货点，则卖方可在目的地选择最合适其目的的交货点。

(2)保险合同

卖方无义务订立保险合同。然而，应买方的要求，卖方必须提供有关取得保险相关风险和费用的信息。

A4 交货

卖方必须在约定日期或交货期限内，在指定的目的地将在交货的运输工具上尚未卸下的货物交给买方或买方指定的其他人处置。

A5 风险转移

除B5规定外，卖方必须承担货物灭失或损坏的一切风险，直至已经按照A4规定交货为止。

A6 费用划分

除B6规定外，卖方必须支付以下费用：

(1)按照A3(1)规定发生的费用，以及按照A4规定交货之前与货物有关的一切费用；

(2)在需要办理海关手续时，货物出口和进口需要办理的海关手续费用，及货物出口和进口时应交纳的一切关税、税款和其他费用，以及交货前货物从他国过境的费用。

A7 通知买方

卖方必须给予买方有关发运货物的充分通知，以及要求的任何其他通知，以便买方能够为受领货物而采取通常必要的措施。

A8 交货凭证

卖方必须自付费用向买方提供按照 A4(B4)规定受领货物可能需要的提货单和(或)通常运输单据,以使买方按照规定受领货物。

A9 查对、包装、标记

卖方必须支付为按照 A4 规定交货所需要进行的查对费用(如核对货物品质、质量、过磅、点数的费用)。

卖方必须自付费用提供为所需要的包装(除非按照相关行业惯例,合同所指货物无需包装即可交货)。包装应作适当标记。

A10 其他义务

卖方必须支付为获取 B10 所述单据或有同等作用的电子信息(A8 所列的除外)所发生的一些费用,并偿付买方因给予协助而发生的费用。

B 买方义务

B1 买方的一般义务

买方必须按照销售合同规定支付价款。

B2 许可证、其他许可和手续

应卖方要求,并由其负担风险和费用,买方必须给予卖方一些协助,帮助卖方在需要办理海关手续时取得货物进口所需的进口许可证或其他官方许可。

B3 运输合同和保险合同

(1)运输合同

买方无义务订立运输合同。

(2)保险合同

买方有义务订立保险合同。

B4 受领货物

买方必须在卖方按照 A4 规定交货时受领货物。

B5 风险转移

买方必须承担按照 A4 规定交货时起货物灭失或损坏的一切风险。如买方没有履行 B2 规定的义务,则必须承担由此发生的货物灭失或损坏的一切额外风险。如买方未按照 B7 规定通知卖方,则必须自约定的交货日期或交货期限届满之日起,承担货物灭失或损坏的一切风险,但以该项货物已正式划归合同项下,即清楚地划出或以其他方式规定为合同项下的货物为限。

B6 费用划分

买方必须支付以下费用:

(1)自按照 A4 规定交货时起与货物有关的一切费用;

(2)如买方未履行 B2 规定的义务,或未按照 B7 规定作出通知,由此而发生的一切额外费用,但以该项货物已正式划归合同项下,即清楚地划出或以其他方式规定为合同项下的货物为限。

B7　通知卖方

一旦买方有权决定在约定期限内的时间和(或)在指定的目的地受领货物的点,买方必须就此给予卖方充分通知。

B8　交货凭证

买方必须接受按照A8规定提供的适当的提货单或运输单据。

B9　货物检验

买方必须支付任何装运前检验的费用,但出口国有关当局强制进行的检验除外。

B10　其他义务

应卖方要求并有其承担风险和费用,买方必须给予卖方一切协助,以帮助卖方取得为按照本规则将货物交付买方需要的,由进口国签发或传递的任何单证或有同等作用的电子信息。

适合于海上和内陆水上运输方式。

八、FAS(装运港船边交货(……指定装运港))

该术语仅用于海上或内陆水上运输方式。

船边交货是指卖方在指定的装运港将货物交到船边,即完成交货。当货物被放置在船边,货物损失的风险便转移,买方必须承担自那时起货物灭失或损失的一切风险。建议双方在合同中精确地规定装运港,以及到达那一点卖方应该承担的风险。

如果要求卖方把货物交到目的地的承运人手中,而不是船边,在这种情况下,FAS术语不适用,应使用FCA术语。FAS术语要求卖方办理出口清关手续。然而,卖方无义务进口报关,缴纳进口关税或履行任何进口手续。

A　卖方义务

A1　卖方的一般义务

卖方必须提供符合销售合同规定货物和商业发票或有同等作用的电子信息,以及合同可能要求的,证明货物符合合同规定的其他任何凭证。

A2　许可证和其他手续

卖方必须自担风险和费用,取得任何出口许可证或其他官方许可,并在需要办理海关出口手续时,办理货物出口所需的一切海关手续。

A3　运输合同和保险合同

(1)运输合同

卖方无义务订立运输合同。

(2)保险合同

卖方无义务订立保险合同。然而,应买方的要求,卖方必须提供有关取得保险相关风险和费用的信息。

A4 交货

卖方必须在买方指定的装运港,在买方指定的装货地点,在约定日期或期限内,按照该港习惯的方式将货物交至买方指定的船边。

A5 风险转移

除 B5 规定外,卖方必须承担货物灭失或损坏的一切风险,直至已按照 A4 规定交货为止。

A6 费用划分

除 B6 规定外,卖方必须支付以下费用:

(1)与货物有关的一切费用,直至已按照 A4 规定交货为止;

(2)在需要办理海关手续时,货物出口应办理的海关手续费用及应交纳的关税、税款和其他费用。

A7 通知买方

卖方必须给予买方说明货物已交至指定的船边的充分通知。

(1)买方没能按照 B7 给出通知;

(2)买方指定的船只没能按时到达,或根据 B7 提前到达,买方承担由此造成的一切风险和费用。

A8 交货凭证

卖方必须给予自付费用的买方提供证明按照 A4 规定交货的通常单据。

除非前项所述单据是运输单据,否则,应买方要求并由其承担风险和费用,卖方必须给予买方一切的协助,以取得运输单据。

A9 查对,包装,标记

卖方必须支付为按照 A4 交货所需进行的查对费用(如核对货物品质、质量、过磅、点数的费用)。

卖方必须自付费用,提供按照卖方订立销售合同前已知的有关该货物运输所要求的包装。包装应作适当标记。

A10 其他义务

应买方要求并由其承担风险和费用,卖方必须给予买方一切的协助,以帮助其取得由装运地国和原产地所签发或传送的,为买方进口货物可能要求的或从他国过境所需的任何单据。

B 买方义务

B1 买方的一般义务

买方必须按照销售合同规定支付价款。

B2 许可证和其他许可和手续

买方必须自担风险和费用，取得任何进口许可证或其他官方许可，并在需要办理海关出口手续时，办理货物进口和从他国过境所需的一切海关手续。

B3　运输合同和保险合同

(1)运输合同

买方必须自付费用订立自指定的装运港运输货物合同。

(2)保险合同

卖方有义务订立保险合同。

B4　受领货物

买方必须在卖方按照 A4 规定交货时受领货物。

B5　风险转移

买方必须按照下述规定承担货物灭失或损坏的一切风险：

(1)自按照 A4 规定交货时起；

(2)由于买方未按照 B7 规定通知卖方，或其指定的船只未按时到达，或未接受货物，或较按照 B7 通知的时间提早停止交货，则自约定的交货日期或期限届满时起，但以该货物已计划划归合同项下，即明确保留或其他方式确定为合同项下的货物为限。

B6　费用划分

买方必须支付以下费用：

(1)按照 A4 规定交货时起与货物有关的一切费用；

(2)由于买方指定的船只未按时到达，或未装载上述货物或按照 B7 通知的时间提早停止装货，或由于买方未按照 B7 规定给予卖方相应的通知而发生的任何额外费用，以该货物已正式划归合同项下，即清楚地划出或以其他方式确定为合同项下的货物为限；

(3)在需要办理海关手续时，货物进口应交纳的一切关税、税款和其他费用，及办理海关手续的费用，以及从他国过境的费用。

B7　通知卖方

买方必须给予卖方有关船名、装船点和要求交货时间的充分通知。

B8　交货凭证

买方必须接受按照 A8 规定提供的交货凭证。

B9　货物检验

买方必须支付任何装运前检验的费用，但出口国有关当局强制进行的检验除外。

B10　其他义务

买方必须支付因获取 A10 所述单据或有同等作用的电子信息所放生的一切费用，并偿付卖方因给予协助而发生的费用。

九、FOB(装运港船上交货(……指定装运港))

该术语仅适用于海运或内陆水上运输。

船上交货是当货物在指定的装运港越过船舷,卖方即完成交货。这意味着买方必须从该点起承担货物灭失或损坏的一切风险。

如果要求卖方把货物交到目的地的承运人手中,而不是船上,在这种情况下,应使用FCA术语。

FOB术语要求卖方办理货物出口清关手续。然而,卖方无义务进口报关,缴纳进口关税或履行任何进口手续。

A　卖方义务

A1　卖方的一般义务

卖方必须提供符合销售合同规定的货物和商业发票,以及合同可能要求的、证明货物符合合同规定的其他任何凭证。

A2　许可证和其他手续

卖方必须自担风险和费用,取得任何进口许可证或其他官方许可,并在需要办理海关手续时,办理出口货物所需一切海关手续。

A3　运输合同和保险合同

(1)运输合同

卖方无义务订立运输合同。

(2)保险合同

卖方无义务订立保险合同。然而,应买方的要求,卖方必须提供有关取得保险相关风险和费用的信息。

A4　交货

卖方必须在约定日期或期限内,在指定的装运港,按照该港习惯方式,将货物交至买方指定的船只上。

A5　风险转移

除B5规定外,卖方必须承担货物灭失或损坏的一切风险,直至货物在指定的装运港越过船舷为止。

A6　费用划分

卖方必须支付以下费用:

(1)货物有关的一切费用,直至货物在指定的装运港越过船舷时为止;

(2)需要办理海关手续时,货物出口需要办理的海关手续费用及出口时应交纳的一切关税、税款和其他费用。

A7 通知买方

卖方必须给予买方说明货物已经按照 A4 规定的充分通知。

A8 交货凭证

卖方必须自付费用向买方提供证明货物已按照 A4 规定交货的通常单据。

除非前项所述单据是运输单据,否则应买方要求并由其承担风险和费用,卖方必须给予买方一切协助,以取得有关运输合同的运输单据。

A9 查对、包装、标记

卖方必须支付为按照 A4 规定交货所需进行的查对费用(如核对货物品质、丈量、过磅、点数的费用)。

卖方必须自付费用,提供按照卖方订立销售合同前已知的该货物运输所要求的包装,除非按照相关行业惯例,合同所述货物无需包装发运。包装应作适当标记。

A10 其他义务

应买方要求并由其承担风险和费用,卖方必须给予买方一切协助,以帮助其取得由装运地国和(或)原产地国所签发或传送的、为买方进口货物可能要求的和必要时从他国过境所需的任何单据。

B 买方义务

B1 支付价款

买方必须按照销售合同规定支付价款。

B2 许可证和其他手续

买方必须自担风险和费用取得任何进口许可证或其他官方许可,并在需要办理海关手续时,办理货物进口和在必要时从他国过境的一切海关手续。

B3 运输合同和保险合同

(1)运输合同

买方必须自付费用订立从指定的装运港运输货物的合同。

(2)保险合同

买方有义务订立保险合同。

B4 受领货物

买方必须在卖方按照 A4 规定交货时受领货物。

B5 风险转移

买方必须按照下述规定承担货物灭失或损坏的一切风险:由于买方未按照 B7 规定通知卖方,或其指定的船只未按时到达,或未接收货物,或较按照 B7 通知的时间提早停止装货,则自约定交货日期或交货期限届满之日起,但以该项货物已正式划归合同项下,即清楚地划出或以其他方式确定为合同项的货物为限。

B6 费用划分

买方必须支付以下费用:

(1)货物在指定的装运港越过船舷之时起与货物有关的一切费用;

(2)由于买方指定的船只未按时到达,或未接收货物,或较按照 B7 通知的时间提早停止装货,或买方未能按照 B7 规定给予卖方相应的通知而发生的一切额外费用,但以该项货物已正式划归合同下,即清楚地划出或以其他方式确定为合同下的货物为限;

(3)需要办理海关手续时,货物进口应缴纳的一切关税、税款和其他费用,及办理海关手续的费用,以及货物从他国过境的费用。

B7 通知卖方

买方必须给予卖方有关船名、装船点和要求交货时间的充分通知。

B8 交货凭证

买方必须接受按照 A8 规定提供的交货凭证。

B9 货物检验

买方必须支付任何装运前检验的费用,但出口国有关当局强制进行的检验除外。

B10 其他义务

买方必须支付因获取 A10 所述单据所发生的一切费用,并偿付卖方因给予协助而发生的费用。

十、CFR(成本加费用(……指定目的港))

该术语仅使用于海运或内陆水上运输。

“成本加运费(……指定目的港)”,是指在装运港货物越过船舷卖方即完成交货,卖方必须支付货物运至目的港所需的运费和费用。但交货后货物灭失或损坏的风险,以及由于各种事件造成的任何额外费用,即由卖方转移到买方。

如果要求卖方把货物交到目的地的承运人手中,而不是船上,在这种情况下,应使用 CPT 术语。

CFR 术语要求卖方办理出口清关手续。然而,卖方无义务进口报关,缴纳进口关税或履行任何进口手续。

A 卖方义务

A1 卖方的一般义务

卖方必须提供符合销售合同规定的货物和商业发票,以及合同可能要求的用于证明货物符合合同规定的其他任何凭证。

A2 许可证和其他手续

卖方必须自担风险和费用,取得任何出口许可证或其他官方许可,并在需要办理海关手续时办理货物出口所需的一切海关手续。

A3　运输合同和保险合同

(1)运输合同

卖方必须自付费用,按照通常条件订立运输合同,经由惯常航线,将货物用通常可供运输合同所指货物类型的海轮,或依情况适合内河运输的船只,运输至指定的目的港。

(2)保险合同

卖方无义务订立保险合同。然而,应买方的要求,卖方必须提供有关取得保险相关风险和费用的信息。

A4　交货

卖方必须在装运港,在约定的日期或期限内,将货物交至船上。

A5　风险转移

除 B5 规定外,卖方必须承担货物灭失或损坏的一切风险,直至货物在装运港过船舷为止。

A6　费用划分

卖方必须支付以下费用:

(1)与货物有关的一切费用,直至已经按照 A4 规定交货为止;

(2)按照 A3(1)规定所发生的运费和其他一切费用,包括货物的装船费和根据运输合同由卖方支付的,在约定卸货港的任何卸货费;

(3)在需要办理海关手续时,货物出口需要办理的海关手续费用及出口时应交纳的一切关税、税款和其他费用,以及如果根据运输合同规定,由卖方支付的货物从他国过境的费用。

A7　通知买方

卖方必须给予买方说明货物已按照规定交货的充分通知,以及要求的任何其他通知,以便买方能够为受领货物采取通常必要的措施。

A8　交货凭证

卖方必须自付费用,毫不迟延地向买方提供表明载往约定目的港的通常运输单据。此单据必须载明合同货物,其日期应在约定的装运期内,使买方得以在目的港向承运人提取货物,并除非另有约定,应使买方得以通过转让单据或通过通知承运人,向其后手买方出售在途货物。

如此运输单据有数份正本,则应向买方提供全套正本。

A9　查对、包装、标记

卖方必须支付为按照 A4 规定交货所需进行的查对费用(如核对货物品质、丈量、过磅、点数的费用)。卖方必须自付费用提供符合其安排的运输所要求的包装(除非按照相关行业惯例该合同所描述货物无需包装发运)。包装应作适当标记。

A10 其他义务

应买方要求并由其承担风险和费用,卖方必须给予买方一切协助,以帮助买方取得由装运地国和(或)原产地国所签发或传送的,为买方进口货物可能要求的和必要时从他国过境所需的任何单据。

B 买方义务

B1 买方的一般义务

买方必须按照销售合同规定支付价款。

B2 许可证和其他手续

买方必须自担风险和费用,取得任何进口许可证或其他官方许可,并在需要办理海关手续时办理货物进口及从他国过境的一切海关手续。

B3 运输合同和保险合同

(1)运输合同

买方无义务订立运输合同。

(2)保险合同

买方有义务订立保险合同。

B4 受领货物

买方必须在卖方按照 A4 规定交货时受领货物,并在指定的目的港从承运人处受领货物。

B5 风险转移

买方必须承担货物在装运港越过船舷之后灭失或损坏的一切风险。如买方未按照 B7 规定给予卖方通知,买方必须从约定的装运日期或装运期限届满之日起,承担货物灭失或损坏的一切风险,但以该项货物已正式划归合同项下,即清楚地划出或以其他方式确定为合同项下的货物为限。

B6 费用划分

除 A3(1)规定外,买方必须支付以下费用:

(1)按照 A4 规定交货时起的一切费用;

(2)货物在运输途中直至到达目的港为止的一切费用,除非这些费用根据运输合同应由卖方支付;

(3)包括驳运费和码头费在内的卸货费,除非这些费用根据运输合同应由卖方支付;

(4)如买方未按照 B7 规定给予卖方通知,则自约定的装运日期或装运期限届满之日起,货物所发生的一切额外费用,但以该项货物已正式划归合同项下,即清楚地划出或以其他方式确定为合同项下的货物为限;

(5)在需要办理海关手续时,货物进口应交纳的一切关税、税款和其他费用,及办理海关手续的费用,以及需要时从他国过境的费用,除非这些费用已包括在运输合同中。

B7 通知卖方

一旦买方有权决定装运货物的时间和(或)目的港,买方必须就此给予卖方充分通知。

B8 交货凭证

买方必须接受按照 A8 规定提供的运输单据,如果该单据符合合同规定的话。

B9 货物检验

买方必须支付任何装运前检验的费用,但出口国有关当局强制进行的检查除外。

B10 其他义务

买方必须支付因获取 A10 所述单据所发生的一切费用,并偿付卖方因给予协助而发生的费用。

十一、CIF(成本、保险费加运费(……指定目的港))

该术语仅适用于海运和内陆水上运输。

“成本、保险费加运费”是指在装运港当货物越过船舷时卖方即完成交货。卖方必须支付将货物运至指定的目的港所需的运费和费用,但交货后货物灭失或损坏的风险及由于各种事件造成的任何额外费用即由卖方转移到买方。但是,在 CIF 条件下,卖方还必须办理买方货物在运输途中灭失或损坏风险的海运保险。因此,由卖方订立保险合同并支付保险费。买方应注意到,CIF 术语只要求卖方投保最低限度的保险险别。如买方需要更高的保险险别,则需要与卖方明确地达成协议,或者自行作出额外的保险安排。

若当事方无意越过船舷交货则应使用 CIP 术语。CIF 术语要求卖方办理货物出口清关手续。然而,卖方无义务进口报关,缴纳进口关税或履行进口手续。

A 卖方义务

A1 卖方的一般义务

卖方必须提供符合销售合同规定的货物和商业发票,以及合同可能要求的、证明货物符合合同规定的其他任何凭证。

A2 许可证和其他手续

卖方必须自担风险和费用,取得任何出口许可证或其他官方许可,并在需要办理海关手续时办理货物出口所需的一切海关手续。

A3 运输合同和保险合同

(1)运输合同

卖方必须自付费用,按照通常条件发、订立运输合同,经由惯常航线,将货物用通常可供运输合同所指货物类型的海轮,或依情况适合内河运输的船只装运至指定的目的港。

(2)保险合同

卖方必须按照合同规定,自付费用取得货物保险,并向买方提供保险单或其他保险证据,以使买方或任何其他对货物具有保险利益的人有权直接向保险人索赔。保险合同应与信誉良好的保险人或保险公司订立,在无相反明确协议时,应按照《协会货物保险条款》(伦敦保险人协会)或其他类似条款中的最低保险险别投保。保险期限应按照 B5 和 B4 规定。应买方要求,并由买方负担费用,卖方应加投战争、罢工、暴乱和民变险,如果能投保的话,最低保险金额应包括合同规定价款另加 10%(即 110%),并应采用合同货币。

A4 交货

卖方必须在装运港,在约定的日期或期限内,将货物交至船上。

A5 风险转移

除 B5 规定外,卖方必须承担货物灭失或损失的一切风险,直至货物在装运港越过船舷为止。

A6 费用划分

卖方必须支付以下费用:

(1)与货物有关的一切费用,直至已经按照 A4 规定交货为止;

(2)按照 A3(1)规定所发生的运费和其他一切费用,包括货物的装船费;

(3)按照 A3(2)规定所发生的保险费用;

(4)在需要办理海关手续时,货物出口所需办理的海关手续费用,及出口应交纳的一切关税、税款和其他费用,以及根据运输合同规定由卖方支付的货物从他国过境的费用。

A7 通知买方

卖方必须给予说明货物已按照规定交货的充分通知,以及要求的任何其他通知,以便买方能够为受领货物而采取通常必要的措施。

A8 交货凭证

卖方应自付费用、毫不延迟地向买方提供表明载往约定目的港的通常运输单据。

此单据必须载明合同货物,其日期应在约定的装运期内,使买方得以在目的港向承运人提取货物,并且,除非另有约定,应使买方得以通过转让单据或通过通知承运人,向其后手买方出售在途货物。如此运输单据有数份正本,则应向买方提供全套正本。

A9 查对、包装、标记

卖方必须支付为按照 A4 交货所需进行的查对费用(如核对货物品质、丈量、过磅、点数的费用)。

卖方必须自付费用,提供符合其安排的运输所需求的包装,除非按照相关行业惯例该合同所描述货物无需包装发运。包装应作适当标记。

A10 其他义务

应买方要求并由其承风险和费用,卖方必须给予买方一切协助,以帮助买方取得由装运地国和(或)原产地国所签发或传送的、为买方进口货物可能要求的和必要时从他国过境所需的任何单据。

B　买方义务

B1　买方的一般义务

买方必须按照销售合同规定支付价款。

B2　许可证和其他手续

买方必须自担风险和费用，取得任何进口许可证或其他官方许可，并在需要办理海关手续时办理货物进口和从他国过境的一切海关手续。

B3　运输合同和保险合同

(1)运输合同

买方无义务订立运输合同。

(2)保险合同

卖方无义务订立保险合同。

B4　受领货物

买方必须在卖方已按照 A4 交货时受领货物，并在指定的目的港从承运人处收受货物。

B5　风险转移

买方必须承担货物在装运港越过船舷之后灭失或损失的一切风险。

如买方未按照 B7 规定给予卖方通知，买方必须从约定的装运日期或装运期限届满之日起，承担货物灭失或损失的一切风险，但以该项货物已正式划归合同项下，即清楚地划出或以其他方式确定为合同项下货物为限。

B6　费用划分

除 A3 规定外，买方必须支付以下费用：

(1)自按照 A4 规定交货时起的一切费用；

(2)货物在运输途中直至到达目的港为止的一切费用，除非这些费用根据运输合同应由卖方支付；

(3)包括驳运费和码头费在内的卸货费，除非这些费用根据运输合同规定由卖方支付；

(4)如买方未按照 B7 规定给予卖方通知，则自约定的装运日期或装运期限届满之日起，货物所发生的一切额外费用，但以该项货物已正式划归合同项下，即清楚地划出或以其他方式确定为合同项下货物为限；

(5)在需要办理海关手续时，货物进口所应缴纳的一切关税、税款和其他费用，及办理海关手续的费用，以及在需要时从他国过境的费用，除非这些费用已包括在运输合同中。

B7　通知卖方

一旦买方有权决定装运货物的时间和(或)目的港，买方必须就此给予卖方充分通知。

B8　交货凭证

买方必须接受按照 A8 规定提供的运输单据，如果该单据符合合同规定。

B9　货物检验

买方必须支付任何装运前检验的费用,但出口国有关当局强制进行的检验除外。

B10　其他义务

买方必须支付因获取 A10 所述单据所发生的一切费用,并偿付卖方因给予协助而发生的费用。

第四节　2010 通则的使用

INCOTERMS 规则规定了一系列在货物销售商业合同实践中使用的三字母系列贸易术语。INCOTERMS 规则主要描述了货物从卖方到买方运输过程中涉及的责任、费用和风险的划分。

一、把 INCOTERMS 2010 规则应用到销售合同中

如果要使合同适用 INCOTERMS 2010 规则,应在合同中明确表明,例如所选择的 INCOTERMS 规则适用 INCOTERMS 2010 规则。

二、选择适宜的 INCOTERMS 规则

所选的 INCOTERMS 规则需要与货物采取的运输方式相适应,最重要的是合同双方是否意欲添加额外的义务,例如将办理运输或保险的义务加于买方或卖方。每个贸易术语的指导性解释中的信息对作出如此的决定非常有帮助。不论选用何种 INCOTERMS 规则,双方应该意识到对合同的解释会受到使用的港口或地址惯例的影响。

三、尽可能精准地描述你方地址或港口名称

只有当事人双方选定特定的一个收货地或港口时,所选术语才能发挥作用。地点或港口名称越精准,INCOTERMS 规则越有效。以下精准描述就是一个很好的例子:

"INCOTERMS 2010,FCA 规则,法国,巴黎,38 Cours Albert 1er。"

在 INCOTERMS 规则中:

EXW　工厂交货

FCA　货交承运人

DAT　目的地交货

DAP　所在地交货

DDP　完税后交货

FAS　船边交货

FOB　船上交货

此处所指地点为交货地点，同时风险也从卖方转移至买方。

在 INCOTERMS 规则中：

CPT　运费付至

CIP　运费、保险费付至

CFR　成本加运费

CIF　成本、保险费加运费

所指地点随交货地不同而不同。在这些 INCOTERMS 规则下，所指地点为运费付至地。为了避免疑问和争议，指定地点或目的地可以进一步阐述为一个精确的地点。

四、谨记 INCOTERMS 规则并没有给当事人提供一份完整的销售合同

INCOTERMS 规则确有阐述销售合同中当事人的特定义务，当卖方将货物运至买方时，承担办理运输和保险的义务。

然而，INCOTERMS 并没有任何关于付款价格或付款方式的规定，或是货物所有权的转移、违约的后果等。这些问题通常是通过销售合同的明示条款和适用的法律条文来解决。当事人需要注意的是，当地强制适用的法律有可能优先于销售合同的内容，包括所选择的 INCOTERMS 规则。

五、INCOTERMS 2010 的主要特征

1. 两个新的贸易术语

DAT 和 DAP 即 DAT 和 DAP 代替了原来 INCOTERMS 2000 的 DAF，DES，DEQ 和 DDU 术语。

贸易术语的数量从原来的 13 个减少到 11 个。INCOTERMS 2010 用两个可以不顾及已议定的运输模式的新术语——DAT（目的地交货）和 DAP（指定地交货）——代替了 INCOTERMS 2000 中的 DAF，DES，SEQ 和 DDU 术语。

DAT 和 DAP 术语都规定需在指定地点交货：在 DAT 情况下，从运输工具上卸下货物交由买方处置（这和先前的 DEQ 术语一样）；在 DAP 情况下同样交由买方处置，但需做好卸货的准备（这和先前的 DAF，DES 和 DDU 术语一样）。

新贸易术语的使用，使 INCOTERMS 2000 中的 DES 和 DEQ 成为多余。DAT 的目的地可以是港口，因此 DAT 可以用于在 INCOTERMS 2000 下 DEQ 适用的情况。同样的，DAP 中运达货物的交通工具可以是轮船，而目的地也可以是港口，因此 DAP 可以用于在 INCOTERMS 2000 下 DES 适用的情况。这两个新的术语，和先前的几个术语一样，是由卖方承担所有费用（除了与进口清算有关的费用）和货物到达目的地前的风险。

2. INCOTERMS 2010 中 11 种贸易术语的分类

INCOTERMS 2010 中的 11 种贸易术语目前被分为以下两类（见表 1－3）：

表 1-3 INCOTERMS 2010

适用于任何运输方式的术语:

EXW 工厂交货

FCA 货交承运人

CPT 运费付至

CIP 运费及保险费付至

DAT 目的地交货

DAP 所在地交货

DDP 完税后交货

适用于海上和内陆水上运输的术语:

FAS 船边交货

FOB 船上交货

CFR 成本加运费

CIF 成本、保险费加运费

第一种分类中的七种贸易术语不用考虑所选用运输方式的种类。EXW,FCA,CPT,CIP,DAT,DAP 和 DDP 都属于第一种分类。它们甚至可以运用于没有海上运输的情况下。谨记只要运输中一个部分运用过船只便可以适用此类术语。

在第二类术语中,交货点和把货物送达买方的地点都是港口,所以只适用于"海上或内陆水上运输"。FAS,FOB,CFR 和 CIF 都属于这一类。最后的三个术语,删除了以越过船舷为交货标准而代之以将货物装运上船。这更准确地反应了现代商业现实,避免了以往风险围绕船舷这条虚拟垂线来回摇摆。

3. 国内贸易和国际贸易的规定

传统的 INCOTERMS 2010 规则只在国际销售合同中运用,此种交易货物运输都需跨越国界。在世界许多地区,商业集团如欧盟使得不同国家间的过关手续不再重要。所以,INCOTERMS 2010 正式认可所有的贸易规则既可以适用于国内交易也可以适用于国际交易。所以,INCOTERMS 2010 在一些地方明确规定,只有在适当的时候,才有义务遵从进口或者出口的手续。

两个新发展使得 ICC 相信向这个方向的改革是适宜的。首先,商人们普遍在国内贸易合同中使用 INCOTERMS 2010 规则。其次,比起先前提到的统一的商业规则中的运输和交付术语,在国内贸易中更多美国人愿意使用 INCOTERMS 2010 中的术语。

4. 引言

在 INCOTERMS 2010 的每条规则前面,都有一条引言。引言用于解释每条贸易规则的基本内容,比如说什么时候被运用到,什么时候风险转移,还有费用在卖方和买方间是怎样分配的等。引言并不是 INCOTERMS 2010 的内容，但是它们能帮助使用者更准确、更有效率地针对特定的贸易运用合适的贸易条款。

5. 电子通信

上一版本的 INCOTERMS 规则已经确定了可以被电子数据交换信息替代的文件。然而 INCOTERMS 规则 2010 中的 A1（B1）赋予电子通信方式和纸质通信相同的效果，只要缔约双方同意或存在国际惯例。这一规定有利于促进 INCOTERMS 规则 2010 中新的电子程序的演进。

6. 保险范围

INCOTERMS 规则 2010 是协会货物条款修订以来的最新版国际贸易术语规则，并就对那些条款的变更作了考虑。INCOTERMS 规则 2010 把关系到保险的信息义务规定在 A3（B3），这涉及到运输和保险合同。这些条款已经从变更为普通的国际贸易术语 2000 中 A10（B10）的文章中删除。为了明确缔约双方的义务，条款 A2（B3）中涉及保险的行文也作了变化。

7. 与安全有关的清关需要的信息

现在人们高度关注货物运输中的安全问题，除了其自身固有的属性外需要确认货物不会对生命和财产有威胁。

因此，INCOTERMS 规则 2010 已经在买家和卖家间分配了义务，在与安全有关的清关获得或者提供帮助，例如在多种多样的国际贸易术语中 A2（B2）和 A10（B10）的监管链相关信息

8. 终点站操作费

在国际贸易术语 CPT，CIP，CIF，DAT，DAP 和 DDP 项下，卖家必须做好安排使货物到达指定目的地。虽然运费是由卖方支付的，但因为运费一般被卖方包含在销售价格中所以实际上运费是由买方支付的。货运费有时包括港口或集装箱码头内的理货和运输费用承运人和终点站运营方也可能向收到货物的买家收取这笔费用。在这种情况下，买家会想要避免对同一服务重复付费：一次付给卖家作为销售价格中的一部分，一次单独地付给承运人或者终点站运营方。INCOTERMS 规则 2010 在相关国际贸易术解释规则的 A6/B6 条款明确的分配此项费用，力求避免重复付费。

9. 连环合同

与工业制成品的销售不同，在农矿产品的销售中，货物经常在沿销售链运转过程中被频繁销售多次。这种情况下，在运输中的卖家不用再运输货物，因为货物已被第一个卖家装船运输了。中途的卖方通过接收货物而非运输货物向买方履行义务。为明确起见，INCOTERMS 规则 2010 在相关规定中把提取已经运输的商品的义务作为运输商品义务的替换。

六、运输方式的规则

1. 国际贸易术语解释通则的变体

贸易各方有时因各自需要意图修改某一国际贸易术语规则的适用。《国际贸易术语解释通则2010》并不禁止这种修改,但是这样做会带来一定的危险。因此双方都应当在合同中明确表明修改意欲达到的效果以避免不愉快的分歧。譬如,假设合同改变了INCOTERMS规则中费用的分配,那么合同各方亦应当明确声明是否改变风险(从卖方到买方)转移的临界点。

2. 本导言的功能地位

本导言只是对《国际贸易术语解释通则2010》的用途和解释的概括提示,并不是这些的组成部分。

3. 对《国际贸易术语解释通则2010》中术语的解释

正如《国际贸易术语解释通则2010》中所述,买方和卖方的共同义务是以对应方式呈现的,也就是说,既能反映出A栏中的买方义务,又能反映出B栏中的卖方义务。这些义务可以由买方或者卖方亲自履行,有时抑或受制于合同或者适用法律中的个别条款的规定,由诸如承运人、转运代理人等中介组织,或者其他由买方或者卖方为了特定目的而委任的人来履行。

《国际贸易术语解释通则2010》正文中条文解析明了。但出于引导辅助(使用者)理解的考虑,编者还是占用了以下篇幅对从《规则》中选取的几个术语进行阐释。

承运人:出于《国际贸易术语解释通则2010》的目的,承运人是指与托运人订立合同,并承担运输义务的一方。

报关单:是指为了遵守海关条例而需要满足的一些要求,包括了单据、安全、信息或者实体检验之义务。

交货:在商法和商事活动中,这个概念有多种含义。但是,在《国际贸易术语解释通则2010》中,交货用来表明在货物由卖方向买方转移的过程中毁损风险在何处转移。

交货单:此术语现在已成为A8条款的标题。交货单,是用于证明已完成交货的凭证。对于《国际贸易术语解释通则2010》中的许多规则,交货单是一种运输单据或相关电子记录。但是对于EXW,FCA,FAS和FOB,交货单只是一种收据。当然,交货单还有其他功能,比如支付程序的一个环节。

电子记录或者程序:由一个或多个可适用的电子信号组成的一组信息库,其功能上等同于相应的纸质文档。

包装一词因语境不同有不同含义:

(1) 符合销售合同要求的货物包装;

(2) 符合运输要求的货物包装;

(3) 集装箱或其他运输工具中已包装货物的理仓。

在《国际贸易术语解释通则 2010》中,“包装”一词有以上(1)和(2)项的含义。INCOTERMS 2010 中并不涉及集装箱内货物的理仓义务,当事人应在销售合同中予以确定。

第二章 货物的品名与品质

第一节 货物的品名

合同中的品名条款通常只是在"商品名称"或品名的标题下,列明交易双方成交商品的名称。在合同中列明商品的名称已成为不可缺少的一项主要贸易条件。按照有关的法律和惯例,对交易标的物的描述关系到买卖双方的权利和义务。若卖方交付的货物不符合约定的品名或说明,买方有权提出损害赔偿要求,甚至可以拒收货物或撤销合同。由此可见,作为销售合同的主要条款,应该在合同中清楚地列明商品具体名称。列出品名时,应尽可能使用双方广泛接受的名称。对某些商品,我们应该仔细使用恰当的名称,以便减少海关关税或节省运费。

第二节 货物的品质

一、货物品质的表示方法

品质是货物销售的最重要部分。卖方必须按照合同规定交货,否则买方有权提出损害赔偿要求,要求交付替代物,甚至拒收货物或撤销合同。合同中的品质条款是卖方交货的依据。国际贸易中常用来表示商品品质的方法如下。

1. 实物表示法

即由卖方在货物工厂向买方展示准备出售的货物,经买方现场检查满意后达成交易。以这种方式达成的交易,货物的品质以检查时的状态为准。卖方只要交付经检查的货物,买方就不得对其品质提出任何异议。一般而言,看货成交是货物数量不太大,买方能够亲临现场的条件下进行的。所以,通常只适用于工艺品等贵重货物。

2. 凭样品买卖

样品可以由卖方提供,但有时也可以由买方提供。前者称为"质量以卖方样品为准",后者称为"质量以买方样品为准"。

(1) 对等样品:凭买方样品的买卖,如果卖方所交货物不符合买方的样品,买方可以拒收货物。为了避免交货时引起争端,卖方可以根据买方样品进行复制或提出与之相似的样品作为"回样"或"样品",不确认作为交货时的品质依据。

(2)密封样品:在送交样品或交货之前,卖方可以选择一些样品在买方和公证人面前密封。密封的样品是将来检验货物的质量依据。

(3)保障条款:在凭买方样品买卖时,为了避免侵犯第三者知识产权,通常在合同中规定保障条款,示例如下:"买方承诺没有侵犯第三方的知识产权。"

(4)参考样品:当凭说明书买卖商品时,卖方或买方可以把真实的商品交到对方手中以便确认。这种样品标注"仅供参考",它并不是交货的依据。

3. 用说明表示的方法

(1)凭标准、等级或规格的买卖:一些主要技术指标,如化学成分、含量、长度、大小能够充分描述商品的质量。商品的规格用来反映商品品质比较方便、准确,所以应用较广。商品按其规格上的差异,将品质分为各不相同的若干等级。

例如:红皮新鲜鸡蛋

一级	每只鸡蛋 60 ~ 65 gm
二级	每只鸡蛋 55 ~ 60 gm
三级	每只鸡蛋 50 ~ 55 gm
四级	每只鸡蛋 45 ~ 50 gm

商品的标准一般由国家或商业组织规定,有的是国家标准,有的是国际标准。许多国家使用自己的标准,例如英国使用 BS 标准,美国和日本使用 ANSI 标准。最典型的国际标准是 ISO 标准。在援引国外标准时,必须注明所援引标准的出版年份。

(2)凭牌号或商标的买卖:有些商品在市场上已经销售多年,并树立了良好的信誉,交易时仅凭牌号或商标即可说明其品质。例如可口可乐、大白兔奶糖。

然而,一些知名品牌的产品由于他们的种类和构成各不相同,也不能仅凭商标和品牌来表示。例如索尼品牌,就有索尼电视机、索尼随身听、索尼 DVD 等,在这种情况下,有必要清楚地描述产品质量指标或者技术成分。

(3)凭说明书和图样的买卖:有些商品,如机械、仪器、设备、运输工具等,由于其结构和性能十分复杂,无法用几个简单的具体指标来反映其品质的全貌,因此,必须凭详细的说明书以及图样来具体说明。按这种办法进行的买卖,合同中的品质条款不仅包括商品品名、牌号,还订有对产品结构和功能的说明书,条款写明"商品品质与技术数据严格符合卖方提交的说明书"。

(4)凭产地名称买卖:有些产品在品质方面具有其他产区的产品所不具有的传统工艺、独特风格或特色。对于这类产品,一般也可用产地名称来表示其品质,如四川榨菜。

二、合同中的品质条款

在品质条款中,商品的品名、规格、登记、序列号和样品的日期等应该清楚地表明。我们可以使用说明书或样品描述商品的质量,既可单独运用,也可以将几种方式结合运用,这取决于商品的特征。

(1)凭样品买卖时,有时卖方所交货物品质难以完全与样品的品质相符。在这种情况下,可以规定这样的条款:“所交货物大致等于样品”。

(2)对有些初级商品的品质规格规定上下限。

(3)品质公差。不可避免地要对一些工业产品,例如工具规定品质公差。例如,“大豆,根据到岸货物含油量增加1%,价格也应该相应上浮2%”。

第三章　货物的数量

第一节　货物数量的计算方法

一、计量单位

在国际贸易中，由于不同的产品具有不同的特点，并且各国采用不同的计算重量和体积的体制，因此计算数量的单位与方法各异。各国度量衡制度不同，所使用的单位也各异。目前常用的度量衡制度，有国际单位制、公制、英制和美制。英制中的长吨等于2200磅，美制中的短吨等于2000磅。此外，在英制和美制中，一些表示容积，如加仑和蒲式耳的计量单位是相同的，但其实际容积是不同的。在国际贸易中有两种表示货物数量的计量单位：一种是计量单位，包括重量、长度、面积、体积和容积；另一种是数字，包括一些习惯性的单位，例如打、令和一些诸如桶（石油、油）、包（棉花）等的包装单位。

二、计算重量的方法

国际贸易中的许多商品是按重量买卖的。按照一般商业习惯，计算重量的方法有以下几种。

1. 毛重

即商品本身的重量加包装的重量，一般适用于低值的商品。

2. 净重

即商品本身的重量，在国际贸易中，大部分以重量计量的商品，都是以净重计价。有些商品在包装后计算重量，包括包装在内的重量称为毛重，一些价值较低的产品也以毛重计价。这种以毛重计价的方法称为“以毛作净”。例如：货物按净重计算时，必须由毛重扣除皮重，计算皮重的方法如下。

（1）实际皮重

即商品包装实际重量。

（2）平均皮重

在皮重相差不大的情况下，从全体商品中抽出若干件包装材料，计算出皮重，然后求出其平均重量。

（3）习惯皮重

有些比较标准化、规格化的包装，其重量已为市场所公认，因此不必逐件重复过秤，而以习惯上公认的包装重量计算，称为习惯皮重。

(4)约定皮重

即买卖双方事先协商约定的皮重。

3. 公量

即用科学方法除去商品中所含的实际水分,再另加标准水分,所求得的重量。这种方法经常用于水分含量不稳定、易受空气湿度影响的商品,如羊毛、生丝、棉花等。

4. 理论重量

即对于有固定规格和固定尺寸的商品,根据其数量经推算所得的重量。计算公式为总重量 = 点数 × 单位重量。

第二节 合同中的数量条款

一、数量条款的重要性

商品数量是买卖合同中不可缺少的主要条件。按照《联合国国际货物销售合同公约》中的规定,卖方所交货物的数量必须与合同规定相符。卖方所交货物的数量如大于合同规定的数量,买方除了可以拒收超额部分外,也可以收取多交部分中的一部分或全部,但应按合同价格付款。

二、溢短装条款

在实践中,尤其是在农副产品和工矿产品的交易中,往往由于商品的供应、加工条件的限制等原因,比较难以准确地按合同规定的数量交货。因此,买卖双方在商定交货数量时应订有一定的机动幅度,即应在合同中明确规定溢短装条款。按照这一规定,卖方在交货时可以溢交或短交合同数量的百分之几。例如,2 000 公吨,卖方可溢交或短交 5%。然而,如果数量与交通状况有关,当船只由买方安排时,也可以规定由承运人决定或者由买方决定。

商品溢短装部分的清算通常以合同价格为基础。如果双方考虑到交货时价格的大幅度波动,他们可以在货物装船时规定这一部分的清算,以合同价格为基础。

第四章 货物的包装

第一节 货物包装的种类

商品通常需要包装,一些包装是产品的构成要素,国际贸易商品的包装更为重要。包装条款是合同中的主要条款。根据在货物流通中的作用不同,包装可以被分为销售包装和运输包装两种。销售包装也被称作小包装、内包装或者方便包装,有利于保护商品,方便使用和促销。内包装要遵守购买国家有关法律法规的规定。运输包装又称大包装或外包装,它的作用主要在于保护商品,便于储存和运输。在这一节,我们主要讨论运输包装。

在运输中,并不是所有的商品都需要包装。随着运输业的发展,越来越多的小圆形货物,例如谷物、水泥和石油这样的液体货物用散装方式,它们不需要机械操作,可以被直接装载到运输车辆上。这种方式节省了运输成本,加快了运输速度。一些货物如钢材,木材等仅仅需要被捆扎,这被称作裸装。但是大多数商品在运输中必须要有包装,运输包装的方式主要有以下两种。

一、单件包装

单件运输包装的种类很多,常见的种类如下。

(1)大包:大包是一堆材料挤压在一起,用绳子或者金属线捆绑,适合纸张、羊毛、棉花和地毯等。小包:小包由棉花、塑料、纸张或亚麻构成,可以包装水泥、肥料、面粉、化学品等。桶:桶的材料有木头、塑料或者金属,适用于液体或油脂货物。盒子:盒子的结构是木头,尺寸各异,一些是不透气的,对设备以及汽车零部件这样的货物有极强的保护性。

(2)玻璃容器:玻璃容器用于盛放诸如酸这样需要仔细处理的危险液体货物。纸板箱:纸板箱是最常见的包装方式。为了促销可以把销售文字印刷在上面。板条箱:介于大包和盒子中间的木质结构,用于盛放如机器设备这样的重量较轻但体积较大的商品。

二、集合包装

集合包装是将一定数量的单件商品组合成一件大的包装或装入一个大的包装容器内。托台,灵活的集装箱和容器都是集合包装。集合包装可以提高港口装卸速度,便于货运,减轻装卸搬运的劳动强度,降低运输成本。

第二节 货物包装的标志

运输包装标志便于识别货物,也有利于顺利地进行工作。根据功能,运输包装标志分为运输标志、指示性标志、警告性标志和重量/体积标志、原产地标志。

一、运输标志

运输标志有利于在装卸、装运和仓储的过程中对商品识别和计数。运输标志可以防止货物被错误运输或装运。运输标志通常由数字、字母和简单的单词组成。联合国制定了一项运输标志向各国推荐使用。该标准运输标志包括收货人的英文缩写字母;参考号,如订单号或发票号;目的地;件号。

例如:ABCCO
SC9750
LONDON
NO.4 -20

运输标志通常被标注在出口单据中,例如发票、提单和保险单。

二、指示性标志

提出某些在装卸搬运操作方面的要求和注意事项,称为指示性标志。例如:"小心轻放""此端向上""保持干燥""禁止使用吊钩"。

三、警告性标志

警告性标志也称为危险性标志,是针对包装内装有爆炸品、有毒品、易燃物品等危险品,由图表、图片和单词组成。

第三节 合同中的包装条款

一、中性包装

中性包装是一种特殊包装,指在商品上和内外包装上不注明原产地。中国出口的商品经常标有"中华人民共和国制造""中国制造",但有时应买方的要求,卖方会接受中性包装。中性包装包括定牌中性包装和无牌中性包装。前者是指包装上仅有买方指定的商标或牌号,但无生产国家名称;后者是指包装上既无原产国名称,又无商标、牌号。中性包装是国际贸易中的一种习惯做法,但近些年来被一些国家严格禁止,出口商应该谨慎采用。

二、合同中的包装条款

在合同中,通常规定包装材料和包装方式。

例如:包装:纸盒箱,每箱30打。

包装:木箱,每箱 50 千克。

在国际贸易中,有些合同如使用"海运包装"和"习惯包装"的术语,此种术语,由于内容不明确,各国理解不同,容易引起争议。因此,在合同中,一般应尽量避免使用,通常由卖方决定,但是如果买方指定包装,则有必要规定详细的运输标志。包装物料和费用一般包括在货价之内,不另计价。如果在买方提出特殊要求的情况下,卖方也可要求另收包装费。

第五章　货物的价格

第一节　作 价 原 则

一、支付货币的选择

价格是交易中最重要以及复杂的任务之一，尤其在出口中。出口商应该以消费者可以接受的价格出售商品，与此同时还要兼顾自己的利润收入。恰当的定价并不容易，这需要技巧并且需要认真谨慎地对待。

记账货币是计算价格的货币，支付货币是结算货币。一般情况下，如果没有在合同中规定，记账货币就是支付货币。记账货币和支付货币可以使用出口国的货币、进口国的货币或第三国的货币，只要这些货币是可以自由兑换的。在选择货币时，出口商和进口商应该考虑外汇汇率，汇率的波动会影响他们的利益。

理论上讲，使用硬货币(币值稳定需求增加的货币)作为支付货币更有利于出口商，而进口商更偏向于选择软货币(不能随时兑换成黄金或者其他货币，需求减少币值不稳定的货币)。

选择哪一种货币取决于买卖双方之间的协商。如果卖方选择了对自己不利的货币作为支付货币，他应该采取一些措施排除或减轻汇率变动的风险。

1. 努力降低进口商品价格，提高出口商品价格

在签订合同时，把汇率波动的趋势考虑在内。如果是进口商，当货币的价格有可能上浮时(注意：这是你的预测)，你应该努力迫使卖方降低价格。如果是出口商，当货币的价格有可能下跌时，你应该努力提高价格。通常这样的措施适合短时期采用，因为长时间内很难预计外汇的走势。

2. 订立保值条款

记账货币和支付货币如果同时选择了相同的软货币，卖方应该考虑当前日期与结算日期之间的汇率变化。为了防止公司遭受损失，卖方应该在合同中提及这类损失，卖方可以在合同中使用另外一种相同金额的硬货币，根据签订合同之日的当天合同货币和其他一种货币的汇率保值。在交割的日期，硬货币应该被相应的兑换成软货币，按比例调整合同价格，这一兑换成的软货币就是买方应该支付给卖方的余额。

二、合同中的价格条款

贸易合同中的价格条款一般包括两项内容，即单价和总值。单价由四部分组成，即计

价货币、单位价格金额、计量单位和价格术语。例如,每桶500美元FOB大连。

1. 固定价格

常用的规定价格的方法是使用双方都赞成的固定价格。固定价格很清楚且便于记账。

2. 浮动价格

因为市场的不确定性,价格可以浮动规定,如“价格在XXX天协定”或者“价格的一部分固定”。

3. 价格调整条款

需要较长时间生产的机器设备合同,“价格调整条款”可以加在固定价格中,也可以在签订合同时使用“初始价格”。此条款根据工资和原材料的价格变动作相应调整。

第二节 佣金和折扣

一、佣金

当一笔交易有中间商介入时要规定佣金。佣金是中间商为提供中介服务而收取的报酬。佣金可以被包含或者不包含在价格中,这是不同的表示方法,例如每公吨1 000美元CFR西雅图包括2%佣金。凡价格中包括佣金的称为含佣价,这种在价格中表明佣金的称为明佣。有时,买卖双方约定的佣金不在价格中表明,习惯上称为暗佣。中国对外贸易一般使用暗佣,也就是作为进出口商的国内代理,佣金的金额不出现在报价中。

二、折扣

折扣是卖方按价格给予买方一定百分比的减让,例如“数量折扣”“现金折扣”和“特殊折扣”。折扣被规定在价格条款中,例如每公吨2 000美元CIF伦敦3%折扣。折扣是促进销售和扩大销售的一种方法。

第六章　货物的运输

第一节　运 输 种 类

国际货物运输是国际贸易的重要连接。运输单据是国际结算的重要单据之一。运输条款是合同中的主要条款。运输时把货物从一个地点传递到另一个地方,没有运输,国际贸易也就不可能实现。运输方式的种类很多,包括海洋运输、铁路运输、公路运输、航空运输、邮政运输、江河运输、管道运输和联合运输。

一、海洋运输

海洋运输是国际贸易中广泛使用的运输方式。在国际贸易总量中,通过海洋运输的货物约占90%以上。在中国,大部分都采用海洋运输。海洋运输不受道路和轨道的限制,通过能力很大,而运输成本较低。然而,与公路运输和空运相比,海洋运输易受恶劣气候的影响,不准时。海洋运输分为班轮运输和租船运输。

1. 班轮运输

(1)班轮运输的特点

① 班轮是指按照固定的航行时间表,沿着固定的航线,停靠固定的港口,收取固定运费的运输船舶。

② 班轮运输包括装货费和卸货费,所以承运人需要负责装卸。

(2)班轮运费

班轮运费被规定在海关关税中,包括基本运费和附加费两部分。

① 基本运费的计收标准

a. 按货物的重量计收,即1重量吨为1公吨作为计算运费单位。在运价表内用W字母表示。

b. 按货物的体积或按尺码吨计收,即1尺码吨以每立方米作为计算运费单位。在运价表内用M字母表示。

c. 按重量或体积来计算运费。例如:在运价表内用"W/M"表示,即指船方可凭货物的重量或体积取收费较高的一种计收运费。

d. 按商品的总值计收,即所谓从价运费。班轮公司在承运黄金、白银、精密仪器、昂贵的皮毛等贵重商品或高价商品时,可以对这类商品收取从价运费,其费率从占货价的1%到5%不等,在运价表上有(A. V.)字样。

e. 若用"W/M or A. V. "表示,即指船方可根据货物的重量、体积或货价三者中取收费较高的一种计收运费。

② 各种附加费用

班轮承运货物除了收取“基本运费”外,往往还要加收种种附加费。

a. 燃油附加费;

b. 港口附加费;

c. 转船附加费;

d. 超重附加费和超长附加费。

2. 租船运输

租船运输通常是指包租整船。租船运输的运费比班轮运输的运费便宜。船方可以选择直接的路线,大宗货物一般都采用租船运输。租船方式主要包括定程租船和定期租船两种。

(1)定程租船

在定程租船方式下,船方必须按租船合同规定的航程完成货物运输任务。定程租船可以被分为单航次、连续单航次等。船方还要负责船舶的经营管理及其在航行中的各项费用开支,租船人则应支付双方约定的运费。租船的运费一般按装运货物的数量计算,也有按船次包租总金额计算的。

定程租船是在一定的时间内签订租用整艘船只在固定的航线内行驶。它提供给双方权利和义务,至于货物在港口的装卸费用,究竟由船方或租方负担,应在租船合同中作出明确规定。如果船主不准备承担这些费用,应该确定装卸费的最后期限或者费率。关于装卸费的收取办法,有下列各种不同的规定:

①船方负担装卸费;

②船方只负担装货费,不负担卸货费(F. O.);

③船方只负担卸货费,不负担装货费(F. I.);

④船方不负担装卸费(F. I. O.)或船方不管理舱和平舱(F. I. O. S. T.)。

(2)定期租船

定期租船即指按一定期限租赁船舶。在租赁期间,租船人根据租船合同规定的航行区域可自行使用和调度船舶。一般定期租船在各自航次中所产生的燃料费、港口费、装卸费等项费用,均由租船人负担。

二、铁路运输

在国际贸易货物运输中,铁路运输占着相当重要的地位,仅次于海洋运输。铁路运输具有许多特点,例如铁路火车运行速度较快,载运量较大,不易受气候条件的影响,能终年正常运行,而且在运输当中遭受的风险较小,但是铁路运输受到铁轨的限制,因此不太灵活。铁路运输分国际铁路联运和国内铁路运输两种。

三、航空运输

1. 航空运输的特点

航空运输是一种现代化的运输方式,航空运输最明显的优势就是速度快。以下是航空运输的利弊分析。

(1)快速、可靠的运输:航空运输节省了大量的仓储费用和急需物资、易损货物和贵重商品的风险。

(2)货物中途破损率小,丰厚的保险费。

(3)消费品的理想运输方式,例如变质腐烂的鲜花和水果,较短销售期的时尚商品,季节性商品或者高价值低重量的贵重商品。

(4)就所运货物数量而言,属于高运营费用和初始成本。飞机的平均载重量仅仅为2 000到25 000公斤。

2. 航空运输的种类

航空运输包括班机运输、包机运输、集中托运三种方式。

(1)班机运输: 是指客、货班机定时、定点、定线的运输,它适用于载运新鲜的,有急需和季节性商品。

(2)包机运输:是指包租整架飞机运输货物,它适用于载运数量较大或不同托运人的货物运往相同的目的地。

(3)集中托运:是指航空货运公司把若干单独发运的货物组成一整批货物,用一份总运单整批发运到预定目的地,由航空货运公司在那里的代理人收货并交给实际收货人。许多托运人喜欢这种运输方式,因为运费费率比班机运输低7% ~10%。

四、集装箱运输

集装箱运输是把货物集中在一起运输,适合于海洋、铁路和多式联运。它是一种最新型的现代运输方式,采用这种工具进行运输,可以大大节省成本,提高货运质量和营运效果。

采用集装箱运输,主要有以下优点。

(1)采用集装箱运输时,可以直接将货物装进特制的标准规格的集装箱内,所以节省了劳动力和装卸费用。

(2)由于集装箱结构坚固,同时货物装箱后,可以避免互相挤压和碰撞,一般不会因包装不同或配载不当而招致货损。

(3)凡采用集装箱运输的货物,包装简易,从而大大节省了包装用料和包装费用。

(4)采用集装箱运输,由于货运手续简便,装卸效率高,船舶运转快,因而大大提高了货运速度,缩短了货运时间。

五、国际多式联运

随着国际运输业的发展，出现了一种崭新的运输方式，即国际多式联运。国际多式联运是指通过两种或两种以上不同的运输方式来完成某项运输任务，在国际贸易中，有些货物是通过(海、陆、空)各种不同的运输方式联合运输的，而多式联运经营人负责从发货人那里取货，运送到收货人。

使用多式联运具有高效率、低成本，货物在原产地和运输地之间的移动时间较短的特点。全程只使用多式联运单据，在单据化过程中既经济又简便。

第二节　运输单据

一、提单

提单是货物承运人在收到货物后签发给托运人的一种证明，它体现了承运人和托运人之间的相互关系。

1. 提单的目的

提单有三个目的：首先，它是承运人签发给托运人的货物收据；第二，它是承运人和托运人双方同意的运输契约的证明；最后，它是代表货物所有权的凭证，占有提单就有支配货物的权利，就等于占有货物。提单是货物装载到船上的收据，由承运人(或其代理人)签发，并且表明货物运输时的状态。

(1)货物收据

提单是表明货物运输时的质量和状态。提单通常由托运人提前填制，之后确保所装载的商品符合提单上的规定，然而，承运人应该负责检查货物的标签和包装没有被损坏。如果证实已按提单记载的事项收到货物，承运人应凭提单所列内容向收货人交货。

(2)运输契约的证明

提单是运输契约的证明。

(3)货物所有权的凭证

由于提单是一种物权证件，是提取货物的凭证，因此占有提单就有支配货物的权利，就等于占有货物。承运人有责任把货物交给提单的合法持有人。

2. 提单的种类

在国际贸易业务中，提单可以从各种不同的角度加以分类，主要有以下几种。

(1)已装船提单和备运提单

已装船提单是指货物装船后，由承运人签发给托运人的提单，它必须载明装货船名和装船日期。装船日期经常以签发提单的日期来证明。由于已装船提单对收货人按时收货有保障,因此,在买卖合同中一般都规定出口商必须提供已装船提单。

备运提单未经承运人加注“已装船”字样,是承运人在收到托运货物等待装船期间,向托运人签发的提单。

(2)清洁提单和不清洁提单

清洁提单是指交运货物的外表状况良好,承运人未加有关货损或包装不良之类批注的提单。在买卖合同中,卖方提交了清洁提单才能取得货款。

凡承运人加注了这类表明货物外表状况不良或存在缺陷的批语的提单,称为不清洁提单。买方和银行为了自身的安全,对不清洁提单一般都拒绝接受。

(3)记名提单、不记名提单和指示提单

记名提单是指发给指定的收货人的提单,在提单中的收货人栏内,具体填明收货人的名称。这种提单只能是指定的收货人提货,不能转让。一般只有在运送贵重物品或特殊用途时,才予采用。

不记名提单又称空白提单,即指在提单收货人栏内不填写收货人或指示人的名称而留空,提单持有人可不作任何背书,就能凭提单转让货物所有权或提取货物,承运人只凭提单交货。由于这种提单风险较大,故国际上一般极少使用。

指示提单被广泛应用在国际贸易中。它是指在提单的收货人栏内只填写:“凭指定书”或“凭某人指定”字样的一种提单。这种提单可以背书转让。指示提单经背书后可转让给其他另一方。注明“凭指定”的提单,在卖方未指定收货人之前,卖方仍保持货物的所有权,如经卖方在提单上空白背书转让后,持有这种提单的人,就有权提货。

(4)直达提单和联运提单

承运人对自装运港直接运到目的港的货物所签发给托运人的提单,称为直达提单。

联运提单是由第一承运人或其代理人在货物起运地签发运往货物最终目的地的提单,并收取全程运费,货物到达转运港后,由前一承运人或其代理人代为将货物交给下一段航程的承运人或其代理人,继续运往目的地。

(5)全式提单和略式提单

全式提单是指通常应用的带有背面条款的提单。

略式提单是指内容简略而不带背面条款的提单。这种提单仅保留其正面的必要项目。

第三节 合同中的运输条款

一、装运期和交货期

在买卖合同中,涉及装运方面的条款主要有装运期、装运港和目的港等项内容。

装运期作为买卖合同中的主要条件,如卖方违反这一条件,买方有权撤销合同,并要求卖方赔偿其损失。关于买卖合同中的装运期,有以下几种规定方法。

(1)明确规定具体装运期限

例如:限于2011年12月装运或交货。

2011年12月31日以前装运或交货。

(2)规定在收到信用证后若干天装运

使用信用证付款的合同,为了避免买方未开出信用证的风险,可以使用此种方法。在这种情况下,卖方需要备货之前等待信用证的到达,所以交货期与收到信用证的日期有关。

二、分批装运和转船

1. 分批装运

凡一笔成交的货物分若干批次装运,称为分批装运。在大宗货物交易时,买卖双方根据交货数量、运输条件和供应需要等因素,可在合同中订立分批装运的条款。根据国际商会的《跟单信用证统一惯例》规定:"除非信用证有不同规定,不准许分批装运。"为了避免发生争论,买卖双方在商订装运条件时,如限一次装运完毕,即应明确规定不准分批装运的限制性条款;如需分批装运,则对分批装运的时间和数量,应在合同中具体订明。分批装运的数量关系到买卖双方的利益,因此,买方一般都要求具体规定每批装运的数量。但卖方在货源无充分把握时,一般不愿作此规定,倘若笼统地规定,则卖方比较主动,因为他可以根据货源情况灵活安排,但这对买方很不利,故买方一般不轻易接受。此外,对一笔货物在短期内分若干批装运的条款,在船源无把握的情况下,不宜轻易接受,因为在规定期内,如无适当的两条以上的船只,就会影响这笔货物的全部装运。当买卖合同规定有分批装运条款时,买卖双方应当严格按照合同和信用证有关规定办理。

2. 转船

当国际贸易货物没有直达船或一时无合适的船舶运输,而需通过某中途港转运时,买卖双方可以在合同中商订允许转船的条款。除非在信用证中禁止转船,否则转船是允许的。如果在合同中如果没有转船是否允许的字样,转船视为不被允许。

第七章　货物的保险

第一节　海 上 风 险

货物有可能遇到各种风险和遭受各种损失。一般来说,海上风险是船长无法控制的,如果货物遭受海上风险,承运人是否要对其负责取决于风险的损失。如果不是由于船长的玩忽职守造成的,承运人不负责补偿货主损失。为了保障货物在遭受损失时能得到经济上的补偿,就需要办理货物的运输保险。这些风险所指的大致内容如下。

(1)自然灾害:所谓自然灾害,是仅指恶劣气候,如雷电、洪水,浮冰、地震、海啸以及其他人力不可抗拒的灾害。

(2)意外事故:海上意外事故所指的主要是船舶搁浅、触礁、沉没、碰撞、火灾、爆炸、船舶失踪或其他类似事故。

(3)外来风险:所谓"外来风险",通常是由外来原因引起的,通常仅指偷窃、破碎、渗漏、沾污、受潮、受热、串味、钩损、短量、锈损等。除上述风险外,保险货物还可能遇到一些特殊军事、政治和行政的风险,如战争、罢工、交货不到、拒收等。

第二节　海 上 损 失

一、全部损失

海运保险货物在海洋运输中由于海上风险所造成的损坏或灭失,称为海损。按照货物损失的程度,海损可以分为全部损失与部分损失。

1. 实际全损

是指被保险货物完全灭失,或指货物完全变质,或货物已不可能归还被保险人而言。实际全损按照定义,可以界定为以下三种情况。

(1)被保险货物完全灭失;

(2)被保险货物的损坏程度已经不能称其为这种货物;

(3)货物已不可能归还被保险人。

2. 推定全损

是指被保险货物受损后,进行施救整理或恢复原状所需的费用。超过恢复后的货价,或者施救及修理费用加上续运至目的地的费用的总和,估计要超过货物在目的地的完好状态的价格。

二、部分损失

部分损失是指货物的损失不及上述全部损失的程度。部分损失可以分为共同海损和单独海损。

1. 单独海损

保险货物遭受海损以后,如未达到全损程度,仅属部分损失,而且这种损失又不属共同海损,不是由多方面的关系人共同分摊,仅由受损方面自己负责,这种损失称为单独海损。例如,由于船只失火,10%的棉线货物被烧毁。

2. 共同海损

在海运途中,载货的船舶遇到危险时,船方为了维护船舶和所有货物的共同安全或使航程得以继续完成,有意采取合理措施所作的某些特殊牺牲或支出某些特殊的额外费用,这些特殊的牺牲和额外费用,称为共同海损。根据以上概念,构成共同海损应具有下列几方面的条件:

(1)必须确实遭遇危险;

(2)措施必须是有意识的、合理的;

(3)必须是为了船、货各方面的共同安全;

(4)牺牲或费用的支出必须是非常性质的;

(5)损失必须是共同海损行为的直接结果;

(6)牺牲或费用的支出必须有效果。

第三节　合同中的保险条款

中国人民保险公司根据1972年颁布,1976和1981年修订的《海上货物保险》条款的规定,保险货物的险别分为基本险和附加险。附加险又包括一般附加险和特殊附加险。

一、基本险

1. 平安险

平安险不负单独海损责任。也就是说,被保险标的所遭受的单独海损的损失,原则上不在保险人承保范围之内。在航运中发生上述意外事故之前或这后等自然灾害所致的部分损失,仍在平安险承保的责任范围之内。

2. 水渍险

水渍险的责任范围比平安险的责任范围大。水渍险负单独海损责任,其责任范围是平安险责任范围以内的全部责任和由于自然灾害引起的部分损失。

3. 一切险

一切险的责任范围是除包括平安险和水渍险的各项责任外，保险人对于被保险货物因遭受所有因意外事故所发生的损失。但是，由于货物本身特性所造成的损失、延迟交货造成的损失，货物内在缺陷或者特殊外来风险，战争险或罢工险不包括在内。

二、附加险

1. 一般附加险

一般附加险的种类很多，其中主要包括以下几类。

（1）偷窃提货不着险。偷窃险指的是货物在运输过程中被偷窃。提货不着险是由于未知原因货物在装卸过程中包装（盒子、箱子、鼓）破裂造成的风险。

（2）淡水雨淋险。是指货物被淡水或者雨淋的风险。

（3）破碎险。易碎的货物由于震荡或挤压造成的破裂风险。

（4）渗漏险。液体货物容器损坏而渗漏的风险。

（5）短量险。货物由于外包装破裂造成数量短缺。运输中正常的数量磨损不包括在内。

（6）污染险。货物彼此污染造成的风险。

（7）串味险。食物、草药、化妆品或原材料有时会串味的风险。

（8）受潮受热险。货物由于气温突然改变或者船上的通风系统故障造成受潮或受热的损失。

（9）生锈险。货物由于海水造成生锈。货物本身的生锈或者瑕疵不包括在内。

（10）包装破裂险。货物的不良处理造成的风险。

（11）钩损险。货物在装卸的过程中由于吊钩造成的损失，例如水泥的包装袋由于吊钩造成的损失。

一般附加险不能单独使用，必须与平安险或水渍险结合使用，它们都包括在一切险中。

2. 特殊附加险

特殊附加险包括由于特殊原因造成的损失风险。例如政治事件、军事事变、国家政策和法案以及行政措施。特殊附加险包括：（1）战争险；（2）罢工险；（3）交货不到险；（4）进口关税险；（5）舱面险；（6）拒收险。

这些特殊附加险通常与平安险、水渍险和一切险结合使用。

第八章　国际货款支付

第一节　支付工具

在国际贸易中,买卖双方很难严格地做到交货和付款同时进行。通常,卖方通过单据交货,银行是中介机构,单据是支付工具,这些是当代国际货款支付的特点。当前非现金支付是全世界普遍接受的方式。其中最主要使用的就是汇票、本票和支票,汇票是最常见的一种。只有货款被安全的转账到出口商的账户,出口交易才是成功的。与国内结算相比,进出口货款如何支付是一个复杂的问题。本章讲述国际货物贸易中的支付工具、方法和术语。

一、汇票

1. 汇票的含义

汇票是一种债权证书,它是由出票人向付款人签发的无条件的书面支付命令。它要求付款人立即或者在一定时间之内,对收款人支付一定的金额。作为国际结算中的一个主要组成成分,汇票允许一方要求另一方对自己、其代理人或者第三方付款。当然,只有付款人确实有义务向出票人付款,汇票才是有效的。这种情况可能发生在出票人借款给受票人,或者出票人把商品出售给受票人,受票人欠出票人的销售货款时,如图 8-1 所示。

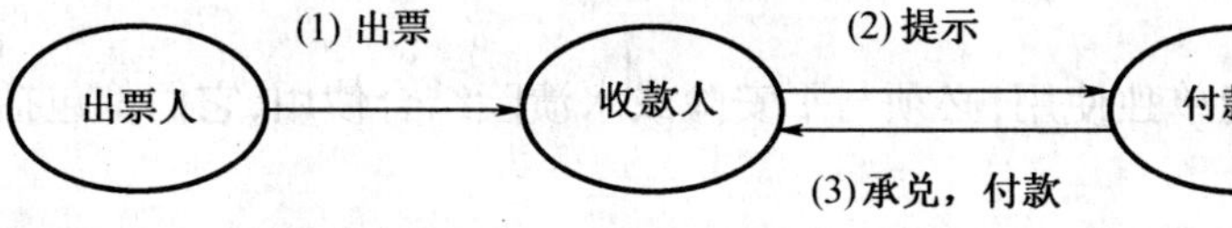

图 8-1　汇票的程序

2. 汇票的基本内容

(1) 汇票的当事人

①出票人——开出汇票的人,在进出口业务中,通常就是出口商。

②受票人——汇票的付款人,在进出口业务中,通常就是进口商。

③收款人——就是受领汇票所规定的金额的人,在进出口业务中,通常就是出口商或其指定的人。

(2) 金额和货币

汇票必须明确具体地规定受票人应付的金额,并注明使用的货币。在国际贸易中,汇票的金额应在合同或信用证金额的范围内,如无特殊规定,其具体金额和货币一般必须与发票金额和货币一致,否则受票人有权拒付。

(3)付款时间

汇票还需规定明确的付款时间,如"见票即付""见票后30天付款"等。

(4)出票和付款地点

汇票一般应注明开票和付款地点。一般分别以汇票上所列的出票人和受票人的所在地表示。

(5)出票人签字

3. 汇票的种类

汇票从不同的角度可分为以下几种。

(1)在国际贸易中,凡由出口商签发,向进口商或银行收取货款或其他款项的汇票,都属商业汇票。由银行开立的汇票,即为银行汇票。付款人和收款人都是银行。

(2)光票是指不附货运单据的汇票。跟单汇票是指附有货运单据的汇票。

(3)凡汇票上规定见票即付款的称即期汇票。

凡汇票上规定付款人在将来一个可确定的日期付款的,称远期汇票。远期汇票的付款日期有三种规定方法:

①规定付款人见票后若干天付款;

②在出票后若干天付款;

③在规定具体日期付款。

4. 汇票的使用

在国际贸易实际业务中,使用汇票支付货款一般需经过出票、提示、付款等程序。如远期汇票,受票人在到期付款之前,还必须办理承兑手续。在汇票拒付时,持票人行使其追索权,所要汇票上的金额、利息和相关费用。如果是远期汇票,付款人必须在汇票正面上写上承兑字样,签上名字以及日期以便汇票到期时付款。承兑是远期汇票到期之前办理的一道手续。远期汇票只有经过付款人承兑,付款人才承担到期付款的义务。汇票到期时,付款人向合法持票人支付足够金额,后者注销汇票并且返还给付款人作为收据。背书就是由原来的收款人、受票人或者持票人在汇票的背面签上自己的名字,表示该汇票已转让出去。在金融市场上,典型的背书是汇票的贴现,例如,持票人把背书后的汇票转让给银行或贴现公司,作为被转让者,银行扣除贴现率后把剩余的金额转让给持票人。汇票被拒付时,持票人有权向出票人及所有"前手"背书人进行追索。拒绝证书是由公证人或其他权威人士起草并签名盖章,为了证明汇票已被提示付款但被拒付的一种书面证明。汇票没有被承兑或拒绝付款时,发出拒付通知,持票人把汇票传递到公正人那里,公证人再次提示汇票要求承兑或付款。当再次被拒付时,公证人起草拒绝证书,拒绝证书是证明拒付并阐明原因的官方证书,以此命令受票人(或承兑人)。

二、本票

本票是出票人对受款人承诺无条件支付一定金额的票据。本票的当事人只有两个,即出票人和收款人。本票的付款人就是出票人本人,如图 8-2 所示。

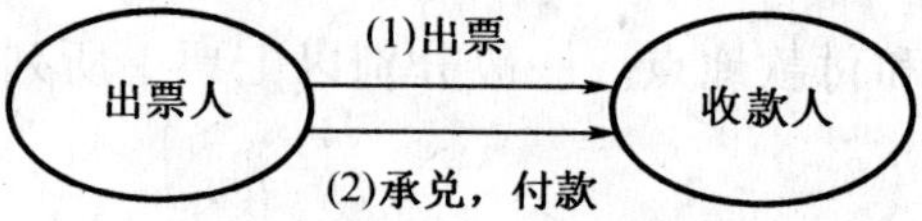

图 8-2　本票的程序

三、支票

支票是一种特殊的汇票,出票人签发支票,受票人是银行,并且出票人在该银行有存款账户,收款人是支票上的受益人。所以,支票是出票人对银行签发的委托银行对受款人在见票时无条件支付一定金额的票据。出票人在签发支票时应在付款银行存有不低于票面金额的存款。如果出票人没有足够的银行存款用于支付支票上的金额,支票会被拒付,这种支票被称作空头支票,是不允许的,如图 8-3 所示。

图 8-3　支票的程序

第二节　支付方式

一、汇付

1. 汇付的概念

汇付指资金从分处不同国家的一方转移到另一方,也就是说,银行(汇付行)应顾客的申请,将款项汇到其海外的分行(付款行),指示将款项汇交居住在海外的指定的个人或公司(收款人为受益人)。银行把客户的资金从本国汇到国外可以采用三种不同的方式。它们是信汇、电汇和票汇,如图 8-4 所示。

2. 汇付的种类

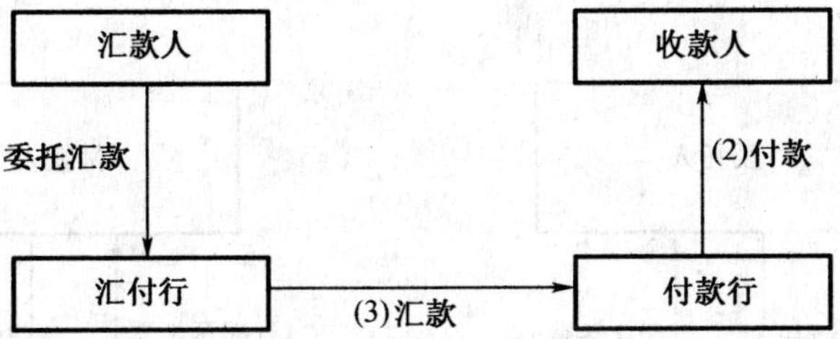

图8-4　汇付的程序

(1)信汇

通过航空邮件汇款称为信汇。信汇是由汇款人将款项交给汇付银行,由银行开具付款委托书,通过邮递寄交付款银行,委托其向指定的个人或者受益人付款。

(2)电汇

电汇是通过电报方式付款。电汇是用电信方式由汇付行通知付款行,其他的程序与信汇相同。这种方法较之信汇快捷,但是却要因此负担较高的费用。当汇款金额较大,并且有时间限制时可以使用电汇。

(3)票汇

票汇是使用银行即期汇票的方式付款。由买方向进口地银行购买银行汇票自行邮寄给卖方,由卖方或其指定的人持汇票向出口地有关银行取款。

从我国对外贸易的实践来看,汇付方式主要用于预付定金、佣金等,并不是主要的支付方式。但是在发达国家普遍使用,原因在于有大量的跨国公司内部交易、可靠的贸易伙伴以及销售网络。随着中国对外贸易的发展,中国外贸企业已经与海外的贸易伙伴建立起相对稳固的关系。随着世界市场竞争的加剧,国外进口商经常要求先出后结的办法,即卖方在没有收到货款以前,先交出单据或货物,然后由买方主动付款。当前,在我国出口贸易中,尤其是与发达国家的贸易中,使用汇付方式结算增多。在部分付款与延期付款中,汇付与银行保证函或者信用证一起使用。

二、托收

1. 托收的概念

在国际贸易中,债权人为出口商,债务人即为进口商。为了结清这种债权债务,出口商出具以进口商为付款人的汇票并通常随发票及货运单据,委托银行收款。托收是债权人出具汇票委托银行向债务人代收款项的一种结算方式。银行充当中间人。

2. 托收的当事人

托收业务通常涉及 4 个当事人,即委托人(出口商)、托收行、代收行和付款人,如

图8－5所示。

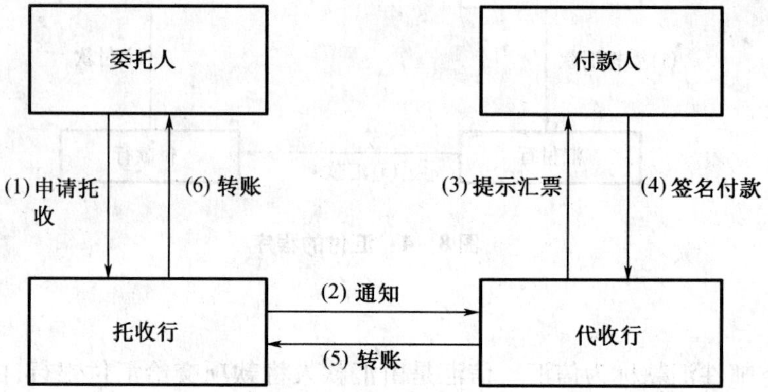

图8－5 托收的程序

(1)委托人

委托人即出口商,是指委托银行办理托收业务的客户。

(2)付款人

付款人是买方或进口商,以最终结清债权债务。

(3)托收行

托收行是指受委托人的委托,办理托收业务的银行。在托收业务中,托收行处于代理人的地位,重要的责任就是依据委托人的指示办理,在向代收行发出业务委托时,其内容要与委托人的委托书一致。

(4)代收行

代收行是指除托收行以外,参与办理托收指示的任何银行,它通常是与进口商同在一地的某家银行。在托收业务中,代收行也处于代理地位,它受托收行委托办事。

3. 托收的种类

(1)光票托收

光票托收是指商业票据不随附像发票、提单、保险单这样的其他单据的托收。

(2)跟单托收

跟单托收是指汇票随附其他单据的托收。跟单托收按其交单方式又分为付款交单和承兑交单。

①付款交单

付款交单是指付款才能放单给付款人,付款人只有在交付货款后才能取得单据凭以提货。按支付时间的不同,付款交单又可分为即期付款交单和远期付款交单两种。

a. 即期付款交单

即期付款交单是指银行提示即期汇票和单据,进口人见票时应立即付款,并在付清货款后取得单据。

b. 远期付款交单

远期付款交单是指银行提示远期汇票,进口人审核无误后在汇票上进行承兑,于汇票到期日付清货款后再领取货运单据。

②承兑交单

承兑交单即汇票付款人承诺到期付款后,代收行可放单给付款人。承兑交单有两个特点,一是付款是远期的,二是有远期汇票,无汇票则无法发生承兑的行为。债权人和债务人的关系既简单又可靠,卖方处于相对有利的位置。

三、信用证

1. 信用证的概念(图 8-6)

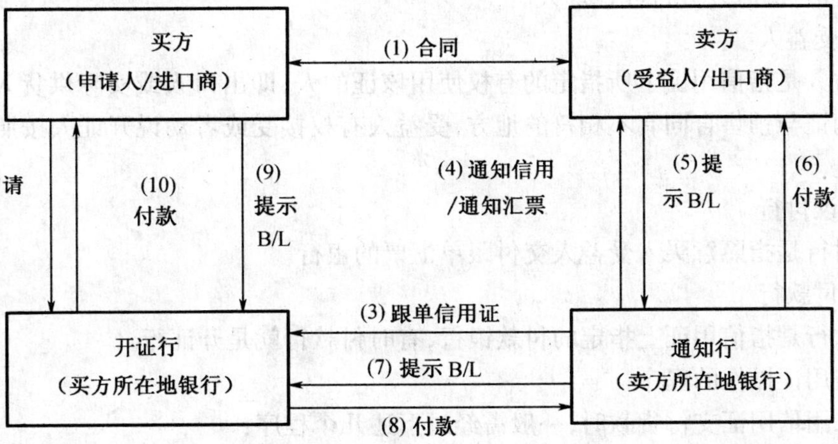

图 8-6 信用证的程序

在国际交易中,卖方无疑希望对方提前付款。但是另一方面,买方希望在付款之前得到如下确认:

(1)货物已经装船;

(2)货物符合合同规定;

(3)在付款之前能够收到货物。依据以上的买卖双方之间的矛盾,在销售合同中要规定相关条件。如果卖方不能确信买方的信用,他可以要求现金支付。如果买方想确认货物已经被装船,可以使用付款交单方式。如果买方坚持在付款之前收货,也可以使用承兑交单方式。但是以上两种方式并不常见。这是因为双方之间彼此不信任。为了避免这种情况，合同双方可以使用信用证，信用证是银行有条件的承担付款义务。

2. 信用证的当事人

信用证可能涉及的当事人有开证行、开证申请人、通知行、受益人，议付行、保兑行等。

(1)开证申请人

一般来说，信用证的申请人为进口商或买方。申请人与开证行之间以开证申请书作为合同，要求银行以出口商或海外的卖方为受益人开出信用证。

(2)开证行

开证行是指接受开证申请人的委托，开立信用证的银行，通常与开证申请人同处一地。开证行在信用证业务中承担向受益人付款的义务，如果受益人在开证行付款之后不能付款，开证行有权出售其商品并向申请人索赔。

(3)通知行

通知行是指接受开证行的委托，将信用证转交出口人的银行。通常与受益人同处一地，是开证行的海外分行或代理人。

(4)受益人

受益人是指信用证上所指定的有权使用该证的人，即出口人或实际供货人。如果所开出的信用证与销售合同有不相符的地方，受益人有权接受或者劝说开证人按照合同修改信用证。

(5)议付行

议付行是指愿意买入受益人交付跟单汇票的银行。

(6)付款行

付款行是指信用证上指定的付款银行，有时付款行就是开证行。

3. 信用证操作的程序

在采用信用证支付货款时，一般需经过下述几个程序：

(1)买卖双方对销售条件协商一致：

①指定跟单信用证作为支付方法；②指定通知行(通常是卖方所在地的银行)；③提供所需单据。

(2)买方向其所在地银行提出申请书，要求银行(开证行)按申请书的内容，向卖方(受益人)开出信用证。

(3)开证行按申请书内容开立以卖方为受益人的信用证，并通过其在卖方所在地的代理行或往来行，通过电汇的方式转交通知行。

(4)在证实信用证的合法性之后，通知行通知信用证的受益人或直接把信用证转交给他。留复印件存档。有两种通知的方法：一种是直接把信用证转交给受益人，附上已经签名的通知单；另一种是通知行把信用证的内容复制在自己的通知单上，然后转交给受益人。

(5)卖方(受益人)发货给买方，从船运公司或代理人那里取得可议付的运输单据(可议付的提单)。

(6)卖方向通知行准备并提交包含商业发票、保险单和检验证书的运输单据。

(7)通知行检查信用证,确认无误后向卖方支付货款。如果信用证是可以议付的,议付行(通知行)向受益人负有追索权的进行议付。议付后,议付行根据信用证中的追索权向开证行行使追索权并向其提供单据。通知行把单据邮寄给开证行。开证行审核单据符合信用证条款,向通知行付款并通知买方单据已经到达。买方审核单据符合信用证条款,以现金或即期汇票的方式向通知行付款,远期汇票需要承兑。开证行通知买方接货。当今,信用证采取电信方式开出,尽管其格式各不相同,但主要内容是相同的。

4. 信用证的特点

(1)银行信用凭据

信用证支付方式是一种银行信用,由开证行以自己的信用作出付款的保证。所以银行承担的是付款的首要债务,而不是次级债务。

(2)银行处理单据

开证行的第一性付款责任在信用证业务中,只要受益人提交了合格单据,无论是议付行拒绝议付或付款行拒绝付款,还是开证申请人破产倒闭,开证行的付款义务都是确实和不可推卸的。在信用证业务中,各有关当事人处理的是单据,而不是与单据有关的货物、服务或其他行为。如果所提供单据与信用证条款不符,不管合同货物是否被装船发运,银行都将拒付货款。

(3)信用证是一种相对独立的文件

信用证与可能作为其依据的销售合同或其他合同是相互独立的交易,即使信用证中含有此类合同的任何援引,银行也与该合同毫不相关,并不受其约束。

5. 信用证的种类

(1)根据信用证是否可以被撤销

信用证可以分为可撤销和不可撤销的。每一个信用证都应该清楚表明可撤销还是不可撤销。如果信用证没有明确注明是可撤销的或是不可撤销的,应视为是不可撤销的。

①不可撤销信用证

不可撤销信用证是指一经开出,未经所有当事人,主要是受益人同意不能撤销,这对受益人是一个确定无疑的付款承诺和保障。

②可撤销信用证

可撤销信用证是指信用证开立后,不必事先通知或征得受益人同意就有权随时撤销或修改的信用证。然而,如果银行在收到撤销通知之前付款、承兑或议付,开证行仍然有追索权。

(2)根据付款方式

所有的信用证都应该清楚地表明是付款、承兑还是议付。

①付款信用证

付款信用证是指指定某一银行付款的信用证，一般不要求受益人开具汇票，而仅凭受益人提供的单据付款。

②承兑信用证

如果信用证规定付款期限为远期，同时要求出具汇票，这种信用证即为承兑信用证。

③议付信用证

议付信用证是指允许受益人向某一指定银行或任何银行交单议付的信用证。

(3)特殊的信用证

①循环信用证

循环信用证是指当受益人全部或部分使用完信用证的金额以后，其信用金额又恢复原金额再被受益人使用，直至达到规定次数或累计总金额为止。

②背对背信用证

背对背信用证是指一个信用证的受益人要求银行以该信用证为保证开出另一信用证。这种方式通常用于第一个信用证的受益人是中间商，需要向实际供货人开出购货的第二个信用证的三角贸易。

6. 合同中的信用证

(1)即期信用证条款

买方应在接到卖方通知×天内或签约后×天内通过××银行开出以卖方为受益人的(由××银行保兑的)不可撤销的(可转让、可分割的)全部发票金额的即期信用证，信用证有效期延至装运日期后15天在中国到期。

(2)远期信用证

买方应在接到卖方通知后×天内或签约后×天内通过××银行开立以卖方为受益人的不可撤销的(可转让的)见票××天(或装船后×天)付款的银行承兑信用证。信用证议付有效期延至上述装运期后15天在中国到期。

四、银行保证书

在国际贸易中，合同中的任何一方都要求对方按照合同做事。银行保证书是由银行开立的担保凭证。银行保证书是当其他个人或者法人实体不能付款的情况下，由银行(担保人)支付债务或履行职责。银行保证书通常是独立于申请人协议的合同，所以银行承担的责任是第二性的。

第九章　检验、索赔、不可抗力和仲裁

第一节　检　　验

一、货物检验的作用

在国际贸易中,检验是卖方向买方交付商品时一个重要环节。《联合国国际货物销售公约》以及各国的法律都有相似的规定,即买方有权检验。实际上,为了澄清责任,必须在合同内规定检验的地点和时间、检验依据、检验组织等。为了防止争议的产生,买卖双方对于索赔的合法性、索赔依据,甚至索赔金额的条款都应在合同中作出明确和详细的规定。然而,如果违反合同属于不可抗力,当事人不需承担责任。为了明确不可抗力事件,我们应该提前规定不可抗力的范围。如果双方就一些事实和条款有不同的理解,或者任何一方故意减轻责任,通常需要调解和仲裁,甚至法律诉讼。在处理国际贸易纠纷时,大多数商人赞成使用仲裁。

在国际贸易中,商品的品质和数量应该符合合同规定的要求。在货物交付中有必要对商品进行检验并提供检验证书。可以是卖方也可以是买方负责检验。但是大多数情况下,卖方不会面对面地把货物交给买方。此外,在长途运输中,货物的装卸,由于各种风险或承运人的过失会造成货物损失。为了分辨责任和确认事实,需要由权威机构检验并开出检验证书。检验证书是国际贸易中交货、付款、索赔的重要依据。

二、检验时间与地点

关于检验时间与地点,通常有下列三种不同的规定方法。

(1)离岸品质、重量

检验发生在卖方的工厂或装运港。在采用这种做法时,买方在货物到达目的港后,虽然可以对货物进行再次检验,但无权提出异义。这种做法对卖方比较有利。

(2)到岸品质、重量

这种条款规定,商品应在目的港卸货后进行检验,这种做法显然是对买方有利。

(3)离岸重量、到岸品质

在装运港检验及货到目的港后,买方有权对商品进行再次检验,货物如果与合同不符,可以提出索赔。这种方法有利于双方,所以广泛使用于国际贸易中。

三、检验机构

从事商品检验的机构主要有两类,即政府和非政府。政府检验机构,例如美国药品委员会专门检验特殊的商品(谷物、药品等)。国际检验机构主要由非政府机构承担,与中介组织具有相同的法律地位。

在我国,进出口商品检验、鉴定工作是统一由国家设立的中国进出口商品检验局办理的,其基本任务如下。

(1)进出口商品的法定检验

进出口商品的法定检验分为两类,即法定检验和非法定检验。为了对外贸易发展的需要,国家检验局规定并调整进出口商品检验清单,对社会和公众利益产生影响的商品也被列入其中。商品清单随着对外贸易的发展而变化。例如1995年7月1日采用的清单有18大类商品,涉及协调制度中的2 012个商品。对进出口商品的法定检验包括以下项目:

①对检验清单上的进出口商品检验;

②出口食品的卫生检验;

③危险品的包装和容器性能的检测和检验;

④适合货物运输工具,例如船舱、出口的易腐烂和冷冻食物的容器;

⑤商品检验总局根据相关国际条约对进出口商品的检验;

⑥根据商品检验规则对进出口商品的检验。

(2)进出口商品的调查

国家检验总局和相关国际贸易当事人、中国的有关单位,对指定范围内的出口商品颁发调查证书。常见的检验证书包括品质证明书、重量证明书、卫生证明书、损坏商品的检验证书和非传染性检验证书。

(3)监督与控制

法律法规规定国家商品检验总局通过检验代理处和指定人员或收货人、寄售人、生产商、贸易单位、进出口商品的仓储和运输单位进行监督与控制。监督与控制的方法主要有:

①进口安全许可证与出口质量许可证制度。没有国家商品检验总局颁发的进口安全许可证,商品不允许进口。没有国家商品检验总局颁发的出口质量许可证,商品不允许出口。

②卫生登记制度。出口食品必须履行国家商品检验总局的卫生登记制度。只有取得国家商品检验总局颁发的卫生许可证,才可以生产、加工或储存出口食品。

③质量证书标记。国家商品检验总局应该根据相关协议或有关外国机构的授权对进出口商品的质量颁发质检证书,并且使用进出口商品质检证书标记。

④商品检验标记。商品检验标记应该被标注在根据标准经过检验后的商品上。

四、检验标准

国家商品检验总局对进出口商品的检验涉及质量、规格、数量、重量、包装和安全卫生。国家商品检验总局应该根据以下标准进行检验。

(1)按生产国的标准进行检验;

(2)按买卖双方协商同意的标准和方法进行检验;

(3)按国际标准或国际习惯进行检验。

第二节 索 赔

索赔通常有三种类型,即针对卖方和买方的索赔、针对船公司的索赔、针对保险公司的索赔。在这一节,将介绍针对卖方和买方的索赔。

一、索赔的含义

(1)卖方违反合同

属于卖方的责任:①延期交货;②原装货物数量短少;③商品不符合合同条款。

(2)卖方违反合同

属于买方的责任:①付款不及时;②延迟接货。

二、合同中的索赔条款

(1)索赔条款

以下是销售合同中经常采用的索赔条款。

①索赔依据和证据;

②索赔期限。

(2)罚金条款

卖方延迟开出信用证或者卖方没能按时交货,可以使用罚金条款。这一条款要求没有履行合同的当事人缴纳罚金,是全部货款的百分比。下面是罚金条款的两个例子。

①有关卖方延迟交货的罚金条款

如延迟交货除人力不可抗拒者外,卖方应付给买方每一星期按迟交货物总值的0.5%的迟交罚款,不足一星期的迟交日数作为一星期计算。此项罚款总额不超过全部迟交货物总值的5%。在议付货款时,由银行代为扣除,或由买方在付款时进行扣除。如延迟交货超过原定期限十个星期时,买方有权终止合同,但卖方仍应向买方缴付以上规定的罚款。

②有关买方延迟开出信用证的罚金条款

如买方由于自己的原因没能按照合同规定开出信用证,买方需要向卖方缴纳罚金。每十天延迟开出信用证,按货物总值的0.5%的迟交罚款,不足十天按照日计算。此项罚款总额不超过全部迟交货物总值的5%。这是此种延迟唯一的惩罚。

第三节 不可抗力

一、不可抗力的含义

不可抗力(法语:优先权),是指在合同签订以后,不是由于当事人的过失或疏忽,发生了当事人所不能预见的、无法预防的意外事故,以致不能履行合同或不能如期履行合同。遭受意外事故的一方可以据此免除履行合同的责任或延迟履行合同,对方无权要求损害赔偿。不可抗力不仅范围狭窄,而且在应用上也很有限。不可抗力包括自然灾害、战争、政府封锁、罢工、禁运和供应商的破产。当事人双方都在努力执行合同,任何一方都没有错,违反合同的一方可以免除赔偿损失。然而他应该采取其他恰当的补救措施,例如延迟履行合同。

不可抗力事故所引起的后果主要有两种:一种是解除合同,一种是延迟履行合同。至于在什么情况下可以解除合同,在什么情况下不能解除合同而只能延迟合同的履行,要看意外事故对履行合同的影响。也可由买卖双方在合同中作具体规定。一般解释为:如不可抗力事故使合同的履行成为不可能,则可解除合同;如不可抗力事故只是暂时阻碍了合同的履行,则只能延迟履行合同。

二、合同中的不可抗力条款

不可抗力条款通常包括以下几方面内容。

(1)不可抗力事件的内容:因为没有对不可抗力事件的确定解释,所以卖方和买方应该在合同中规定不可抗力事件的范围。不可抗力事件包括自然灾害、火灾、洪水、暴风雨、大雪、地震等以及社会动荡,例如战争、罢工、制裁等。

(2)通知对方的时间期限:一旦发生不可抗力,当事人应该使用不可抗力条款立即通知对方。

(3)提供有关机构的证明:遭受到不可抗力事故后,提供有关机构的证明。出证机构应在合同中规定。

第四节 仲 裁

一、解决争议的方法

在国际贸易中,买卖双方发生争议后的解决方式有友好协商、仲裁和诉讼等。采用友好协商的方法,气氛比较友好,可以节省仲裁或诉讼的费用,有利于双方贸易的开展。这是买卖双方解决争议所常用的方法。如果这两种方式不能解决时,才采用仲裁或诉讼的方式。仲裁是由买卖双方根据双方达成的书面协议自愿把双方之间的争议提交双方同意的第三者进行裁决。裁决对双方都有约束力。凡采用仲裁方式处理争议时,双方当事人必须订有仲裁协议。

(1)自愿。双方自愿把争议交给仲裁员解决。仲裁员可以是个人、非利益方或非官方政府组织。

(2)仲裁协议是双方当事人表示愿意将他们之间的争议交付冲裁解决的一种书面协议,它是仲裁机构受理争议案件的依据。

(3)仲裁比法律诉讼程序简单、费用较少、处理案件时间较短。

(4)仲裁的结果是终局性的,对双方均有约束力。

二、仲裁程序

仲裁程序主要指进行仲裁的手续和做法,包括仲裁的申请、仲裁员的指定、仲裁条件的审理、仲裁裁决的效力和仲裁费用的支付等内容。各国常设的仲裁机构都定有自己的仲裁程序规则。为便于仲裁进行,仲裁条款应明确规定采用哪个仲裁机构的仲裁规则进行仲裁。

仲裁的裁决应由当事人自动执行。对于由我国的对外经济贸易仲裁委员会的裁决,一方如果逾期不予执行,另一方可申请中国人民法院依法执行。外国仲裁机构的裁决可以根据具体情况向仲裁所在地国家的法院或向与仲裁地国家订有相互承认和执行仲裁公约或条约的国家申请执行。

三、仲裁地点

仲裁地点可以是在卖方国家、买方国家,或者在第三国。在仲裁协议中仲裁地点的选择与仲裁机构同等重要。仲裁国家就是外国在仲裁裁决的地点,所以仲裁地点对于仲裁裁决的确认和执行至关重要。

四、仲裁机构

国际贸易仲裁机构有临时机构和常设机构两种。临时仲裁机构是为了解决特定的争议而组成的仲裁庭。争议处理完毕,临时仲裁庭即告解散。中国国际贸易促进委员会附设的对外经济贸易仲裁委员会,也属于全国性的常设仲裁机构,总部设在北京,分部在深圳和上海,联络办公室在大连、福州、长沙、成都和重庆等地,接受案件时,使用统一的仲裁规则和仲裁员小组。为方便仲裁在仲裁条款中通常都选用适当的常设机构。

五、合同中的仲裁条款

国际贸易合同中的仲裁条款,主要包括仲裁地点、仲裁机构、仲裁程序、仲裁效力和仲裁费用等。我国对外贸易合同中的仲裁条款常用的有下列三种。

(1)规定在我国仲裁的条款

凡因执行本合同所发生的或与本合同有关的一切争议,双方应通过友好协商解决;如果协商不能解决,应提交北京中国国际贸易促进委员会对外经济贸易仲裁委员会根据该会的《仲裁程序暂行规则》进行仲裁,仲裁的裁决是终局的,对双方都有约束力。

(2)规定在被诉方所在国仲裁的条款

凡因执行本合同所发生的或与本合同有关的一切争议,双方应通过友好协商解决;如果协商不能解决,应提交仲裁。仲裁在被诉人所在国进行,如在中国,由中国国际贸易促进委员会对外经济贸易仲裁委员会根据该会《仲裁程序暂行规则》进行仲裁。如在某国,由某仲裁机构根据该机构的仲裁程序规则进行仲裁。仲裁裁决是终局的,对双方都有约束力。

(3)规定在第三国仲裁的条款

凡因执行本合同所发生的或与本合同有关的一切争议,双方应通过友好协商解决;如果协商不能解决,应提交某国某仲裁机构根据该仲裁机构的仲裁规定进行仲裁。仲裁裁决是终局的,对双方都有约束力。

第十章　国际货物销售合同的商订

第一节　交易磋商的程序

合同是在买卖双方之间通过磋商签订的。交易磋商程序大致可分为询盘、发盘、还盘和接受,其中发盘和接受是必不可少的两个基本环节。国际销售合同的商订可以通过书信、传真、电子邮件等方式操作,也可以面对面进行谈判。不管选择哪一种方法,通常包括4个环节。

一、询盘

询盘也称要约邀请。买方和卖方都可以发出询盘,是指交易的一方欲出售或购买某种货物,向另一方发出的探询买卖该项货物有关交易条件的一种表示。

卖方应该高度重视买方发出的询盘,买方可能会成为卖方的潜在顾客。每一次询盘都代表一次销售机会,巩固潜在的长期关系的机会。以下是一个询盘的例子。

电报:对你方蝴蝶牌缝纫机感兴趣,请报价。

二、发盘

发盘是指交易的一方向另一方提出一定交易条件,并愿意按照提出的交易条件达成买卖该项货物的交易,并签订合同的一种表示。

买方和卖方都可以发盘,前者称为"卖方发盘",后者被称为"买方发盘",也称为报价。以下是一个发盘的例子。

电报:发盘2000打运动衫,3月5日邮寄样品,每打90美元,CIF纽约,使用标准出口包装,5月/6月装船,不可撤销即期信用证,请在20日回复

三、还盘

所谓还盘,是受盘人对发盘内容不完全同意而提出要求更改的表示。例如,卖方收到

了买方的发盘，但是通知买方商品将是不同的颜色，这就是还盘。

实际上，还盘是发盘人发出的新发盘。原始发盘无效，不再具有约束力。还盘可以在买卖双方之间重复多次。一笔交易往往经过还盘及往返多次的再还盘才能达成。以下是一个还盘的例子。

发送的电报：很抱歉不能接受你方第3次电报，因为竞争者的相类似质量产品报价55美元，请立即回复。

收到的电报：我方第3次更新发盘将于我们时间的10日回复。

四、接受

接受是交易的一方完全同意对方发盘中全部交易内容的肯定表示。微小的更改不会影响发盘的实质性条件。以下是一个接受的例子。

"你方14日电我接受（或确认）。"

第二节　合同的订立

一、发盘

发盘是对发盘人具有约束力的"要约"，发盘人在发盘的有效期限内不得撤回或修改，是发盘人向受盘人提出各项主要交易条件，并愿按这些条件达成交易的肯定表示。发盘一经对方在有效时限内表示无保留的接受，交易即成立。

1. 发盘的构成

（1）向一个或一个以上的特定人发出

发盘是由发盘人向受发盘人发出的。因此，这里所谓特定的人是指受发盘人须为特定人。向公众的建议则只能视作邀请。例如，报纸上商品销售的广告会使广告商陷入尴尬的境地，因为大量的需求，需要供应更多的货物，或者在广告登出的时间时产生大量的损失。

（2）发盘的内容必须十分确定

应当载明货物的名称，应明确规定货物的数量和价格，如果没有确定规定其他条件，也应该被加在合同上。

2. 发盘的有效期

发盘的有效时限是发盘人受所发盘约束的期限，在此期限内不得任意撤销，也是受盘人表示接受的期限。在此期限内作出答复，才算有效。在国际贸易中，发盘通常都规定有效时间。规定发盘有效期的方法如下。

（1）最新时间：请于15日以前回复。

（2）有效时限：发盘有效期为3天。

3. 发盘的撤回与撤销

(1)撤回

只有发盘到达受发盘人那里发盘才有效。发盘的撤回是指发盘人在发出发盘之后,在其尚未到达受发盘人之前,即在发盘尚未生效之前,将该项发盘收回,使其不发生效力。

(2)撤销

发盘的撤销是指发盘人在其发盘已经到达受发盘人之后,即在其发盘已经生效之后,将该项发盘取消,从而使发盘失去效力。

二、接受

接受是指受盘人在发盘有效期之内同意发盘的全部内容。受盘人声明或作出其他行为表示同意一项发盘,即为接受。

1. 接受的构成

(1)接受必须是被受盘人作出。除此之外,任何其他人表示接受均无法律效力。

(2)接受的必须是发盘内容。

原则上说,当接受中含有对发盘内容的增加、限制或修改,接受均不能成立。

《公约》第19条明确规定:

①对发盘表示接受但载有添加、限制或其他更改的答复,即为拒绝该项发盘,并构成还盘。然而,这一条款并不意味着受发盘人接受时不允许你添加、限制或其他更改的答复,问题是这种更改是不是实质性的。

②对发盘表示接受但载有添加或不同条件的答复,如所载的添加或不同条件在实质上并不变更该项发盘的条件,除发盘人在不过分迟延的期间内以口头或书面通知反对其间的差异外,仍构成接受。如果发盘人不作出这种反对,合同的条件就以该项发盘的条件以及接受通知内所载的更改为准。

③有关货物价格、付款、货物质量和数量、交货地点和时间、一方当事人对另一方当事人的赔偿责任范围或解决争端等的添加或不同条件,均视为在实质上变更发盘的条件。

(3)接受必须在一项发盘的有效期限之内或一段合理的时间内作出。

(4)接受必须由受盘人采用声明或作出实际行动来表示,并且在传达给发盘人时生效。

2. 接受的撤回

《公约》第22条规定:"接受也可以撤回,如果撤回通知应于接受生效之前或同时,送达发盘人。"接受通知一经到达发盘人合同即告成立。

附录1 国际贸易实务常用词汇(英汉对照)

A

accelerate trade payment(ATP) 加速贸易付款

acceptance 承兑,接受

acceptance letter of credit(acceptance L/C) 承兑信用证

accepting bank 承兑行

acceptor 承兑人

acknowledgement of insurance declaration 投保声明的回执

actual delivery 实际交货

actual quality 实际品质

actual tare 实际皮重

actual total loss 实际全损

Ad. val (拉丁语)从价

advanced bill of lading (advanced B/L) 预借提单

advanced payment 预付货款

advising bank 通知行

aflatoxin risk 黄曲霉素险

agency 代理

agent 代理商

agreement 协议书

agreement of consignment 寄售协议

Air Express 急件传送

air transportation all risks 航空运输一切险

air transportation cargo war risks 航空运输货物战争险

air transportation risks 航空运输险

air way bill 航空货运单

aligned document system 套合一致的单证

all risks 一切险

all risks for shipment of frozen products 冷藏货物运输一切险

alteration charge 变更卸货港附加费

American Association of Textile Chemists and Colorists(AATCC)美国纺织化学师与印染师协会标准
American Society of Testing Materials (ASTM)美国材料试验协会的标准
announcement of tender 发布招标公告
anticipatory letter of credit (anticipatory L/C)预支信用证
ante-dated bill of lading (ante-dated B/L) 倒签提单
antirust packaging 防锈包装
applicant 开证申请人
application for credit 开证申请书
arbitration 仲裁
arbitration agreement 提交仲裁协议
arbitration application 仲裁申请
arbitration clause 仲裁条款
arbitration procedure 仲裁程序
arrival contract 到达合同
artificial harbor 人工港
assembling with customer's parts 来件装配
assignment of proceed 款项让渡或款项过渡
Association of Official Analytical Chemists (AOAC) 美国公职分析化学师协会标准
assortment list 花色搭配单
at buyer's option 由买方决定
at seller's option 由卖方决定
auction 拍卖
auctioneer 拍卖人
authority to purchase(A/P) 委托购买证
automatic revolving letter of credit (automatic revolving L/C)自动循环信用证
available by negotiation 议付兑现
available by payment 付款兑现
average price 平均价
average tare 平均皮重
avoidance of delay 防止延迟

B

back to back letter of credit（back to back L/C）对背信用证
bale packing 捆包装
bank credit card 银行信用卡
bank guarantee 银行保证函
banker's acceptance bill 银行承兑汇票
banker's acceptance letter of credit（banker's acceptance L/C）银行承兑信用证
banker's bill 银行汇票
banker's cheque 银行支票
banking charges 银行费用
barter trade 易货贸易
base port 基本港
beneficiary 受益人
benefit of insurance 保险利益
berth terms 船方负担装卸费
bid 递盘
bid bond 投标保证金,投标押金
bidding documents 编制招标文件
bill for collection(B/C）托收汇票
bill of exchange 汇票
bill of lading（B/L）海运提单
bill of lading weight 提单货量
blank endorsement 空白背书
bona fide holder 善意持有人
book 订购
booking note 托运单
both to blame collision clause（B. B. clause）船船互撞条款
breach of condition 违反要件
breach of contract 违反合同
breach of innominate terms 违反无名条款
breach of intermediate terms 违反中间性条款
breach of warranty 违反担保或违反随附条件
brief cable 简电本

British standard(BS) 英国(工业)标准
bulk cargo 散装货物
bunker adjustment factor(BAF) 燃油附加费
business negotiation 交易磋商
buy back 回购
buyer's sample 买方样
buyer's usance credit 买方远期信用证
buying hedging 买期保值
buying offer 购货发盘

C

cable address (C/A) 电挂
cable confirmation 电报证实书
cable credit 电开信用证
call of tender 招标
Canadian Standards Association (C. S. A) 加拿大标准协会
canceling date 解约日
cargo in bulk 散装货物
cargo manifest 货物舱单
cargo plan 积载图(又名船图)
cargo receipt 承运货物收据
carriage and insurance paid to (... named place of destination)(CIP) 运费、保险费付至(……指定目的地)
carriage paid to (... named place of destination)(CPT) 运费付至(……指定目的地)
carton 纸箱
cash against documents 凭单付款
cash discount 现金折扣
cash in advance(C. I. A) 预付现款
cash in order(C. I. O) 订货时付款
cash on delivery (C. O. D) 交货付款
cash with order (C. W. O) 附订单付现
certificate for dispatch of documents 寄单证明
certificate for dispatch of shipment samples 寄样证明
certificate in regard to handlooms textile handcrafts and traditional textile products of the cottage

industry 手工制纺织品产地证
certificate of age of vessel 船龄证明书
certificate of classification 船舶船级证明
certificate of compliance 明白证明书
certificate of date of sailing 开船证明书
certificate of delivery 交货证明书
certificate of departure from port 离港证明书
certificate of load line 船舶载重线证明
certificate of vessel's nationality 船舶国籍证明
certificate of origin 产地证明书
certificate of textile products 纺织品产地证
certificate of ownership 所有权证书
certificate of weight 重量证书
certified cheque 保付支票
certified invoice 证实发票或签证发票
CFR ex ship's hold CFR 舱底交货
CFR ex tackle CFR 吊钩下交货
CFR landed CFR 卸到岸上
CFR liner terms CFR 班轮条件
CFS to CFS（集装箱运输）站到站
CFS to CY（集装箱运输）站到厂
CFS to door（集装箱运输）站到门
China Council for the Promotion of International Trade（C. C. P. I. T）中国国际贸易促进委员会
China Council for the Promotion of International Trade Certificate of Origin（CCPIT certificate of origin）中国国际贸易促进委员会产地证
China Exit and Entry Inspection and Quarantine Bureau（CIQ）中国出入境检验检疫局
China National Foreign Trade Transportation Corporation（SINOTRANS）中国外贸运输公司
China Ocean Shipping Agency（COSA）中国外轮代理公司
China Ocean Shipping Company（COSCO）中国远洋运输公司
CIF ex ship's hold CIF 舱底交货
CIF ex tackle CIF 吊钩下交货
CIF landed CIF 卸到岸上
CIF Liner terms CIF 班轮条件
claim 索赔

clash and breakage risks 碰损、破碎险
Class Rate Freight Tariff 等级运价表
classification of commodities 货物分级表
clean bill 光票
clean bill of lading (clean B/L) 清洁提单
clean letter of Credit (clean L/C) 光票信用证
clean report of findings 清洁报告书
closed bids 密封递价
closed policy 总括保险单
collecting bank 代收行
collection 托收
collection advice 托收委托书
colour sample 色彩样品
combined bill of lading (combined B/L) 并提单
combined certificate 联合凭证
combined certificate of value and origin 估价和原产地联合证明书
combined documents 联合单据
combined offer 复合发盘
combined transport bill of lading (CTB/L) 联合运输提单
commercial acceptance bill 商业承兑汇票
commercial bill 商业汇票
commercial documents 商业单据
commercial invoice 商业发票
commercial paper letter of credit (commercial paper L/C) 商业票据信用证
commercial technology transfer 商业性技术转让
commission 佣金
commission agency 佣金代理
commission agent 佣金代理商
commodity exchange 商品交易所
Commodity Futures Trading Commission 商品期货交易委员会
commodity inspection 商品检验
commodity inspection corporation (C. I. C) 商检公司
common license 普通许可
communicate to all address 分送电

compensation agreement 补偿协定
compensation system 补偿制
compensation trade 补偿贸易
complete knock down（C. K. D）全拆卸
complete set bill of lading（complete set B/L）全套提单
Comprehensive Import Supervision Scheme（C. I. S. S）全面进口监督计划
computed tare 约定皮重
conciliation 调解
concurrent terms 对流条件
conditional sale lease 销售租赁
conditioned weight 公量
confirm 保兑
confirmation 确认书
confirmed letter of credit（confirmed L/C）保兑信用证
confirming bank 保兑行
confirming sample 确认样
consecutive days 连续日
consideration 对价
consignee 收货人,代销商
consignment 寄售
consignment bill for highway transportation 公路货物运输托运单
consignor 寄售人
constructive delivery 推定全损
constructive total loss 推定全损
consular invoice 领事发票
consular visa 领事签证
consulting engineers 咨询工程公司
consulting service 顾问咨询
container bill of lading（container B/L）集装箱提单
container freight station（C. F. S）集装箱货运站
container load 集装箱装载
container load plan（C. L. P）装箱单
container number（container no.）集装箱号
container yard（CY）集装箱堆场

contingency insurance ,covers seller's interest only 卖方利益险
contract 合同
contract for the international sale of goods 国际货物销售合同
Convention on the Recognition and Enforcement of Foreign Arbitral Award 承认及执行外国仲裁裁决公约
cover note 暂保单
co-production 合作生产
copy of bill of lading (copy B/L) 副本提单
correspondent bank 代理行
cost and freight (... named port of destination)(CFR) 成本加运费(……指定目的港)
cost, insurance and freight ...(named port of destination)(CIF) 成本加运保费(……指定目的港)
couriers receipts 快邮收据
counter offer 还盘,还价
counter purchase 互购
counter sample 对等样品
counter trade 对等贸易
counter card 信用卡
counter to expire abroad 国外到期信用证
crew list 船舶船员名单
cross license 交叉许可
cross offer 交叉发盘
crossed cheque 划线支票
currency adjustment factor (CAF) 币值附加费
customary packing 习惯包装
customary tare 习惯皮重
cutting sample 剪样
CY to CFS (集装箱运输)场至站
CY to CY (集装箱运输)场至场
CY to door (集装箱运输)场至门

D

Dalsey ,Hilbolom , Lind ,Courier's Service DHL 信使专递
dampproof packing 防潮包装

date of issue 出票日期
date of draft 出票日期
dead freight 空舱费
dead weight 总载重量
dead-weight cargo 重货
dead-weight tonnage 载重量吨位
debit note(D/N) 借款账单
declaration of country of origin 原产地声明书
deductible 绝对免赔率
deferred payment 延期付款
deferred payment letter of credit (deferred payment L/C) 迟期付款信用证
delivered at frontier(... named place)(DAF) 边境交货(……指定地点)
delivered duty paid(... named place of destination)(DDP) 完税后交货(……指定目的港)
delivered duty unpaid(... named place of destination)(DDU) 未完税交货(……指定目的地)
delivered ex quay (... named port of destination)(D.E.Q) 目的港码头交货(……指定目的地)
delivered ex ship (... named port of destination)(D.E.S) 目的港船上交货(……指定目的港)
delivery 交货
delivery order (D/O) 提货单
demand draft (D/D) 汇票
demise charter 光船租船
demurrage money 延期费,滞期费
deposit receipt (D/R) 押金收据
description of goods 货物说明
desk to desk express service 桌到桌快递服务
dispatch money 速遣费
destination of discharge 目的地
detail airmail 详见航邮件
detailed invoice 详细发票
detailed packing list 详细装箱单
Diners Club international 大莱卡
direct additional 直航附加费
direct barter 直接易货
direct bill of lading(direct B/L) 直运提单
direct price 直接价

discount 贴现
discrepancy and clam clause 异议与索赔条款
dishonor 拒付行为
Disinfection Inspection Certificate 消毒检验证书
displacement tonnage 排水量吨位
disponent owner 船东
dock receipt（D/R）码头收据，场站收据
documentary bill 跟单汇票
documentary letter of credit（documentary L/C）跟单信用证
documentary against acceptance（D/A）承兑交单
documentary against payment（D/P）付款交单
documentary against payment with trust receipt（D/P. T/R）付款交单凭信托收据借单
domestic credit 国内信用证
door to CFS（集装箱运输）门到站
door to CY（集装箱运输）门到场
door to door（集装箱运输）门到门
D/P at . . . days after sight 远期付款交单
D/P at sight 即期付款交单
draft 汇票
drawee 受票人，付款人
drawee bank 付款行
drawer 出票人，收款人
duplicate sample 复样
dutch auction 减价拍卖
duty paid value 完税价格

E

EDI message 电子信息
Electronic Data Interchange（EDI）电子数据通信
Electronic Data Processing（EDP）电子数据处理
enclosure 附件
endorsement 批单，背书
engineering contracting 工程承包
enquiry 询盘

equipment lease 设备租赁
errors and omissions excepted (E. &O. E) 有错当查,错误或遗漏不在此限
establishing bank 开证行
estimated time of arrival(E. T. A) 预定到达时间
estimated time of departure(E. T. D) 预定开航时间;预定离港时间
ex works (... named place)(EXW) 工厂交货(……指定地点)
except as otherwise noted (E. A. O. N) 除非另有记载
exclusive agency 独家代理
exclusive agency agreement 独家代理协议
exclusive agent 独家代理商
exclusive distributor 包销商
exclusive License 独占许可
exclusive sale 包销
exclusive sale agreement 包销协议
expected time of finishing discharging (E. T. F. D) 预计卸完时间
expected time of finishing loading(E. T. F. L) 预计装完时间
export declaration(E/D) 出口申报书
export freight manifest 出口载货运费清单或运费舱单
export licence 出口许可证
export licence textile products 纺织品出口许可证
export manifest 出口载货清单
exporter 出口人
extraneous risks 外来风险

F

failure to deliver risk 交货不到险
fair average quality (F. A. Q) 良好平均品质
false bill of lading (false B/L) 伪造提单
feedback 技术反馈
finance lease 融资租赁
financial documents 资金单据
fire risk extension clause for storage of cargo at destination HongKong, including Kowloon, or Macao(F. R. E. C) 货物出口到香港(包括九龙)或澳门存仓火险责任扩展条款
first beneficiary 第一收益人

fixed price 固定价
fixed scale royalty 固定提成率
flexible container 柔性集装袋
FOB liner term FOB 班轮条件
FOB stowed(FOBS) FOB 包括理舱
FOB stowed and trimmed(F. O B. S. T) FOB 包括平舱和理舱
FOB trimmed(FOBT) FOB 包括平舱
FOB under tackle FOB 钓钩下交货
FOB vessel(... named port of shipment)指定运港船上交货
Food and Drug Administration(FDA) 美国食品及药品管理局
for reference only 仅供参考
force majeure 不可抗力
force majeure clause 不可抗力条款
fortuitous accidents 意外事故
forward price 期货价格
forward cargo receipt(FCR) 运输代理人的承运货物收据
forwarding agents 发货代理或货运代理
foul bill of lading(foul B/l) 不清单提单
franchise 相对免赔率
free all average(F-A-A) 不计一切海损
free alongside ship(... named port of shipment)(FAS) 船边交货(……指定装运港)
free carrier(... named place)(FCA) 货交承运人(……指定地点)
free from particular average (F-P-A) 平安险
free in(F-I) 船方管卸不管装
free in and out(F-I-O) 船方不管装和卸
free in and out, stowed and trimmed(F-I-O-S-T) 船方不管装卸、理舱和平舱
free on board(... named port of shipment) 装运港船上交货(……指定装运港)
free out 船方管装不管卸
free perimeter 自由边境区
free port 自由港
free trade zone 自由贸易区
freight agent 货运代理人
freight bill 运费账单
freight manifest 运费舱单

freight prepaid 运费已付
freight to collect 运费到付
freight ton 运费吨
fresh water and /or rain damage(F-W-R-D) 淡水雨淋险
fresh water road line 淡水载重线
frustration of contract 合同落空
full cable 全电本
full container load(F-C-L) 整箱货
full packed 全部包装
full payout 完全付清
fill set bill of lading(full set B/L) 全套提单
full set of clean on board bill of lading made out to order and endorsed in blank 全套清洁已装船作成凭指示和空白背书的提单
fundamental breach 根本违反合同
future contract 期货合同
futures market 期货市场
future transaction 期货交易

G

general additional 一般附加险
General Administration of Civil Aviation China (AAC) 中国民航总局
general agency 总代理
general agent 总代理人
general average(G-A) 共同海损
general average contribution 共同海损分摊
general conditions of delivery of goods 交货共同条件
general terms and conditions 一般交易条件
generalized system of preference certificate of origin Form A(G-S-P Form A) 普惠制产地证格式
Geneva uniform law on cheque 日内瓦统一支票法规
Good merchantable quality(G-M-Q) 上好可销品质
goods quality 商品品质
grade of goods 商品等级
green clause credit 绿条款信用证
gross bills of lading weight 毛提单货量

gross for net 以毛作净
gross registered tonnage(G-R-T) 注册总吨
gross terms 船方担负装卸费
grounded 搁浅
groundage bill of lading 成组提单
guarantee letter of credit(guarantee L/C) 担保信用证,保证信用证
guarantor 保证人
gunny bags 麻袋

H

Hamburg Rules 海牙规则
hard ware 硬件
heavy lift additional 超重附加费
heavy weather 恶劣气候
hedging 套期保值
hire purchase 租购式租赁
hook damage 钩损险
house air way bill 分运单
house bill of lading 运输代理行提单

I

immediate shipment 立即装运
import declaration 进口申请书
import duty risk 进口关税险
importer 进口人
indent 订单
indicative marks 指示性标志
industrial activity 实用性
industrial property 工业产权
initial payment 初付费,入门费
initial price 初步价格
injured party 受害方
inland depot 内陆货运站
inland extended cover 内陆附加险

inland waterway bill of landing 内陆提单
inspection and claim clause 检验与索赔条款
Inspection Certificate of Health 健康检验证书
Inspection Certificate of Origin 产地检验证书
Inspection Certificate of Quality 品质检验证书
Inspection Certificate of Quantity 数量检验证书
Inspection Certificate of Value 价值检验证书
Inspection Certificate of Weight 重量检验证书
Inspection Certificate on Cargo Weight and Measurement 货物衡量证书
Inspection Certificate on damaged Cargo 验残检验证书
Inspection Certificate on Tank /Hold 验舱证书
Inspection of goods 货物检验
Institute Cargo clauses(ICC) 协会货物险条款
Institute Cargo clauses A(ICC(A)) 协会货物(A)险条款
Institute Cargo clauses B(ICC(B)) 协会货物(B)险条款
Institute Cargo clauses C(ICC(C)) 协会货物(C)险条款
Institute strikes clauses-Cargo 协会罢工险条款(货物)
Institute War clauses-Cargo 协会战争险条款(货物)
Insurable interest 保险利益,可保权益
Insurance certificate 保险凭证
Insured amount 保险金额
Insurer 承保人,保险人
Intellectual property 知识产权
Interim measures of protection 保全措施又称临时保护措施
International Chamber of Commerce(ICC) 国际商会
International code of conduct on the technology transfer 国际技术转让行动守则
International competitive bidding 国际竞争性招标
International combined transport 国际多式联运
International express mail service(EMS) 国际特快专递
International multimodal transport 国际多式联运
International railway through transport 国际铁路货物联运
International rules for the interpretation of trade terms(INCOTERMS) 国际贸易术语解释通则
International standard organization 国际标准化组织
International trading certificate(ITC) 国际贸易证书

Intrinsic quality 商品内在素质
Inventive activity 创造性
Invitation to make offer 邀请发盘
Invitation to tender 招标
Irrespective of percentage(I-O-P) 不论损失程度
Irrespective letter of credit(irrevocable L/C) 不可撤销信用证
Issue 出票
Issuing bank 开证行
Insurance policy 保险单
Insurance value 保险价值

J

Japanese Industrial Standard(JIS) 日本工业标准
Jettison and/or washing over board 抛掷,海水冲击险

K

Kite mark 风筝标志
Knocked-down in carloads 拆散成整车皮装货物
Knocked-down shipment (货物)分运
Know how 专有技术

L

Land bridge transport 大陆桥运输
Landed terms 起货条件
Landing account 卸货报告
Landing quality ,weight as final 以到岸品质、重量为准
Landing weight 卸货重量,到岸重量
Last pay certificate 最后付款证明书
Late acceptance 逾期接受
Law and practice 法律惯例
Lay time 装卸时间
Lay days date 受载时间
Leakage risk 渗漏险
Lease trade 租赁贸易

Licensor's share on licensee's profit(LSLP) 利润分成原则
Legal net weight 法定净重
Legal weight 法定重量
Less than container load(LCL) 拼箱货
Lessee 承担人
Lessor 出租人
Letter of credit(L/C) 信用证
Letter of guarantee(L/G) 银行保证函
Letter telegramme 书信电报
Leverage lease 杠杆租赁
Licensing 许可证贸易
Licensing agreement 许可证协议
Lien 扣押权
Light displacement 空船排水量或清排水量
Liner 班轮
Liner shipping 班轮运输
Liner terms 班轮条件,船方负担装卸费
Liner' s freight tariff 班轮运价表
Liquidated damages 预定损害赔偿
Litigation 诉讼
Load line 船舶载重线
Loaded displacement 满载排水量、重排水量或总排水量
Loading list 装货清单
Local freight agent 当地运输代理商
Local vanning 当地装箱
Log book 航行日志
London Metal Exchange 伦敦五金交易所
London Stock Exchange 伦敦证券交易所
Long form bill of lading(long from B/L) 全式提单
Long length additional 超长附加费
Loss and/or damage caused by breakage of packing 包装破裂险
Lot tolerance rate 批内允许破损率
Lot tolerance defective 批内允许次品费
Lowest price limit 最低售价

Lump sum payment 一次总算

M

Mail confirmation to follow 随寄证实书
Mail credit 信开信用证
Mail transfer(M/T) 信汇
Main mark 主要标志
Major causes 重大意外事故
Malicious damage clauses 恶意损害险条款
Manufacture's certificate of origin 生产商原产地证明书
Manufacture's invoice 厂商发票
Marine bill of lading 海运提单
Marine insurance policy 水运保险单
Marker capacity 标定容量
Master airway bill 民航运单
Master Card 万事达卡
Master document 总单证
Master receipt 大副收据
Material breach 重大违约
Mate's receipt 大副收据
Measurement and weight mark 体重和重量标志
Measurement cargo 轻货
Measurement list 尺码单
Measurement ton(M/T) 尺码吨
Memorandum 备忘录
Method of dispatching documents 寄单方法
Method of reimbursement 索汇方法
Mildew proof packaging 防霉包装
Mini land bridge(M-L-B) 小路桥
Minimum bill of lading(minimum B/L) 起码提单
Minimum freight 起码运费
Minimum premium 最低保险费
Minimum rate 起码费率
Minimum weight 最低重量

Minor breach 轻微违法
Mixed agreement 混合协议
Mixed policy 混合保险单
Mode of shipment 运输方式
Money of account 计价货币
Money of payment 支付货币
More or less clause 溢短装条款
Multimode transport documents(MTO) 多式联运单据
Multimode transport operator(MTO) 多式联运经营人
Multiple country declaration 多国家产地声明书

N

Name of commodity 品名
National harbors 天然港
Natural calamity 自然灾害
Negotiable calamity 流通证券
Negotiated bidding 谈判招标
Negotiating bank 议付行
Negotiation 议付
Negotiation letter of credit 议付通行证
Net bills of lading weight 净提单货量
Net dead weight 净载重量
Net net weight 净净重
Net registered tonnage(NRT) 注册净吨
Net weight 净重
Neutral invoice 中性发票
Neutral packing 中性包装
New York Commodity Exchange 纽约商品交易所
No commercial value(N-C-V) 无商业价值
No mark(N/M) 无唛头
No orders(N/O) 无指示,无订单,不指定人
Non-acceptance(N/A) 拒绝承兑,拒绝接受
Non-automatic revolving letter of credit Non-base port 非自动循环信用证
Non-commercial technology transfer 非基本港

Non-cumulative revolving letter of credit 非商业性技术转让
Non-payout 非累计循环信用证
Non-vessel operating carrier(NV OC) 不完全付清
Non-vessel operating common carrier(NVOC C) 无船承运人
Non-vessel owning common carrier(NVOCC)无船承运人
Notice of abandonment 委付通知
Notice of readiness 备装通知
Notify party 被通知人
Notifying bank 通知行
Novelty 新颖性
Nuded cargo 裸装货物

O

Ocean bill of lading (ocean B/L) 海运提单
Ocean marine insurance frozen products 海洋运输冷藏货物保险
Ocean marine insurance wood oil bulk 海洋运输散装桐油保险
Ocean waybill 海上货运单或海运单
Off set 抵消贸易
Offer 发盘
Offer without engagement 不受约束的发盘
Omnibus bill of lading(omnibus B/L) 并提单
On board bill of lading(on B/L)已装车提单
On deck risk 舱面险
Once on demurrage a 一旦滞期,始终滞期
Open account transaction 赊账交易
Open bidding 公开招标
Open by airmail 信开
Open by telecommunication 电开
Open policy 预约保单
Open negotiation letter of credit 公开议付信用证
Opener 开证人,开证申请人
Opening bank 开证行
Opening of tender 开标
Operating lease 经营租赁

Operative instrument 有效文本
Optional charges 选港费
Optional fees 选择卸货港附加费
Optional port 选择港
Order 订货,订单
Order bill of lading (order B/L) 指示提单
Original mark 原产地标志
Outturn sample 船样
Overland common points(O-C-P) 内陆地区
Overland transportation all risks 陆运一切险
Overland transportation cargo war risks-by train 路上运输货物战争险
Overland transportation frozen products 路上运输冷藏货运险
Overland transportation risks 陆运险

P

Pack slip 装箱单
Packaging 销售包装
Package number mark 件号标志
Package list 装箱单
Packed cargo 包装货物
Packing 运输包装
Packing documents 包装单据
Packing loan 打包放款
Packing specification 包装证明
Packing summary 包装提要
Paper bags 纸袋
Parcel post all risks 邮包一切险
Parcel post risk 邮包险
Parcel post war risks 邮包战争险
Part packed 局部包装
Partial loss 部分损失
Partial shipment 分批装运
Particular average 单独海损
Patent 专利

Pattern sample 款式样品
Pay by installment 分期付款
Payee 受款人
Payer 付款人
Paying bank 付款行
Payment 付款
Payment in advance 预付条款
Penalty clause 罚金条款
Performance bond 履约保证金
Performance guaranty 履约保证函
Performance letter of credit 履约信用证
Perils of the sea 海上风险
Physical delivery 实际交货
Place of departure 起运地
Place of issue 出票地点
Place of payment 付款地点
Place of receipt 收货地
Port of call 挂靠港
Port congestion surcharge 港口拥挤附加费
Port of destination 目的港
Port of discharge 卸货港
Port of loading 装货港
Port of shipment 装运港
Port of transshipment 转运港
Port surcharge 港口附加费
Port to port 港到港
Postal money order 邮政汇票
Presentation for acceptance 承兑提示
Presentation for payment 付款提示
Presenting bank 提示行
Price adjustment clause 价格修正条款
Price terms 价格条件,价格术语
Principal 委托人
Processing with customer's materials 来料加工

Product buyback 产品返销
Product sharing 产品分成
Performa invoice 形式发票
Progress 先进性
Progression payment 分期付款
Promissory note 本票
Prompt shipment 即期装运
Protest 拒付证书
Provisional price 暂作价
Public certificate 公务证书
Purchase order 购货订单
Purchase confirmation 购货确认书
Purchase contract 购货合同

Q

Quality sample 品质样品
Quality latitude 品质机动幅度
Quality of goods 商品品质
Quality to be about equal to the sample 品质与样品大致相同
Quality tolerance 品质公差
Quote 报价

R

Real tare 实际皮重
Receipt for the goods 货物收据
Receipt invoice 收妥发票
Received for shipment bill of lading 备运提单
Reciprocal letter of credit 对开信用证
Red clause letter of credit 红条款信用证
Reference sample 参考样品
Registered tonnage 注册吨
Regular shipping liner 班轮
Reimbursing agent 偿付代理人
Reimbursing bank 偿付行

Reissuing bank 转开行
Rejection risk 拒收险
Related product 相关样品
Remittance 汇付
Remittance against documents 凭单付汇
Remitting bank 托收行
Repayment guarantee 还款保证函
Representative sample 代表性样品
Restricted negotiation letter of credit 限制议付信用证
Restrictive endorsement 限制背书
Resultant product 直接产品
Return sample 回样
Return voyage charter 来回航程次
Revised American Foreign Trade Definitions 1941 一九四一年美国对外贸易定义修正本
Revocable letter of credit 可撤销信用证
Revoke 撤销
Revolving around time letter of credit 按时间循环信用证
Revolving around value letter of credit 按金额循环信用证
Revolving letter of credit 循环信用证
Right of exclusive sale 独家经销权利
Right of recourse 追索权
Right of subrogation 代位追偿权,代位权
Risk for shipment of frozen products 冷藏险
Risk of intermixture and contamination 混杂,沾污险
Risk of odour 串味险
Risk of shortage 短量险
Risks clause 风险条款
Risks covered 承保范围
Risks of strikes, riots and civil commotion(SRCC) 罢工,暴动,民变险
Rules for Pre-arbitral Referee Procedures 仲裁前公断程序规则
Ruling price 现行价
Running days 连续日
Running working days 连续工作日
Rust-inhibiting packaging 防锈包装

Rusting risk 锈损险

S

Safty-mark 安全标志
Sailing date 开航日期,船期
Sale and lease back 回租
Sale by brand name or trade mark 凭牌名或商标销售
Sale by buyer's sample 凭买方样品销售
Sale by description 凭文字说明销售
Sale by grade 凭等级销售
Sale by illustration 凭说明书销售
Sale by sample 凭样销售
Sale by seller's sample 凭卖方样品销售
Sale by specification 凭规格销售
Sale by standard 凭标准销售
Sales confirmation 销售确认书
Sales contract 销售合同
Salvage charge 救助费用
Sanitary Inspection Certificate 卫生检验证书
Scheduled airline 班机运输
Sea protest 海事报告
Sea water damage 海水损失险
Sea waybill 海运单或海上货运单
Seal number(seal no.) 封号
Sealed bid 密封发盘,密封递价
Sealed sample 封样
Seaworthy packing 适合海运包装
Second beneficiary 第二受益人
Secondary credit 从属信用证或对背信用证
Selected bidding 选择性招标
Seller's sample 卖方样
Seller's usual packing 卖方惯用包装
Selling hedging 卖期保值
Selling offer 售货发盘

Semi knock down(S. K. D) 半拆卸
Semi-automatic revolving credit 半自动循环信用证
Separate bill of lading 分提单
Settlement of exchange 结汇
Shipment 装运
Shipment as soon as possible 尽快装运
Shipment certificate 装船证明
Shipment certificate textile products 纺织品装船证明
Shipment contract 装运合同
Shipment request 装货申请
Shipped bill of lading 已装船提单
Shipper 托运人
Shipping advice 装船通知
Shipping agent 船务代理
Shipping mark 运输标志
Shipping note 装货通知单
Shipping order(S/O) 装货单
Shipping package 运输包装
Shipping quality, weight or quantity as final 以离岸品质、重量或数量为准
Shipping sample 装船样品
Ship's classification 船级
Shockproof packing 防震包装
Short delivery 短交,短交获
Short from bill of lading(short from B/L) 略式提单
Show how 技术示范
Sight 见票
Sight draft 即期汇票
Sight letter of credit 即期信用证
Sight payment letter of credit 即期付款信用证
Signature of the drawer 出票人签字
Similar credit 套证
Single country declaration 单一国家声明
Simple license 普通许可
Single rate freight tariff 单相费率运价表

Single voyage charter 单程航次
Sliding price 滑动价
Soft ware 软件
Sole agency 独家代理
Sole agent 独家代理商
Sole license 排他许可
Special additional risk 特别附加险
Special drawing rights（SDRs）特别提款权
Special endorsement 特别背书
Special order 特别订单
Special policy 逐笔保险单
Specification list 规格明细单
Specification of goods 商品规格
Speed post receipt 快递收据
Standby letter of credit 备用信用证
Stowage factor 积载系数
Stowage plan 积载图,船图
Straight bill of lading 记名提单
Straight lease 直接租赁
Strand 触礁
Strikes risk 罢工险
Subject matter insured 保险标的物
Sub-license 分许可
Submission of arbitration agreement 提交仲裁协议
Submission of tender 投标
Subsidiary credit 从属信用证或对背信用证
Sue and labour expense 施救费用
Summer load line 夏季载重险
Survey report 检验报告
Sweat and heating risks 受潮受热险
Switch bill of lading 交货提单
Switcher 转手商
Symbolic delivery 象征性交货

T

Technical and clause committee 技术与条款委员会
Technical servicing and assistance 技术服务与协助
Technology continuing assistance 技术继续援助
Technology transfer agreement 技术转让协议
Technology transfer transaction 技术转让
Telegraphic transfer (T/T) 电汇
Tender guarantee 投标保证书
Terminal devanning (集装箱)区内拆箱
The British System 英制
The doctrine of strict compliance 严格符合的原则
The metric system 米制
The People's Insurance Company of China (PICC) 中国人民保险公司
The U. S. Export Quotations and abbreviations 美国出口报价及其缩写条例
The U. S. System 美制
Theft ,pilferage and non-delivery 偷窃,提货不着险
Theoretical weight 理论重量
Through bill of lading (through B/L) 联运提单
Time charter 定期租船
Time draft 远期汇票
Time letter of credit (time L/C) 远期信用证
Time policy 定期保险单
To draw 出票
To order 凭指定
To order of 凭某某指定
To order of (* *)Bank 凭某某银行指定
To order of shipper 凭托运人指定
Tonnage certificate 船舶吨位证书
Total amount 总值
Total loss 全部损失
Total quality control 全面质量控制
Trade and payment agreement 贸易和支付规定
Trade discount 贸易折扣

Trade mark 商标

Trade terms 贸易条件,贸易术语

Transferable letter of credit 可转让信用证

Transfering bank 转证行

Transshipment bill of lading 转船提单

Transshipment risk 转运费

Transshipment surcharge 转船附加费

Transshipment to be allowed 允许转船

Transit Siberian land bridge container service traffic（TSCS）西伯利亚大陆桥集装箱运输

Transit storage 转运仓库

Transmitting bank 转递行

Transport document 运输单据

Traveler's cheque 旅行支票

Traveler's letter of credit 旅行信用证

Trip charter 定程租船

Tropical fresh water load line 热带地区淡水载重线

Tropical load line 热带地区载重线

True lease 正式租赁

Trust receipt（T/R）信托收据

T/T reimbursement 电报索赔条款

Turn key project 交钥匙项目

Twenty-foot equivalent unit（TEU）20 英尺(集装箱)等量单位

Two-stage bidding 两段招标

Type sample 标准样品

U

Unclean bill of lading 不清洁提单

Unconditional guarantee 无条件函

Unconfirmed letter of credit 不保兑信用证

Underwriter laboratories Inc.（U.L）美国保险人公会安全认证标志

Uniform customs and practice for commercial documentary credit（UCP）商业跟单信用证统一惯例

Uniform Rules for Collection 托收统一规则

Unit load device 成组装运设备

Unit packing list 成组(货物)装箱单

Unit price 单价
United Nations Conference on Trade and Development (UNCTAD) 联合国贸发会议
United Nations Layout Key for Trade Documents 联合国贸易单据设计样式
Universal bulk ship 通用散装货船
Universal products code (UPC) 通用产品符号
Unlimited competitive bidding 不限竞争性招标
Unlimited price 不限价
Unvalued policy 不定值保险单
Usance credit 远期信用证
Usual risks 通常险
Utility 实用性

V

Value added tax 增值税
Value policy 定值保险单
Verification certificate 验单
Veterinary Inspection Certificate 兽医检验证书
Visby Rules 维斯比规则
Voyage charter 定程租船
Voyage policy 船程保单

W

War risk 战争险
Warehouse receipt 仓库收据
Warehouse stock 仓库存货
Warehouse to warehouse clause (W/W clause) "仓至仓"条款
Warf-owner's liability 码头主责任
Warning marks 警告性标志
Warsaw-Oxford Rules 1932 1932 年华沙－牛津规则
Waterproof packaging 防雨包装
Weather working days 晴天工作日
Weather working days of 24 consecutive hours 连续 24 小时晴天工作日
Weather working days of 24 hours 24 小时晴天工作日
Weight certificate 重量证书

Weight list 重量单
Weight memo 磅码单
Weight note 重量单
Weight ton（W/T）重量吨
Winter load line 冬季载重线
Winter north Atlantic load line 北大西洋冬季载重线
With average（W. A）水渍险
With particular average（W. P. A）水渍险
With recourse credit 有追索权信用证
Withdraw 撤回
Without engagement 不受约束
Without recourse 不受追索
Without recourse credit 无追索权信用证
Wooden cakes 木桶
Wooden cases 木箱
Working days 工作日
Written statement 书面声明

Y

York-Antwerp Rules 约克·安特卫普(共同海损理算规则)

附录2 国际贸易单证

附表2-1

PACKING LIST

1) SELLER	3) INVOICE NO.	4) INVOICE DATE
	5) FROM	6) TO
	7) TOTAL PACKAGES (IN WORDS)	
2) BUYER	8) MARKS & NOS.	

9) C/NOS.	10) NOS. & KINDS OF P	12) QTY. (pcs.	13) G. W. (kg)	14) N. W. (kg)	15) MEAS(m3)

附表 2-2

中国人民保险公司
THE PEOPLE'S INSURANCE COMPANY OF CHINA

总公司设于北京 一九四九年创立
Head Office: BEIJING Established in 1949

发票号码 **保 险 单** 保险单号码
Invoice No. INSURANCE POLICY Rolicy No. ST16/

中国人民保险公司(以下简称本公司)
This Policy of insurance witnesses that The People's Insurance Company of China (hereinafter called " The Company ")
根据
at the request of ______
(以下简称被保险人)的要求,由被保险人向本公司缴付约定
(hereinafter called the " Insured ") and in consideration of the agreed premium paying to the Company by the
的保险费,按照本保险单承保险别和背面所载条款与下列
Insured , undertakes to insure the undermentioned goods in transportion subject to the condition of this policy
特款承保下述货物运输保险,特立本保险单。
as per the Clauses printed overleaf and other special clauses attached hereon.

标 记 Marks & Nos.	包装及数量 Quantity	保险货物项目 Description of Goods	保险金额 Amount Insured

保险金
Total Amount insured: ______

保费 费率 装载运输工具
Premium as arranged Rate as arranged Per conveyance S. S. ______

开行日期 自 至
Sig. On or abt. ______ From ______ to ______

承保险别

Condition.

所保货物,如遇出险,本公司凭本保险单及其他有关证件给付赔款。

Claims, if any, payable on surrender of this Policy together with other relevant documents.

所保货物,如发生本保险单项下负责赔偿的损失或事故。

In the event of accident where by loss or damage may result in a claim under this Policy immediate notice applying for

应立即通知本公司下述代理人查勘。

survey must be given to the Company's Agent as mentioned hereunder:

赔款偿付地点:

CLAIM PAYABLE AT/IN ____________________

日期 深圳

DATE ________________ SHENZHEN

地址:深圳罗芳路 122 号南方大厦 25 楼

25F NANFANG BUILDING 122# LUOFANG ROAD

SHENZHEN, CHINA

中国人民保险公司深圳分公司

THE PEOPLE'S INSURANCE CO. OF CHINA

SHENZHEN BRANCH

附表 2 – 3

进出口货物代理报关委托书

编号：

委托单位		十位编码	
地　　址		联系电话	
经 办 人		身份证号	

我单位委托＿＿＿＿＿＿＿＿代理以下进出口货物的报关手续，保证提供的报关资料真实、合法、与实际货物相符，并愿意承担由此产生的法律责任。

货物名称		商品编号		件　数	
重　　量		价　　值		币　制	USD
贸易性质	一般贸易	货物产地			
是否退税	是	船名/航次			
委托单位开户银行		账号			

随附单位名称、份数及编号：

1. 合同	份；	6. 机电证明	份、编号；
2. 发票	份；	7. 商检证	份；
3. 装箱清单	份；	8.	
4. 登记手册	本、编写；		9.
5. 许可证	份、编号；		10.

（以上内容由委托单位填写）

被委托单位	十位编码
地　　址	联系电话
经 办 人	身份证号

（以上内容由被委托单位填写）

代理（专业） 报关企业章及 法人代表章：	委托单位章及 法人代表章：

附表 2-4

产地证明书
CERTIFICATE OF ORIGIN

SHENZHEN ____________

兹证明下列商品系中华人民共和国生产/制造

(This is to certify that the mentioned commodities were produced/manufactured in the People's Republic of China)

标记及号码 (Mark & No.)	品名 (Commodity)	数量 (Quantity)	重量 (Weight)

附表 2 – 5

中华人民共和国海关出口货物报关单

预录入编号：　　　　　　　　　　　　　　　　　　　　海关编号：

出口口岸		备案号	出口日期	申报日期
经营单位		运输方式	运输工具名称	提运单号
发货单位		贸易方式	征免性质	结汇方式
许可证号	运抵国（地区）	指运港		境内货源地
批准文号	成交方式	运费	保费	杂费
合同协议号	件数	包装种类	毛重（公斤）	净重（公斤）
集装箱号	随附单据			生产厂家
标记唛码及备注				

项号	商品编号	商品名称、规格型号	数量及单位	最终目的地（地区）	单价	总价	币制	征免

税费征收情况

录入员　　录入单位	兹声明以上申报无讹并承担法律责任	海关审单批注及放行日期（签章）	
报关员		审单	审价
单位地址	申报单位（签章）	征税	统计
邮编　　电话	填制日期	查验	放行

附表 2 – 6

中华人民共和国海关进口货物报关单

预录入编号：　　　　　　　　　　　　　　　　　　　　　　海关编号：

进口口岸		备案号	进口日期	申报日期
经营单位		运输方式	运输工具名称	提运单号
发货单位		贸易方式	征免性质	征税比例
许可证号	起运国(地区)	装货港		境内目的地
批准文号	成交方式	运费	保费	杂费
合同协议号	件数	包装种类	毛重(公斤)	净重(公斤)
集装箱号	随附单据			用途
标记唛码及备注				

项号	商品编号	商品名称、规格型号	数量及单位	最终目的地(地区)	单价	总价	币制	征免

税费征收情况

录入员　　录入单位	兹声明以上申报无讹并承担法律责任	海关审单批注及放行日期(签章)
报关员		审单　　　　审价
单位地址	申报单位(签章)	征税　　　　统计
邮编　　电话	填制日期	查验　　　　放行

附表 2－7

中华人民共和国出入境检验检疫

入境货物通关单

编号：

1. 收货人			5. 标记及号码
2. 发货人			
3. 合同/提(运)单号	4. 输出国家或地区		
6. 运输工具名称及号码	7. 目的地		8. 集装箱规格及数量
9. 货物名称及规格	10. H. S. 编码	11. 申报总值	12. 数/重量、包装数量及种类
13. 证明 上述货物业已报检/申报，请海关予以放行。 签字：　　日期：　　年　　月　　日			
14. 备注			

①货物通关　[2－1－1(2000.1.1)]

附表 2－8

山 东 省 丝 绸 进 出 口 公 司
SHANDONG SILK IMP. & EXP. CORP.
6, FUZHOU ROAD, QINGDAO, CHINA

发票
INVOICE

发票号码
Invoice No. ______________________
青岛，日期
Oingdao, ______________________

TO: ______________________

装船口岸
From ______________________

目的港
to ______________________

开证银行
Drawn Under ______________________

信用证号码
L/C No. ______________________

唛头及号码 Marks & Numbers	数量与货品名称 Quantity & Descriptions	金额 Amount

山东省丝绸进出口公司
SHANDONG SILK IMP. & EXP. CORP.

____
Manager

附表 2 – 9

COMMERCIAL INVOICE

1) SELLER	3) INVOICE NO.	4) INVOICE DATE
	5) L/C NO.	6) DATE
	7) ISSUED BY	
2) BUYER	8) CONTRACT NO.	9) DATE
	10) FEOM	11) TO
	12) SHIPPED BY	13) PRICE TERM

14) MARKS	15) DESCRIPTION OF GOODS	16) QTY.	17) UNIT PRICE	18) AMOUNT

附表 2 – 10

中华人民共和国出入境检验检疫
出境货物报验单

报检单位(加盖公章): Admin 87812345 *编　号

发货人	(中文)	澳威斯机械发展有限公司
	(外文)	AOWEISI MACHINERY DEVELOPMENT CO. ,LTD
收货人	(中文)	
	(外文)	ROSE FRANCE IMPORT AND EXPORT CO. ,24 SANT MART RUE PARIS

货物名称(中/外文)	H. S. 编码	产地	数/重量	货物总值	包装种类及数量
MACHINERY	234566. 6677		5000PCS	17000. 00	30CTNS

运输工具名称号码		贸易方式	一般贸易	货物存放地点	
合同号	20020001	信用证号		用途	
发货日期		输出国家(地区)	FRANCE	许可证/审批号	
起运地	SHANGHAI	到达口岸	HONGKONG	生产单位注册号	
集装箱规格、数量及号码					

合同、信用证订立的检验检疫条款或特殊要求	标记及号码	随附单据(划"√"或补填)
		合同　包装性能结果单 信用证　许可/审批文件 发票 换证凭证 装箱单 厂检单

需要证单名称(划"√"或补填)		*检验检疫费	
品质证 __正__副 重量证书 __正__副 数量证书 __正__副 兽医卫生证书 __正__副 健康证书 __正__副 卫生证书 __正__副 运输卫生证书 __正__副	植物检疫证书 __正__副 熏蒸/消毒证书 __正__副 出境货物换证凭条	总金额(人民币元)	
		计费人	
		收费人	

报检人郑重声明:	领　取　凭　证	
1. 本人被授权报检。 2. 上列填写内容正确属实,货物无伪造或冒用他人的厂名、标志、认证标志,并承担货物质量责任。 签名:__________	日期	
	签名	

注:有" * "号栏由出入境检验检疫机关填写　　◆国家出入境检验检疫局制

附表 2－11

中国民用航空总局
GENERAL ADMINISTRATION OF CIVIL AVIATION OF CHINA
国际货物托运书
SHIPPER'S LETTER OF INSTRUCTION

货运单号码
NO. OF AIR WAYBILL

始发站 AIRPORT OF DEPARTURE	到达站 AIRPORT OF DESTINATION	供承运人用 FOR CARRIER USE ONLY
SHANGHAI	HONGKONG	航班/日期 FIGHT/DATE ; 航班/日期 FIGHT/DATE

线路及到达站
ROUTING AND DESTINATION

至 TO:	第一承运人 FIRST CARRIER	至 TO:	至 TO:	至 TO:	至 TO:	至 TO:	至 TO:

已预留吨位
BOOKED

收货人账号 CONSIGNEE'S ACCOUNT NUMBER	收货人姓名及地址 CONSIGNEE'S NAME AND ADDRESS

ROSE FRANCE IMPORT AND EXPORT CO.,

24 SANT MART RUE PARIS

唛头：

另请通知 ROSE FRANCE IMPORT AND EXPORT CO.,

ALSO NOTIFY 24 SANT MART RUE PARIS

托运人账号 SHIPPER'S ACCOUNT NUMBER	托运人姓名及地址 SHIPPER'S NAME AND ADDRESS

SINOTEX UNITED IMPORT & EXPORT LTD

3208 32FL.,JINMAO BUILDONG PUDONG NEW DISTRICT SHANGHAI

托运人声明的价值 SHIPPER'S DECLARED VALUE		保险金额 AMOUNT OF INSURANCE	所附文件 DOCUMENT ACCOMPANY TO AIR WAYBILL
供运输用 FOR CARRIAGE	供海关用 FOR CUSTOMS		

件数 NO. OF	实际毛重(公斤) ACTUAL	运价类别 RATE	收费重量 CHAGEABLE WEIGHT	费率 RATE/CHARGE	货物品名及数量(包括体积或尺寸) NATURE AND QUANTITY OF GOODS
30CTNS	840.00KGS				LEATHER SLIPPERS

在货物不能交收货人时，托运人指示处理方法
SHIPPER'S INSTRUCTION IN CASE OF INABLITY TO DELIVER SHIPMENT AS CONSIGNED

处理情况(包括包装方式，货物标志及号码等)
HANDLING INFORMATION (INCL. METHOD OF PACKING, INDENTIFY MARK AND NUMBERS ETC.)

托运人证实以上所填全部属实并愿意遵守承运人的一切载运章程
THE SHIPPER CERTIFIES THAT THE PARTICULAR ON THE FACE HEREOF ARE CORRECT AND AGREE TO THE CONDITIONS OF CARRIAGE OF THE CARRIER.

托运人签字 SHIPPER'S SIGNATURE　　日期 DATE　　经手人 AGENT

附表 2－12

中国外轮代理公司
CHINA OCEAN SHIPPING AGENCY
收 货 单
MATE'S RECEIPT

S/O No. ________

船名 M. S/S ____________ 航次 Voy. ____________ 目的港 For ____________

托运人 Shipper ______________________________

受货人 Consignee ______________________________

通知人 Notify ______________________________

下开完好状况之货物业已收妥无损

Received on board the following goods apparent in good order and condition

标记及号码 Marks & Nos.	件数 Quantity	货名 Description of Goods	毛重量公斤 Gross Weight in Kilos	尺码(Cu. M.) M 立方公尺

共 件 计 数 (大 写)

Total Number of Packages in Writing ______________________________

日期 Date ____________ 时间 Time ____________

装入何仓 Stowed ______________________________

实收 Received ______________________________

理货员签名 Tallied By ____________ 大副 Chief Officer ____________

附表 2－13

B/L No. ________

托运人
Shipper

收货人或指示
Consignee or order

通知地址
Notify address

	转船港 Port of transhipment
船名 Vessel	装货港 Port of loading
卸货港 Port of discharge	最后目的地 Final destination

直运或转船提单

BILL OF LADING

DIRECT OR WITH TRANSHIPMENT

中国对外贸易运输总公司

CHINA NATIONAL

FOREIGN TRADE TRANSPORTATION CORP.

Cable: SINOTRANS BEIJING

Telex: 22153 TRANS CN

22154 TRANS CN

22265 TRANS CN

附表 2-13(续)

标志和号码 Marks and Nos.	件数和包装种类 Number and kind of packages	货名 Description of goods	毛重(公斤) Gross weight(kgs.)	尺码(立方米) Measurement(m^3)

以上细目由托运人提供

ABOVE PARTICULARS FURNISHED BY SHIPPER

运费和费用 Freight and charges	SHIPPED on board in apparent good order and condition(unless otherwise indicated) the goods or packages specified herein and to be discharged at the mentioned port of discharge or as near thereto as the vessel may safely get and be always afloat. The weight, measure, marks and numbers, quality, contents and value, being partculars funished by the Shipper, are not checked by the Carrier on boading. The Shipper, Consignee and the Holder of this Bill of Loading hereby expressly accept and agree to all printed, written or stamped provisions, exceptions and conditions og this Bill of Lading, including those on the back hereof. IN WITNESS whereof the number of original Bill of Lading stated below have been signed, one of which being accomplished, the other(s) to be void.	
	运费支付地 Freight payable at	签章地点和日期 Place and date of issue
	正本提单份数 Number of original Bs/L	代表船长签字 Signed for or on benalf of the Master 代 理 as Agents

SUBJECT TO THE TERMS AND CONDITIONS ON BACK

附表 2 – 14

Shipper

COSCO

ORIGINAL

Consignee

B/LNo. ________ OR

中国远洋运输公司
CHINA OCEAN SHIPPING COMPANY

Notify Party

Cable:		Telex:
COSCO	**BEIJING**	22264 CPCPK CN
	GUANGZHOU	44080 COSCA CN
	SHANGHAI	33057 COSCO CN
COSCO	**QINGDAO**	32037 TOSCO CN
	TIANJIN	23221 TOSCO CN
	DALIAN	86162 DOSCO CN

Pre carriage by		Port of Receipt
Ocean Vessel	Voy No.	Port of loading
Port of Discharge		Place of Delivery

Container No.	Seal No. Marks & Nos.	No of containerers or P kgs.	Kind of Packages: Description of Goods Final Description (of the goods not the ship)	Gross Weight	Measurement

附表 2－14(续)

TOTAL NUMBER OF CONTAINERS
OF PACKAGES (IN WORDS)

Freight & charges	Revenue Tons	Rate	Per	Prepaid	Collect

Ex. Rate	Prepaid at	Payable at	Place and date of Issue
	Total, Prepaid	No, of Original B(s)/L	Signed for the Carrier

LADEN ON BOARD THE VESSEL

Date:

BY: ------------------------------

(COSCO STANDARD FORM 07)　　(TERMS CONTINUED ON BACK HEREOF)

附表 2－15

海运出口货物投保单

1）保险人：　　　　2）被保险人：

3）标记	4）包装及数量	5）保险货物项目	6）保险货物金额
7）总保险金额：（大写）			

8）运输工具：　　（船名）　　（航次）

9）装运港：　　10）目的港：

11）投保险别：　　12）货物起运日期：

13）投保日期：　　14）投保人签字：

附表 2－16

中国外轮代理公司深圳分公司

落驳地点 B/LNO.

托 运 单

起运港 船名 开期 转运港
转运船名 开期 目的港 所属公司
托运人
受货人及地点
通知人及地点

唛头	件数及包装式样	货 名	净重(KGS.)	毛重(KGS.)	尺吨
合计					

信用证 NO.	装船期限	结汇期限	缴运费方式	付运费港	提单份数 正本 副本

货值 C. I. F/F. O. B.	第一程船运费	转船运费

特殊条款	
备注	

托运人签章:

参 考 文 献

[1] 刘毅,郭琛. 国际贸易实务[M]. 哈尔滨:哈尔滨工程大学出版社,2008.
[2] 张素芳. 国际贸易理论与实务[M]. 北京:对外经济贸易大学出版社,2007.
[3] 徐景霖. 国际贸易实务[M]. 大连:东北财经大学出版社,2010.
[4] 刘舒年. 国际贸易实务[M]. 北京:中国人民大学出版社,2006.
[5] 国际商会. 跟单位用证统一惯例及关于电子交单的附则[S]. 国际商会中国国家委员会,译. 北京:中国民主法制出版社,2006.